MILTON STUDIES

XLII

MILTON STUDIES

XLII ☙ *Edited by*
Albert C. Labriola
and *David Loewenstein*

Paradise Regained
in Context: Genre,
Politics, Religion

UNIVERSITY OF PITTSBURGH PRESS

MILTON STUDIES

is published annually by the University of Pittsburgh Press as a forum for Milton scholarship and criticism. Articles submitted for publication may be biographical; they may interpret some aspect of Milton's writings; or they may define literary, intellectual, or historical contexts—by studying the work of his contemporaries, the traditions which affected his thought and art, contemporary political and religious movements, his influence on other writers, or the history of critical response to his work.

Manuscripts should be upwards of 3,000 words in length and should conform to *The Chicago Manual of Style*. Manuscripts and editorial correspondence should be addressed to Albert C. Labriola, Department of English, Duquesne University, Pittsburgh, Pa., 15282–1703. Manuscripts should be accompanied by a self-addressed envelope and sufficient unattached postage.

Milton Studies does not review books.

Within the United States, *Milton Studies* may be ordered from the University of Pittsburgh Press, c/o Chicago Distribution Center, 11030 South Langley Avenue, Chicago, Ill., 60628, 1-800-621-2736.

Published by the University of Pittsburgh Press, Pittsburgh, Pa. 15260

Copyright © 2003 by the University of Pittsburgh Press

Manufactured in the United States of America

Printed on acid-free paper

10 9 8 7 6 5 4 3 2 1

ISBN 0-8229-4187-2

ISSN 0076-8820

CONTENTS

IN MEMORIAM
LOUIS L. MARTZ, 1913–2001

O N   T H E   O C C A S I O N of the tercentenary of *Paradise Lost,* Louis L. Martz was invited by the founding editor of *Milton Studies,* James D. Simmonds, to give a lecture at the University of Pittsburgh. He and seven other distinguished Miltonists who lectured on *Paradise Lost, Paradise Regained,* and *Samson Agonistes* became contributors to the inaugural volume of *Milton Studies* (1969). In that volume, Professor Martz's essay, "Chorus and Character in *Samson Agonistes,*" is the only one to deal with Milton's dramatic poem. From the inception of *Milton Studies* and until his death on December 18, 2001, Professor Martz served on the Editorial Board.

Professor Martz's contribution as a Miltonist derives chiefly from his book *Poet of Exile: A Study of Milton's Poetry* (1980), reissued as *Milton: Poet of Exile,* with a new introduction (1986). That book deals with the poems in the 1645 edition of Milton's works, then focuses on *Paradise Lost,* and ends with analyses of *Paradise Regained* and *Samson Agonistes.* Reviewers acknowledge the value and validity, not to mention the influence and impact, of the insights that Professor Martz develops in this work.

Professor Martz established his reputation as a scholar in Renaissance and seventeenth-century studies with *The Poetry of Meditation* (1954), later reissued in a revised edition (1962). The impact of that work cannot be overestimated, for the book highlights how and why meditation and spirituality inform religious literature. The idea of the book first emerged in his essay on Donne's *Anniversaries,* which was published in *ELH* in 1947. Thereafter, Professor Martz in his book applies the paradigm of meditation to the works of authors such as Southwell, Herbert, Crashaw, and Vaughan, while attending to the writings of Sidney, Marvell, Milton, and Bunyan. By 1960, in another essay in *ELH,* Professor Martz perceives the agonistic struggle of Christ and Satan in *Paradise Regained* as "meditative combat." This essay became one of the building blocks of the monumental *Poet of Exile.*

Professor Martz completed his essay for the present volume as he lay in a hospital bed. His essay on the Georgic form and style of *Paradise Regained* urges us to reexamine Milton's brief epic against certain major classical analogues. The method is comparative study or intertextual analysis, whereby the traditions or precedents deriving from Milton's forebears become the frame of reference for appraising the individual talent of the major poet of the English Renaissance and Restoration.

At the time of his death, Martz was Sterling Professor Emeritus of English at Yale University, where he educated generations of graduate students whose loyalty, gratitude, and indebtedness to him are legendary. To others, he was a mentor and friend, whose unfailing courtesy and whose constructive outlook on their research provided both reward and incentive for their labors.

To the lasting memory of Louis L. Martz, we dedicate the present volume.

Albert C. Labriola and David Loewenstein

MILTON STUDIES

XLII

INTRODUCTION

David Loewenstein

MILTON'S EARLY BIOGRAPHERS record that the poet could not bear the suggestion that *Paradise Regained* might be considered an inferior poem to *Paradise Lost*. Edward Phillips observes that *Paradise Regained* "is generally censur'd to be much inferiour to the other, though [Milton] could not hear with patience any such thing when related to him," and John Toland, the radical Whig and religious thinker, repeats this remark adding: "yet this occasion'd som body to say wittily enough that *Milton* might be seen in *Paradise Lost,* but not in *Paradise Regain'd.*"[1] One of course could counter this last observation in diverse ways, noting for example that a great deal of Milton "might be seen" in this contentious religious poem, especially in its portrait of an austere, precocious, and inward-looking Jesus who remains unmoved in the midst of his many trials; Milton's Jesus responds polemically and scornfully to Satan's rhetoric and alluring temptations, while also presenting the "dictates" and "ways of truth" in a manner that combines religious meanings and aesthetic expression (1.480, 478), much as Milton himself attempted to do throughout his career as poet and polemicist.[2] Rather than consider *Paradise Regained* as "inferior" to *Paradise Lost,* the following essays attempt to provide new perspectives on Milton's "brief epic," especially its generic, political, and religious concerns, in order to define its distinctive achievement in Milton's career and the Restoration culture when it was written and published. Moreover, several essays—especially the concluding pieces by David Norbrook and John Coffey—provide fresh perspectives on *Paradise Regained* in relation to the politics of both *Samson Agonistes* and *Paradise Lost.*

This volume is the first extra issue of *Milton Studies* devoted explicitly to *Paradise Regained* and its literary, religious, and political contexts; it thus complements *The Miltonic Samson,* the recent special issue of *Milton Studies* presenting new perspectives on *Samson Agonistes.*[3] These new essays on *Paradise Regained* also appear at a moment when scholars have begun reconsidering the poem in its historical and cultural contexts. Some of the most notable characteristics and themes of *Paradise Regained*—its contentiousness as well as its concerns with spiritual inwardness, obedience, constant perseverance, adversity, and temptation—take on a more urgent resonance when

1

placed in the political and religious contexts of Restoration England. Consequently, a distinctive feature of this volume is that a cluster of its essays (those by Laura Knoppers, N. H. Keeble, Thomas Corns, David Norbrook, and John Coffey) add new perspectives to recent historical work on *Paradise Regained*.[4] Despite being "fully tried / Through all temptation" (1.4–5), the solitary, inward-looking Jesus of *Paradise Regained* remains "unmoved" (3.386, 4.109) as he asserts that his time "is not yet come" (3.397); in this imaginative portrait of Jesus led by the Spirit and tempted in the wilderness of the world, Milton has created a model for unseduced, unshaken radical Puritan saints in the uncertain world of Restoration England. The conflict between the kingdom of Christ and glorious worldly monarchies was especially keen during the Restoration when, in the words of one of Milton's Quaker friends, Isaac Penington the younger, the radical godly were "brought lower than ever, and [were] in greater danger . . . than ever."[5] Indeed, the Conventicle Act of 1670, issued the year before Milton published his poem, was a vicious new penal law against Dissenters and considered by Andrew Marvell "the Quintessence of arbitrary Malice"; its penalties (including heavy fines), its empowerment of a solitary justice to convict on confession, and its invitation to would-be informants to spy on Nonconformists aimed to provide "further and more speedy remedie against the growing and dangerous practices of seditious sectaries and other disloyal persons."[6] In the words of Thomas Ellwood, the Quaker who claimed he prompted Milton to write *Paradise Regained,* this was a particularly "stormy time" for Dissenters under siege in Restoration England.[7] Consequently, this issue of *Milton Studies* offers a number of essays that specifically address the Restoration contexts of Milton's spiritual poem and illuminate freshly its political concerns.

Other essays in this issue provide new perspectives on the poem's genre and theology (including its heretical dimensions). Some years ago Barbara Lewalski's magisterial study of the genre of *Paradise Regained* demonstrated exhaustively Milton's attempt to write a "brief epic" on the Jobean model.[8] However, as Louis L. Martz reminds us again in this volume, there is another important generic model for the poem: Virgil's *Georgics*.[9] Albert Labriola and I feel especially fortunate to include Louis Martz's essay which he completed just before his death. This new piece extends and refines his argument in *Poet of Exile* that *Paradise Regained* bears some analogy to the style and form of the *Georgics* with its four-book structure, while also allowing Milton to fulfill his early plan for a brief epic modeled on the Book of Job.[10] Milton's interest of the four-book division of the *Georgics* expressed in *The Art of Logic,* published the year after *Paradise Regained,* strengthens Martz's case. His essay compares in detail the styles and themes of both poems, while also making a larger point about the importance of the analogy for Milton's poetic career: it completes for Milton the crucial Virgilian triad of pastoral, georgic, and epic. Toward the end of his essay, Martz reminds us as well of the implications of both Virgil and Milton writing during and after periods of civil war, while hoping for leaders (Octavian in the first instance and Cromwell in the second) who might bring peace and stability to troubled lands. The comparison adds a political dimension to Martz's comparative study of the two poems. His argument also reminds us that for all the emphasis on the authority of Hebraic models—both poetry and prophecy—in *Paradise Regained,* classical literary modes continued to exert an important influence on the poems of Milton's 1671 volume.

The two subsequent essays in this issue, by Regina Schwartz and John Rumrich, examine the theological dimensions of *Paradise Regained* from different perspectives. Schwartz addresses the subject of redemption in *Paradise Regained,* asking specifically how Paradise is re-gained and how man is redeemed. She discovers that, beyond obedience to the will of God, there is no explicit definition of salvation in the poem, and that instead of turning (as we might expect) to the positive theology of the cross, Milton's vision of redemption is indebted to the tradition of negative theology and that apophatic theology is the absent center at the heart of *Paradise Regained.* In "Milton's *Theanthropos:* The Body of Christ in *Paradise Regained,*" John Rumrich explores the distinctive heretical theology underpinning the problem of the Son's identity. In this sense, Rumrich extends his recent work on the heretical Milton, showing the unorthodox nature of Milton's union of divine and human—the *theanthropos*—in the Son of *Paradise Regained.*[11] The essay builds its case by considering earlier orthodox church views of the incarnate Son, by drawing upon *De doctrina Christiana* (whose heresies Rumrich firmly believes are Milton's), and by making a number of revealing comparisons with the anti-Trinitarian Son of *Paradise Lost.*

The remaining five essays in this special issue all explore, in one way or another, *Paradise Regained* in relation to Restoration contexts, as well as Milton's controversial political and religious writings. Laura L. Knoppers provides the first essay-length treatment of the poem in terms of the seventeenth-century English fear of popery. What characterized that fear of popery, as Jonathan Scott has recently stressed, was "its range and power: it spanned the century" and was fueled by the struggle against the European Counter-Reformation since popery meant not just Catholicism but anti-Protestantism.[12] In "Satan and the Papacy in *Paradise Regained,*" Knoppers explores the impact of the opulent culture, power, and religious relics of papal Rome on Milton's late poetry and particularly *Paradise Regained.* As Knoppers shows, the Son of *Paradise Regained* rejects popish appropriations of art, architecture, classical learning, military might, and fame only to reappropriate beauty, art, and learning for a radical Protestant inwardness and spiritual discipline in an age of persecution.

N. H. Keeble's essay focuses on the wilderness as a central motif in *Paradise Regained,* exploring it in the context of seventeenth-century applications, including those by Nonconformist writers during the 1660s and 1670s. The Miltonic desert of *Paradise Regained* is both a refuge from and a challenge to the cultural and religious world of Restoration England. The wilderness topos and narrative became politically charged in a new way after the Restoration as Nonconformists were subject to severe persecution and constraints, including social and political exclusion, and thus experienced a kind of internal exile. Yet, as Keeble shows, the wilderness was a contested site—the royalists had used it to convey the trials of Charles II—and *Paradise Regained* needs to be understood in terms of the cultural and political contest over this major topos. In the course of addressing the wilderness topos, Keeble also considers the quietist emphasis of the poem—an issue taken up by John Coffey later in the volume—while exploring the language of combat and patient endurance in a poem concerned with offering consolation to Nonconformists exiled by the Restoration.

In "'With Unaltered Brow': Milton and the Son of God," Thomas N. Corns complements the essays on *Paradise Regained* and Restoration contexts by exploring the similarities between the arguments of the Son of God and the daring arguments and language of Milton's political prose and occasional verse. Corns links the militant imagery of the prose, notably *Areopagitica, Eikonoklastes,* and the *Second Defence,* with the language of combat and protracted disputation in *Paradise Regained.* Corns thus shows how the connections between Milton's polemical exertions and military conflict carry over into *Paradise Regained.* Moreover, he reveals how the military and civic arguments of the political sonnets to Fairfax and Cromwell are further developed in *Paradise Regained.* The result is a fresh political reading of the brief epic, including the Son's analyses of national corruption and civic virtue, in the context of Milton's career as a controversialist and political poet. The essay reminds us how much *Paradise Regained* remains a politically contentious poem after the Restoration.

David Norbrook's essay, "Republican Occasions in *Paradise Regained* and *Samson Agonistes,*" offers another fresh political reading of the poem, this time in the context of republican discourse and Milton's 1671 volume as a whole. The essay extends Norbrook's major recent study of early modern English literary republicanism, *Writing the English Republic,* which concludes with a lengthy chapter on *Paradise Lost* and Lucan's influence.[13] This new essay links republican issues with religious ones and places the politics of

Milton's 1671 poems in republican Puritan context by bringing into the discussion such writers as Lucy Hutchinson, Robert Overton, George Wither, and George Sikes, the early biographer of the republican parliamentarian Sir Henry Vane the younger. In Norbrook's account, the key term is "occasion" or *occasione,* a rich term in Machiavelli that evokes not only a more secular sense of political calculation, but also a notion of an effective, flexible political agency that would have appealed to republican Puritans. In examining the 1671 volume, Norbrook considers the issue of seizing the right "occasion" for action. As he shows, the two poems of the 1671 volume were seen in their own time as "oppositional speech-acts" (Norbrook's term); seizing the *occasione* could thus include speech-acts and the resourceful use of language. Moreover, like John Coffey's essay concluding this volume, Norbrook's piece complicates and questions the opposition between political quietism and violent activism in Milton's late poems and in republican discourse of the Restoration.

John Coffey's essay provides a fitting conclusion to the volume because it reconsiders, from the perspective of a historian of Restoration culture, some of the political themes of the previous essays and because it situates *Paradise Regained* in the context of Milton's other great poems. Coffey's account of Milton builds on the recent work of Blair Worden and other scholars of republicanism, yet also asserts his own point of view regarding the controversial issue of whether or not the post-Restoration Milton was a pacifist or patient militant. In "Pacifist, Quietist, or Patient Militant? John Milton and the Restoration," Coffey reassesses the debate concerning Milton's post-Restoration politics. Like David Norbrook, he shows that post-Restoration radical writers—including Milton, John Goodwin, Henry Vane, Algernon Sidney, and Edmund Ludlow—were deeply concerned with the timing and means of their deliverance. As Coffey argues, the issue in *Paradise Regained* of the retiring Jesus waiting and acting in "due time" (3.182), rather than acting *now* (as Satan urges him to do), is a concern that would have resonated deeply with other godly republicans after the Restoration. Providing a fresh assessment of issues of war and violence in the great poems, Coffey challenges the common argument for pacifism in *Paradise Regained* (and the other late poems) and discusses the brief epic as a poem concerned with how the godly should respond to the persecuting regime of the 1660s. His essay, like the preceding ones on the historical contexts of *Paradise Regained,* enables us to appreciate more richly the achievement of Milton's spiritual poem, which dared to challenge, in its unique and disputatious way, the political, religious, and aesthetic culture of Restoration England.

University of Wisconsin, Madison

NOTES

1. *The Early Lives of Milton*, ed. Helen Darbishire (London, 1932), 75–76, 185.

2. References to *Paradise Regained* are from *Milton: Complete Shorter Poems*, 2d ed., ed. John Carey (London, 1997).

3. See *Milton Studies* 33, *The Miltonic Samson*, ed. Albert C. Labriola and Michael Lieb (Pittsburgh, 1997).

4. See, for example, David Quint, *Epic and Empire: Politics and Generic Form from Virgil to Milton* (Princeton, 1993), chap. 8; Laura L. Knoppers, *Historicizing Milton: Spectacle, Power, and Poetry in Restoration England* (Athens, Ga., 1994), chaps. 1 and 5; David Loewenstein, *Representing Revolution in Milton and His Contemporaries: Religion, Politics, and Polemics in Radical Puritanism* (Cambridge, 2001), chap. 8.

5. Isaac Penington the Younger, *Concerning Persecution* (1661), in *The Works of the Long-Mournful and Sorely Distressed Isaac Penington* (London, 1681), pt. 1, p. 344. On Milton's respect for Penington, see Thomas Ellwood, *The History of the Life of Thomas Ellwood*, ed. C. G. Crump (London: Methuen, 1900), 89.

6. *The Poems and Letters of Andrew Marvell*, 3d ed., ed. H. M. Margoliouth, rev. by Pierre Legouis with the collaboration of E. E. Duncan-Jones, 2 vols. (Oxford, 1971), 2:314; *The Stuart Constitution: Documents and Commentary*, 2d ed., ed. J. P. Kenyon (Cambridge, 1986), 356.

7. Ellwood, *The Life of Thomas Ellwood*, 169–71; for Ellwood and *Paradise Regained*, see 145. On England in the early 1670s, see John Spurr, *England in the 1670s: "This Masquerading Age"* (Oxford, 2000).

8. Barbara K. Lewalski, *Milton's Brief Epic: The Genre, Meaning, and Art of "Paradise Regained"* (Providence, R.I., 1966). On the genre of the brief epic, see also John T. Shawcross, *"Paradise Regain'd": Worthy T'Have Not Remain'd So Long Unsung* (Pittsburgh, 1988), chap. 7.

9. Lewalski had challenged this model in part because it is not mentioned in Milton's famous discussion of poetic kinds in *The Reason of Church-Government* where the Book of Job is classified as a brief epic. See *Milton's Brief Epic*, 37–38.

10. See the first appendix to *Poet of Exile: A Study of Milton's Poetry* (New Haven, 1980), 293–304; see also Martz, *The Paradise Within: Studies in Vaughan, Traherne, and Milton* (New Haven, 1964), 172–77.

11. John Rumrich, *Milton Unbound* (Cambridge, 1996); and *Milton and Heresy*, ed. Stephen Dobranski and John Rumrich (Cambridge, 1998).

12. Jonathan Scott, *England's Troubles: Seventeenth-Century Political Instability in European Context* (Cambridge, 2000), 29–31, 56–57, 170–73.

13. David Norbrook, *Writing the English Republic: Poetry, Rhetoric, and Politics, 1627–1660* (Cambridge, 1999).

PARADISE REGAINED: GEORGIC FORM, GEORGIC STYLE

Louis L. Martz

T HE OUTPOURING OF excellent studies of the *Georgics* over the past twenty years has encouraged me to try, after several earlier attempts, to persuade readers of *Paradise Regained* that Milton's poem bears a strong analogy with Virgil's four-book poem of similar length.[1] All these new studies, by classically trained scholars writing in English, combine to suggest many different ways in which the *Georgics* may have appealed to Milton as a model for his poem on the temptation of Jesus.[2]

First of all, these studies remove what for many readers may be the prime difficulty in accepting the analogy: the assumption that the *Georgics* is a treatise on agriculture. As Michael Putnam observes: "Only when we eradicate from our minds any lingering notions that the poem is utilitarian, fostered though they be by the poet's overt subject and by the genre, can we begin to come to grips with the *Georgics'* extraordinary qualities. To expound agrarianism is, for Virgil, to ponder some of the major recurrent themes in literature" (7). Later studies, such as those by Miles, Ross, and Perkell, bear out in various ways the truth of this position. Thus Perkell stresses the rich complexity of the poem: "In sum, while the poem purports to be didactic and to teach *praecepta,* it embodies, in fact, a whole range of values that function in tension with the conventional, material, and Iron Age values upon which a georgic poem might be expected to be based. . . . It enlarges and deepens the reader's appreciation of those spiritual and artistic values that do not lead to quantifiable progress" (199). Surely John Milton, with his deep knowledge of the classics, would have realized the larger implications of the poem.

My first effort to argue the analogy, forty years ago, relied primarily on stylistic analogies in the "middle style" of the two poems.[3] But I made a strategic error in citing with approval Tillyard's vehement statement about Milton's poem—"It is not an epic, it does not try to be an epic, and it must not be judged by any kind of epic standard"[4]—thus alienating those readers (nearly all the community of Milton scholars) who were accustomed to regarding the poem as a "brief epic."[5] I should have realized that Tillyard's statement was extreme, since in the subsequent discussion of "styles" I stressed the epic qualities in Milton's presentation of the temptations of Parthia, Rome, and Greece. At the same time, while mentioning the several councils of supernatural beings in Milton's poem, I ought to have recognized that these were part of the epic tradition. There was no need to fight the phrase "brief epic," since Virgil's poem also has its epic moments. Indeed, we might conjecture that these epic qualities in the *Georgics* may explain why Milton used a georgic format in realizing his dream of writing a brief epic.

At last strong support appeared in the form of Anthony Low's 1983 essay, adapted for the final chapter of his *The Georgic Revolution* (1985).[6] Here Low found a thematic correspondence in the "georgic spirit" represented by the Virgilian farmer's perseverance in arduous labor—similar to Milton's presentation of the patient and persevering Son of God: "The georgic condition of fallen Adam is precisely what the Son has come to remedy, but scarcely in such a sudden and easy fashion as Satan proposes. Instead of removing the curse of labor, Jesus himself is to undergo it, and thus to ennoble and transform it" (339). Classical scholars have stressed this aspect of "labor" in Virgil's poem, as Palmer Bovie has done in the introduction to his translation of the *Georgics:* "Over the whole work there glows a burnished contrast between the art of peace, whereby the indomitable farmer moves his curved plough through the earth, and the uncontrollable violence that would dispossess man of his rewards or distort the sanity of his behavior."[7] Such is the essence of the contest between Jesus and Satan in Milton's poem, with the indomitable figure of the Son of God on the one hand and, on the other, the violence of Satan's efforts to distort the sanity of the Son's behavior.

Milton's interest in the four-book structure of the *Georgics* is shown in a treatise that is in a peculiar way contemporary with the writing of *Paradise Regained*. As Anthony Low has noted,[8] Milton twice refers to the four-book division of the *Georgics* in his *Art of Logic,* the Latin textbook published in 1672: first, in his chapter "On Distribution from Subjects," where he cites the opening lines of the *Georgics* as an example of "a division into four parts distinguished by their appropriating subjects, namely fields, trees, livestock and bees"; and later, in his chapter on "Method," where he describes the structure of the whole poem:

Thus Virgil in the *Georgics* divides his proposed subject matter into four parts, as was said before; in the first book he deals with general matters, such as astrology and meteorology, and he treats of crops and their cultivation, which is the first part of his work. And then at the beginning of the second book there is a transition:
Thus far the cultivation of fields, etc.

Then he writes in a general way about trees, and then specifically about vines. Thus in the whole work, he endeavors to put the most general matter in the first position, the subordinate things in an intermediate position, and the most specialized things last.[9]

This textbook, scholars have conjectured, was probably written during the 1640s, for use in Milton's own teaching at that time; but the fact that it was published in the year after the appearance of *Paradise Regained* brings these remarks about the four-book structure of the *Georgics* into a close proximity with that poem.[10] Milton would hardly have sent his treatise to the press without in some measure reviewing its contents. However this may be, the *Art of Logic* provides valuable evidence for Milton's interest in the structure of the *Georgics*.

The best evidence for similarity between the poems lies in their styles or in what I earlier called "the contest of styles." Since the time of Servius, the *Georgics* has been taken as the model for the "middle style": "tres enim sunt characteres, humilis, medius, grandiloquus: quos omnes in hoc invenimus poeta. nam in Aeneide grandiloquum habet, in georgicis medium, in bucolicis humilem."[11] But the term "medius" bears several interpretations. First of all, it may be taken to refer to the direct, didactic style in which the precepts for nurturing crops, trees, and animals are delivered, the middle style established in the opening books of both the *Georgics* and *Paradise Regained*. Virgil establishes this style by sharp contrast with the epic style displayed in the prologue and in the conclusion of his first book.

Virgil's poem opens with what is, in effect, an epic invocation of the gods, extending to forty-two lines and rising in the middle to an invocation of Caesar as one destined to become a god. "Whatever form you take," Virgil concludes,

> Smooth my path, condone this enterprise
> Of bold experiment in verse, and share
> Concern with me for uninstructed farmers:
> Grow used to prayers appealing to your name.   (Bovie, 4–5)

[quidquid eris . . . da facilem cursum, atque audacibus adnue coeptis, / ignarosque viae mecum miseratus agrestis / ingredere et votis iam nunc adsuesce vocari.] (1.36, 40–42)[12]

Then at once the poem drops to the lower style of didactic verse:

> Vere novo, gelidus canis cum montibus umor
> liquitur et Zephyro putris se glaeba resolvit,
> depresso incipiat iam tum mihi taurus aratro
> ingemere, et sulco attritus splendescere vomer.   (1.43–46)

[When Spring is new, and frozen moisture thaws
On white-clothed mountainsides, and crumbling soil
Is loosened by the West Wind, let your bull
Begin to groan beneath the pressing plough
And the well-worn ploughshare gleam from the rub of the furrow.]

(Bovie, 5)

After four hundred lines of careful directions, sprinkled here and there with variations upward toward a higher mode, the book concludes with an epic memory of the disturbances in nature that marked the assassination of Julius Caesar, followed by an epic invocation of the gods, imploring their help in aiding this new young Caesar to cure the many ills besetting his world:

quippe ubi fas versum atque nefas: tot bella per orbem,
tam multae scelerum facies; non ullus aratro
dignus honos, squalent abductis arva colonis
et curvae rigidum falces conflantur in ensem.
hinc movet Euphrates, illinc Germania bellum;
vicinae ruptis inter se legibus urbes
arma ferunt; saevit toto Mars impius orbe:
ut cum carceribus sese effudere quadrigae,
addunt in spatia, et frustra retinacula tendens
fertur equis auriga neque audit currus habenas.

(1.505–14)

[For right and wrong change places; everywhere
So many wars, so many shapes of crime
Confront us; no due honour attends the plough,
The fields, bereft of tillers, are all unkempt,
And in the forge the curving pruning-hook
Is made a straight hard sword. Euphrates here,
There Germany is in arms, and neighbour cities
Break covenants and fight; throughout the world
Impious War is raging. As on a racecourse,
The barriers down, out pour the chariots,
Gathering speed from lap to lap, and a driver
Tugging in vain at the reins is swept along
By his horses and heedless uncontrollable car.][13]

Thus Virgil brings home the basic theme of his poem: the virtues of the sturdy, patient, humble, dedicated farmer, the virtues that made Rome great, are being lost as the fabric of society disintegrates. The powerful simile at the close is the only such simile that appears in this book, and it serves to stress the epic grandeur of this conclusion.

In *Paradise Regained* Milton also establishes the middle style of his poem in the opening book by contrast with the epic style. But Milton has no need to present the contrast of styles within the first book itself. He needs only to remind the reader of his earlier achievement in epic and of the contrast of the opening book of this new poem with the epic similes and epic allusions that dominate the first book of *Paradise Lost:*

> I who e're while the happy Garden sung,
> By one mans disobedience lost, now sing
> Recover'd Paradise to all mankind,
> By one mans firm obedience fully tri'd
> Through all temptation, and the Tempter foil'd
> In all his wiles, defeated and repuls't,
> And *Eden* rais'd in the wast Wilderness.   (*PR* 1.1–7)

One is bound to compare this quiet, normal idiom with the great suspended sentence that opens *Paradise Lost,* with its epic inversion and allusion. Indeed, the first book of *Paradise Regained* contains no epic similes, no classical allusions, except when, near the end, Jesus declares that the pagan oracles have ceased, "at *Delphos* or else where" (1.456–58). Then, with a wry and witty touch, Milton seems to stress the georgic parallel by presenting Satan in the guise of one of the hard-pressed farmers in Virgil's first book—"Men to much misery and hardship born" (*PR* 1.341):

> But now an aged man in Rural weeds,
> Following, as seem'd, the quest of some stray Ewe,
> Or wither'd sticks to gather; which might serve
> Against a Winters day when winds blow keen,
> To warm him wet return'd from field at Eve,
> He saw approach.   (1.314–19)

Thus Milton establishes the middle, didactic style of his poem.

There is, however, another implication attached to the word "medius." It can mean "midway between"; that is, midway between two other styles, the humble and the grand, with frequent movements upward and downward. This action occurs constantly in the *Georgics,* as the common, earthy details of agriculture and animal culture intersect with movements toward the *grandiloquus.* That action is foreshadowed at the very outset of the poem, which begins with an informal, conversational address to his patron, summing up the contents of the four books in unassuming style:

> Quid faciat laetas segetes, quo sidere terram
> vertere, Maecenas, ulmisque adiungere vites
> conveniat, quae cura boum, qui cultus habendo
> sit pecori, apibus quanta experientia parcis,
> hinc canere incipiam.   (1.1–5)

Then, in the middle of a line, Virgil moves to an epic invocation of the gods:

> vos, o clarissima mundi
> lumina, labentem caelo quae ducitis annum,
> Liber et alma Ceres. (1.5–7)

> [What makes the crops rejoice, beneath what star
> To plough, and when to wed the vines to elms,
> The care of cattle, how to rear a flock,
> How much experience thrifty bees require:
> Of these, Maecenas, I begin to sing.
> You, sun and moon, our world's resplendent lights,
> Who lead the year revolving through the skies;
> And Bacchus and kind Ceres. (Bovie, 3)

This peculiar action of contrasting styles is then manifested throughout the following books, which display in each an increasingly stronger development toward the grand style, reaching a climax in Book Four. *Paradise Regained* develops a similar ascending movement toward the grand style.

Book One of the *Georgics* has throughout been devoted to the condition of humankind decreed by Jove (*pater ipse*) when he abolished the Golden Age and brought in the Age of Iron, with its harsh necessities:

> pater ipse colendi
> haud facilem esse viam voluit, primusque per artem
> movit agros, curis acuens mortalia corda,
> nec torpere gravi passus sua regna veterno. (1.121–24)

[The great Father himself has willed that the path of husbandry should not be smooth, and he first made art awake the fields, sharpening men's wits by care, nor letting his realm slumber in heavy lethargy.] (Fairclough, 89)

As a result, "Toil conquered the world, unrelenting toil, and want that pinches when life is hard" [labor omnia vicit / improbus et duris urgens in rebus egestas] (1.145–46).[14] Those famous lines set the tone for the opening book: how hard and demanding the life of the farmer is, a theme perfectly suited to the introduction of the frugal style of the poem.

Abruptly, in a way characteristic of this poem, Book Two opens with a gentler, more hopeful, indeed a joyous theme, as the poem celebrates the bounty of Bacchus. Now, says Virgil in another address to his patron, I will embark upon the open sea, but he at once draws back: he will sail close to shore. He will for the time being retrench his epic tendencies:

> non ego cuncta meis amplecti versibus opto,
> non mihi si linguae centum sint oraque centum,

ferrea vox. ades et primi lege litoris oram;
in manibus terrae: non hic te carmine ficto
atque per ambages et longa exorsa tenebo.   (2.42–46)

[I choose not to enfold
All things within my verse, not though I had
A hundred tongues and mouths, a voice of iron.
Now come with me and cruise along the shore;
Land is in reach: I'll not detain you here
With fancied themes, digressions, overtures.]   (Bovie, 31)

His witty extension of Homer's "ten tongues and ten mouths"[15] to an extrava-
gant hundred prepares the way for an equally humorous promise that he will
not keep, for this book contains the three most famous of all his "digressions":
the praise of Italy, the praise of spring, and lastly, most extravagantly, the
famous praise of the farmer's happy life:

O fortunatos nimium, sua si bona norint,
agricolas! quibus ipsa, procul discordibus armis,
fundit humo facilem victum iustissima tellus.   (2.458–60)

[O happy husbandmen! too happy, should they come to know their blessings! for
whom, far from the clash of arms, most righteous Earth, unbidden, pours forth from
her soil an easy sustenance.] (Fairclough, 149)

Thus, Book Two qualifies the arduous, precarious way of life presented in
Book One. Here, as we see, nature's bounty flows freely, almost overwhelm-
ing the farmer with abundance: life is "facilis," not "improbus." Virgil is
presenting two sides of the coin: sometimes nature can be harsh; at other
times an easy, happy collaboration can exist.

   Although constant work and care are needed to take advantage of nature's bounty, the stress falls upon the immense variety of nature's gifts, as the
poem ranges over all the known spaces of the earth, rising to epic grandeur in
its style as Virgil approaches the praise of Italy:[16]

Sed neque Medorum silvae, ditissima terra
nec pulcher Ganges atque auro turbidus Hermus
laudibus Italiae certent, non Bactra neque Indi
totaque turiferis Panchaia pinguis harenis.

. . . .

nec galeis densisque virum seges horruit hastis,
sed gravidae fruges et Bacchi Massicus umor
implevere; tenent oleae armentaque laeta.   (2.136–44)

[But] not the groves of Media, wealthy land,
Nor lovely Ganges, nor the golden streams

Of Lydia match Italy in praise;
Not India, Afghanistan, nor isles
Of Araby with incense-bearing sands.

. . . .

No human warriors sprang full-armed from her fields:
But teeming fruit and wine of the Campagna
Filled our Italian fields; fat herds and olives
Found their place in Italy's rich land.]   (Bovie, 35)

Then follow some thirty lines of epic praise, concluding with this eloquent apostrophe:

salve, magna parens frugum, Saturnia tellus,
magna virum: tibi res antiquae laudis et artis
ingredior, sanctos ausus recludere fontis,
Ascraeumque cano Romana per oppida carmen.   (2.173–76)

[All hail, Saturnian Land, our honored Mother!
For thee I broach these themes of ancient art
And dare disclose the sacred springs of verse,
Singing Hesiod's song through Roman towns.]   (Bovie, 37)

Then abruptly the style drops down to the didactic level:

Nunc locus arvorum ingeniis, quae robora cuique,
quis color et quae sit rebus natura ferendis.   (2.177–78)

[Now for the innate qualities of soils:
The color, strength, productive powers of each.]   (Bovie, 37)

Thus throughout Book Two the "digressions" rise from the middle style toward an epic expression of joy at nature's variety and generosity: the "digressions" carry the heart of the whole book's message, as Virgil creates his idealized version of country life as a vehicle for satire against the debilitating excesses of his corrupt society.

The second book of *Paradise Regained* displays a similar upward movement in style, as Satan presents his masque of temptation arising from an apparently pastoral or georgic setting: "a pleasant Grove, / With chaunt of tuneful Birds resounding loud" (2.289–90). From here bursts upon us the gorgeous feast, composed of dishes drawn from the four corners of the earth, accompanied by beauteous physical beings and music and smells that appeal to all the varied senses in a rich Spenserian medley of myth and assonance:

Nymphs of *Diana's* train, and *Naiades*
With fruits and flowers from *Amalthea's* horn,
And Ladies of th' *Hesperides,* that seem'd

> Fairer then feign'd of old, or fabl'd since
> Of Fairy Damsels met in Forest wide,
> By Knights of *Logres*, or of *Lyones*,
> *Lancelot*, or *Pelleas*, or *Pellenore*.   (2.355–61)

Is it simply a coincidence that this degenerate celebration of earth's bounty should appear in the same book as Virgil's celebration of the bounty of Italy? Perhaps so, but then Milton may well be inspired by Virgil's example to present this profane version of the misuse of earth's bounty. In any case, as in Virgil, the gorgeous scene is cut down by the brusque reply of Jesus:

> To whom thus Jesus temperately reply'd:
> Said'st thou not that to all things I had right?
> And who withholds my pow'r that right to use?   (2.378–80)

Thus the middle style of the poem comes to represent the self-control of the hero, as he answers Satan's increasingly elaborate temptations "patiently," "calmly," "unmov'd," "sagely," or, at one point, "fervently" (see *PR* 2.432, 3.43, 3.385, 4.109, 4.285, 3.121).

Near the end of his second book Virgil turns abruptly to indicate that the ethical principles of the good life in the farmer are indeed his own, as he intervenes with a highly personal appeal to the Muses, asking them to show him the deep causes of natural manifestations (2.475–82). Here is another sign of his ambition to write poetry that goes beyond his present limited effort. But if he cannot reach "those realms of nature," then he will be content to live in happy harmony with the surface joys of nature's abundance: "let my delight be the country, and the running streams amid the dells—may I love the waters and the woods, though fame be lost" (Fairclough, 149, 151).[17] After this digression within a digression, he returns to the praise of the farmer's life, lashing out at length against the evils of war and all varieties of worldly ambition:

> quos rami fructus, quos ipsa volentia rura
> sponte tulere sua, carpsit, nec ferrea iura
> insanumque forum aut populi tabularia vidit.
> sollicitant alii remis freta caeca, ruuntque
> in ferrum, penetrant aulas et limina regum;
> hic petit excidiis urbem miserosque penatis,
> ut gemma bibat et Sarrano dormiat ostro;
> condit opes alius defossoque incubat auro.   (2.500–507)

[The boughs by their own virtue bear him fruit,
He {the farmer} gathers what the willing fields supply;
Has not made contact with our ironclad laws,

Our frantic Forum, our Public Record Office.
Others lash the unknown seas with oars,
Rush at the sword, pay court in royal halls.
One destroys a city and its homes
To drink from jeweled cups and sleep on scarlet;
One hoards his wealth and lies on buried gold.]   (Bovie, 52)

Against these follies and corruptions, "The farmer drives his curved plough through the earth":

His year's work lies in this; thus he sustains
His homeland, his diminutive descendants,
His herds of stock, his much-deserving bullocks.   (Bovie, 52)

[agricola incurvo terram dimovit aratro: hinc anni labor, hinc patriam parvosque nepotes sustinet, hinc armenta boum meritosque iuvencos.] (2.513–15)

"Such a life," Virgil concludes, "the Sabines once embraced, / And Romulus and Remus; in this way / Etruria grew strong; thus Rome was formed" (Bovie, 53):

hanc olim veteres vitam coluere Sabini,
hanc Remus et frater, sic fortis Etruria crevit
scilicet et rerum facta est pulcherrima Roma.   (2.532–34)

Thus the last eighty-four lines of Virgil's second book are devoted to this climactic assertion of the moral and ethical values from which Romans have lapsed, and which must be restored if the empire is to recover its strength.

In *Paradise Regained* Milton likewise devotes the last fifty-four lines of his second book to a resounding assertion of similar values in the spiritual realm; the Son of God rejects the temptation of wealth by "patiently" replying that without the "Virtue, Valour, Wisdom" that Satan scorns, "Wealth" is "impotent,"

To gain dominion or to keep it gain'd.
Witness those ancient Empires of the Earth,
In highth of all thir flowing wealth dissolv'd:
But men endu'd with these have oft attain'd
In lowest poverty to highest deeds.   (2.434–38)

And he offers as examples not only Gideon, Jephtha, and David, but also "*Quintius, Fabricius, Curius, Regulus*":

For I esteem those names of men so poor
Who could do mighty things, and could contemn
Riches though offer'd from the hand of Kings.   (2.446–49)

Thus earlier in Book Two of the *Georgics* Virgil had set forth a similar list of four family names, examples of how Italy "has mothered a vigorous breed of men"—"the Decii, the Marii, the great Camilli, the Scipios" (Fairclough).[18] In this context, Milton's list seems to call forth the sort of classic virtue that Virgil celebrates and that Milton proceeds to explain in Socratic terms:

> Yet he who reigns within himself, and rules
> Passions, Desires, and Fears, is more a King;
> Which every wise and vertuous man attains:
> And who attains not, ill aspires to rule
> Cities of men, or head-strong Multitudes,
> Subject himself to Anarchy within
> Or lawless passions in him which he serves.   (2.466–72)

This is the principle that Cornford describes as Socrates's "discovery of the soul":

And by the soul he meant the seat of that faculty of insight which can know good from evil and infallibly choose the good. Self-knowledge implies the recognition of this true self. Self-examination is a discipline constantly needed to distinguish its judgment from the promptings of other elements in our nature, closely attached to the body and its distracting interests. Self-rule is the rule of the true self over those other elements.[19]

Both Milton and Virgil, exactly in the center of their poems, set forth the ethical ideals upon which their poems are based.

Milton then opens his third book with the temptation of military glory, with an epic roll of classical military heroes:

> Thy years are ripe, and over-ripe, the Son
> Of *Macedonian Philip* had e're these
> Won *Asia* and the Throne of *Cyrus* held
> At his dispose, young *Scipio* had brought down
> The *Carthaginian* pride, young *Pompey* quell'd
> The *Pontic* King and in triumph had rode.   (3.31–36)

In a similar vein, Virgil opens his third book with a mock-heroic celebration of Roman military glory. First Virgil presents an allegorical account of his epic plans, under the image of an elaborate temple with Caesar as its deity. He then describes his projected temple (poem) in hyperbolic terms that seem to create a parody of the heroic style. Here is what you want me to do, he seems to be saying to his friends; well, here is a sample of what I can do in the epic vein:

in foribus pugnam ex auro solidoque elephanto
Gangaridum faciam victorisque arma Quirini,
atque hic undantem bello magnumque fluentem
Nilum ac navali surgentis aere columnas.
addam urbes Asiae domitas pulsumque Niphaten
fidentemque fuga Parthum versisque sagittis
et duo rapta manu diverso ex hoste tropaea
bisque triumphatas utroque ab litore gentes.   (3.26–33)

On the temple doors, from gold and solid ivory
I will carve the Ganges, overpowered by Rome;
Elsewhere the swelling Nile, full flood with war,
And columns formed from prows of captured ships.
The sculpture I design will show the vanquished
Asian and Armenian mountain heights,
Retreating Parthians, shooting arrows back,[20]
The double trophies seized from far-flung foes
Of both worlds: Roman wins in East and West.   (Bovie, 58)

After this high-flung passage, Virgil draws back: he is not yet ready to undertake the epic mission that his friends expect him to perform. Later, when the time is ripe, he will pursue the epic model:

mox tamen ardentis accingar dicere pugnas
Caesaris et nomen fama tot ferre per annos,
Tithoni prima quot abest ab origine Caesar.   (3.46–48)

Later, I shall don the epic robes,
To sing of Caesar's fiery wars, extend
His name as far in future years as now
It traces back to Troy its origins.   (Bovie, 59)

I am stressing Virgil's reluctance, indeed refusal, to proceed with the writing of his epic until the time is ripe, for here is another aspect of the *Georgics* that bears some resemblance to *Paradise Regained*. Milton's Son of God constantly rejects temptations to achieve the promised goal of Israel's kingship on the oft-repeated grounds that the time has not yet come: trials and tribulations must precede the promised victory, which will of course be gained in the spiritual realm, not in terms of worldly reign.

Virgil's refusal to accept the epic role prematurely is enforced by a contest of styles similar to that which prevails in Milton's poem. One might even say, to press the point hard, that Virgil's flights into epic style in the *Georgics,* recognized by all classical scholars, represent a temptation to display his epic wings; but after each such display, the poem is drawn back to earth by an abrupt return to the didactic, lower style. Thus here in Book Three, after his hyperbolic display of epic promise, he abruptly moves down to a rude description in a lower style, indeed *humilis:*

> Seu quis Olympiacae miratus praemia palmae
> pascit equos, seu quis fortis ad aratra iuvencos,
> corpora praecipue matrum legat. optima torvae
> forma bovis, cui turpe caput, cui plurima cervix,
> et crurum tenus a mento palearia pendent;
> tum longo nullus lateri modus; omnia magna,
> pes etiam; et camuris hirtae sub cornibus aures.   (3.49–55)

> Whoever raises horses to compete
> In games or breeds stout bullocks for the plough
> Should choose the mothers' bodies carefully.
> The best-formed cow looks fierce, her head is coarse,
> Her neck is large, her dewlaps hang down loose
> From throat to shank; flanks rangy as you wish,
> And largeness through the limbs, including feet,
> Are preferable, and look for shaggy ears
> Below the crooked horns.   (Bovie, 59)

Thus throughout the *Georgics* Virgil creates his poem through the placement of contrasting "panels," as Brooks Otis likes to call them—panels in contrasting styles that may well have served Milton as a model for presenting his patterns of temptation and rejection in contrasting styles.[21]

Despite Virgil's apology to his patron, epic style is far from being rejected in his third book, which displays many panels in a high style, mingled with the didactic middle voice. Thus we have the vivid account of chariot racing (103–22), the description of the warhorse (179–208), the mock-heroic battle of the bulls (219–41), the account of frozen Russia (349–83), and, strongest of all, the long concluding account of the fearful plague that struck the animals in Noricum (478–566). Through such passages the level of style is raised far above that of the second book.

A similar development may be observed in *Paradise Regained*. The temptation of the banquet is done in Spenserian style, but the temptation of the Parthian empire in Book Three (269–344) is done overtly in the manner of classical epic, including an epic catalog with long rolls of proper names (signifying worldly power) and an epic simile as conclusion.

Virgil then in his fourth book rises to the highest level of the grand style, first in the mock-heroic warfare of the bees (69–87) and, climactically, in the sustained epic style of the story of Aristaeus's visit to his mother, the river nymph Cyrene, and the subsequent tale of his struggle with Proteus (315–452). The passage contains several Homeric echoes, as Otis has shown (194–97), and indeed it is told in a style so strongly inflated that it seems almost a parody of epic manner. Virgil is perhaps again teasing his friends by giving them this final elaborate example of epic prowess. Similarly, Milton in his fourth book rises to a climactic example of epic style in his account of the power and glory of ancient Rome, with its abundant stream of proper names, followed by the equally grand account of ancient Greece.

One final congruence remains to be considered. Virgil in the middle of Book Four (at line 281 in a book of 566 lines) changes the mode of procedure: he shifts from didactic to narrative, with the tales of Aristaeus and Orpheus, presented in tripartite arrangement: the sad tale of Orpheus is folded within two aspects of the tale of Aristaeus. Emphasis falls upon discovery of the *bougonia,* the method of restoring a swarm of bees by beating the carcass of a calf or bullock: life emerging from death. Otis in particular sees all this as a myth of "resurrection," though of "tragically flawed resurrection" in the case of Orpheus (211–12). Otis has been taken to task by younger critics for "christianizing" the poem by using terms like "sin," "atonement," and "resurrection." Surely, as Perkell points out, the *bougonia* does not involve resurrection: the old swarm is dead and cannot be recovered, but a new swarm can be created; thus life continues.[22] Still, we may ask, may not Milton, with the medieval and Renaissance background of "christianizing" Virgil, have read the poem in a way similar to Otis's reading?[23]

In any case, Milton, shortly past the middle of his last book (at line 394 in a book of 639 lines), also changes his mode of procedure, moving from the panels of temptation and rejection to narrative; and he does so in a tripartite manner, giving first the ordeal of the storm; next, the triumph of the Son's standing on the pinnacle of the temple; and lastly, the banquet and heavenly hymn by which the angels celebrate his victory. One might apply to Milton's ending some of the words that Otis gives in concluding his account of Virgil's ending: "What stands out and is meant to stand out is the central Orpheus panel, where the elliptical, concentrated, emotional style" comes "at exactly the point where we are led to expect revelation" (214). "Tempt not the Lord thy God, he said and stood. / But Satan smitten with amazement fell" (4.561–62). Through that elliptical, concentrated citation, Satan is struck by the revelation that he has been tempting a man endowed with supernatural powers.

All these similarities, together with Milton's interest in the four-part structure of the *Georgics,* as displayed in his *Art of Logic,* combine to suggest that Milton in *Paradise Regained* is engaged in creating an example of the Renaissance art of creative imitation, evoking and transcending classic form and classic style. Despite the derogation of classical poetry so vehemently expressed by the Son of God in Book Four, the form and style of the poem indicate the enduring value of classical models.

We should also consider the meaning of the *Georgics* analogy in relation to Milton's whole poetical career, for acceptance of this analogy completes for Milton the traditional Virgilian triad: pastoral, georgic, and epic, the Virgilian *rota*—as the Middle Ages and the Renaissance interpreted Virgil's career.[24] As Neuse, Low, and Hale have recognized, *Paradise Regained* may be regarded as Milton's way of declaring his participation in this great tradition of poetical achievement. Tillyard long ago suggested that some sort of Virgilian allusion seemed to be implied in the opening line of *Paradise Regained:* "I who e'er while the happy Garden sung." He interpreted the line as a reference to the discarded opening of the *Aeneid:*[25]

> Ille ego, qui quondam gracili modulatus avena
> carmen, et egressus silvis vicina coegi
> ut quamvis avido parerent arva colono,
> gratum opus agricolis.

[I am he who once tuned my song on a slender reed, then, leaving the woodland, constrained the neighbouring fields to serve the husbandmen, however grasping—a work welcome to farmers.] (Fairclough, 241)

Milton seems certainly to echo this passage, contained in Renaissance editions of Virgil; but a similar allusion to Virgil's writings in the pastoral and georgic kinds is contained in the envoi that concludes the *Georgics:*

> Haec super arvorum cultu pecorumque canebam
> et super arboribus, Caesar dum magnus ad altum
> fulminat Euphraten bello victorque volentis
> per populos dat iura viamque adfectat Olympo.
> illo Vergilium[26] me tempore dulcis alebat
> Parthenope, studiis florentem ignobilis oti,
> carmina qui lusi pastorum audaxque iuventa,
> Tityre, te patulae cecini sub tegmine fagi.   (4.559–66)

> [All this I've sung of cultivating fields,
> Of tending flocks and caring for the trees,
> While by the deep Euphrates noble Caesar
> Thunders triumph, grants the reign of law
> To grateful subjects, clears his path to heaven.
> All this time sweet Naples nourished me,
> Her Virgil, in the flower of humble peace,
> In study: I who played at shepherd's songs
> In callow youth, and sang, O Tityrus,
> Of you at ease beneath your spreading beech.]   (Bovie, 111)

The last line of the *Georgics* thus repeats, almost verbatim, the opening line of Virgil's *Eclogues*. In view of Virgil's promise to write an epic in praise of Caesar's conquests, the famous triad or *rota* is already potentially here.

Milton, in reminding his readers of the pastoral of Paradise in his great epic, is not, I think, in any way denigrating his achievement there, but, through the Virgilian echo, is implying that this new "Poem in IV Books" will complete the famous triad by dealing with a *subject* that is "Above Heroic." He does not imply, however, that this higher subject will be pursued in a high style; quite the contrary: as we have seen, the opening book sets forth the middle style for which, since Servius, the *Georgics* has been the model.

Thus acceptance of the *Georgics* analogy will explain why Milton, in his second edition of 1674, changed *Paradise Lost* from its original ten-book division into a poem in twelve books—to enforce the analogy with the Virgilian triad. Of course Milton's sequence in this triad does not follow the chronological pattern of Virgil, but does this matter? The essential thing is that he has, at long last, and quite unexpectedly, completed the triadic pattern. Yet the question remains: Why did Milton choose to follow the ten-book division in 1667, when the redivision of Books Seven and Ten was so easy to perform because of their clear subdivision into two parts? Did Milton at some earlier point intend to have a twelve-book division? But he chose to issue *Paradise Lost* in 1667 as "A Poem Written in Ten Books." By choosing this division Milton announced his work as a modern poem, not one that adheres to ancient tradition, not a poem in the Homeric and Virgilian divisions of twenty-four and twelve. Instead he chose to align his epic with the modern poems that observed great freedom in dealing with Homer and Virgil: the twenty-book epic of Tasso, or the ten-book epic of Camoens.[27]

We may well believe that when Milton had at last completed his epic, "In darkness, and with dangers compast round," and in declining health, he had no thought of filling out the Virgilian triad with a georgic poem. But as he recovered from his enormous effort, the possibility of filling out the traditional triad seems to have emerged, perhaps in part through the famous question of Thomas Ellwood: "Thou hast said much here of *Paradise Lost*; but what hast thou to say of *Paradise found?*"[28]

Finally, we should note that Virgil was writing the *Georgics* during or at the very end of the turbulent period of civil wars in the Roman empire, with Octavian at last emerging as victor in the internecine conflicts. Milton is writing his own four-book poem in the late 1660s, after the period of the civil wars in England, when Cromwell had appeared to Milton as the only hope of bringing peace to the troubled land. It would seem that this historical parallel could hardly have escaped Milton's notice. But Milton's faith in the power of mortal men to bring peace has been dissolved, just as the hope of Virgil has been betrayed by the corruptions that followed the rule of Augustus, as both Satan and Jesus describe them in the fourth book of *Paradise Regained*. Thus Satan offers the Roman empire in decay:

> This Emperour hath no Son, and now is old,
> Old and lascivious, and from *Rome* retir'd
> To *Capreae* an Island small but strong
> On the *Campanian* shore, with purpose there
> His horrid lusts in private to enjoy,
> Committing to a wicked Favourite
> All publick cares, and yet of him suspicious,
> Hated of all, and hating; with what ease
> Indu'd with Regal Vertues as thou art,
> Appearing, and beginning noble deeds,
> Might'st thou expel this monster from his Throne
> Now made a stye, and in his place ascending
> A victor people free from servile yoke?   (4.90–102)

But the Son of God rejects this temptation with words that sound like an echo of Virgil's own laments for the loss of ancient virtue in his people:

> Let his tormenter Conscience find him out,
> For him I was not sent, nor yet to free
> That people victor once, now vile and base,
> Deservedly made vassal, who once just,
> Frugal, and mild, and temperate, conquer'd well,
> But govern ill the Nations under yoke,
> Peeling thir Provinces, exhausted all
> By lust and rapine.   (4.130–37)

Milton's bitter experience has taught him not to place his hopes in any mortal man, but only in "The Son of God, with Godlike force indu'd" (4.602).

Yale University

NOTES

1. The *Georgics* has 2,188 lines, *Paradise Regained*, 2,070 lines.

2. Michael C. J. Putnam, *Virgil's Poem of the Earth: Studies in the Georgics* (Princeton, 1979); Gary B. Miles, *Virgil's Georgics: A New Interpretation* (Berkeley and Los Angeles, 1980); David O. Ross Jr., *Virgil's Elements: Physics and Poetry in the Georgics* (Princeton, 1987); Christine G. Perkell, *The Poet's Truth: A Study of the Poet in Virgil's Georgics* (Berkeley and Los Angeles, 1989); *Virgil: Georgics*, 2 vols., ed. Richard F. Thomas (Cambridge, 1988). Many other valuable books and essays have appeared; I list here only those which I have used.

3. *"Paradise Regained:* The Meditative Combat," *ELH* 27 (1960): 223–47; reprinted with

minor revisions in *The Paradise Within* (New Haven, 1964). My frequent use of the words "meditation" and "meditative" in this essay gave the editor of the *Variorum* volume on *Paradise Regained* the impression that I was regarding the *Georgics* as a meditative poem—something I never had in mind. Starting with this misapprehension, he proceeded to reject the analogy; see *A Variorum Commentary on the Poems of John Milton*, vol. 4, ed. Walter MacKellar (New York, 1975), 15. In revising this essay for my book on Milton, *Poet of Exile* (New Haven, 1980), I expunged nearly all occurrences of the terms "meditative" or "meditation" and removed all reference to the *Georgics*, reserving discussion of the analogy for an appendix in which, with the help of classical scholarship, the variations in Virgil's style could be considered as analogous to Milton's variations in his poem. By these drastic revisions I hoped to place the emphasis upon the main point, the "contest of styles."

4. E. M. W. Tillyard, *Milton* (London, 1930), 316. Tillyard was, I believe, the first to suggest the *Georgic* analogy (322).

5. The arguments for regarding the poem as a brief epic have been ably presented by Barbara Lewalski in *Milton's Brief Epic: The Genre, Meaning, and Art of "Paradise Regained"* (Providence, R.I., 1966).

6. Anthony Low, "Milton, *Paradise Regained*, and Georgic," *PMLA* 98 (1983): 152–69; Low, *The Georgic Revolution* (Princeton, 1985).

7. *Virgil's "Georgics": A Modern Verse Translation*, trans. Smith Palmer Bovie (Chicago, 1956), xi.

8. Low, *Georgic Revolution*, 325.

9. *Complete Prose Works of John Milton*, 8 vols., ed. Don M. Wolfe et al. (New Haven, 1953–82), 8:308, 394. Hereafter designated YP and cited by volume and page number in the text. Quotations of Milton's poetry are from *The Riverside Milton*, ed. Roy Flannagan (Boston, 1998), and are cited by book and line number parenthetically in the text.

10. See Walter Ong's discussion of the dating in YP 8:144–47.

11. *Servii Grammatici Qui Feruntur in Vergilii Carmina Commentarii*, 4 vols., ed. G. Thilo and H. Hagen (Leipzig, 1881–1902), vol. 3, fasc. 1, pp. 1–2.

12. For the Latin text I have used the Loeb edition, *Virgil: Eclogues, Georgics, Aeneid, 1–6*, rev. ed., trans. H. Rushton Fairclough (1935; reprint, Cambridge, Mass., 1974).

13. *Georgics*, trans. L. P. Wilkinson (Hamondsworth, 1982), with introduction and notes, 73.

14. Translation from Fairclough, 91. For the controversy over the implications of the word "improbus," see Richard Jenkyns, *Virgil's Experience* (Oxford, 1998), 335–40, and the appendix, 678–84.

15. *The Iliad of Homer*, trans. Richard Lattimore (Chicago, 1951), 2.489–90. Thomas says of lines 45–46: "The very claim is itself a piece of ironical fiction." See Thomas, ed., *Georgics*, 1:164.

16. For a detailed analysis of the *laus Italiae*, see Jenkyns, *Virgil's Experience*, 341–69.

17. "Rura mihi et rigui placeant in vallibus amnes, / flumina amem silvasque inglorius" (2.485–86).

18. "Haec genus acre virum . . . / haec Decios, Marios magnosque Camillos, / Scipiadas" (2.167–70).

19. F. M. Cornford, *Before and After Socrates* (Cambridge, 1950), 50–51.

20. It seems possible that this allusion to Parthian archery, along with a similar allusion in Book Four (313–14), may lie behind Milton's lines toward the end of Book Three: "How quick they wheel'd, and flying behind them shot / Sharp sleet of arrowie showers against the face / Of thir pursuers, and overcame by flight" (323–25).

21. Brooks Otis, *Virgil: A Study in Civilized Poetry* (Oxford, 1964), 184, 208. Hereafter cited in the text by page number.

22. Perkell, *Poet's Truth,* 139–48.

23. See the essay by Colin Burrow, "Virgils, from Dante to Milton," in *The Cambridge Companion to Virgil,* ed. Charles Martindale (Cambridge, 1997), 79–90. This collection also contains a valuable essay on the *Georgics* by William Batstone (125–44), with a helpful summary of scholarship on the poem.

24. Milton's *Poems* of 1645 represent his pastoral youth. On *rota,* see Richard Neuse, "Milton and Spenser: The Virgilian Triad Revisited," *ELH* 45 (1978): 606–39. Neuse cites the account of the *rota* by Ernst Curtius, *European Literature and the Latin Middle Ages,* trans. Willard Trask (New York, 1953), 231–32. See also Low, *Georgic Revolution,* 3–4; and Albert C. Labriola, "Portraits of an Artist: Milton's Changing Self-Image," in *Milton Studies* 19, *Urbane Milton: The Latin Poetry,* ed. James A. Freeman and Anthony Low (Pittsburgh, 1984), 179–94.

25. Neuse, "Milton and Spenser," 615; Low, *Georgic Revolution,* 328–29; John K. Hale,"*Paradise Lost:* A Poem in Twelve Books, or Ten?" *Philological Quarterly* 74 (1995): 131–49, esp. 140–41; Tillyard, *Milton,* 322.

26. Classical scholars writing in English almost universally adopt the spelling "Virgil" even though the Latin text here reads "Vergilium" and the *Oxford Classical Dictionary* (Oxford, 1949), under the entry "Virgil," notes that "inscriptions prove *Vergilius* as the Latin form."

27. For the many efforts to explain Milton's ten-book division, see Hale, "A Poem in Twelve Books, or Ten?" Milton's admiration for Tasso is recorded in his famous account of his hopes to write an epic in *The Reason of Church-Government* (1641): "Whether that Epick form whereof the two poems of *Homer,* and those other two of *Virgil* and *Tasso* are a diffuse, and the book of *Job* a brief model" (YP 1:813). The latter reference to the Book of Job is of course the site from which the theory of the "brief epic" has been developed. For Milton's familiarity with the ten-book *Lusiad,* see C. M. Bowra, *From Virgil to Milton* (London, 1945), 238–39; and my *Milton: Poet of Exile,* chap. 9.

28. See *The Early Lives of Milton,* ed. Helen Darbishire (1932; reprint, New York, 1965), liv–lvii. Ellwood continues: "He made me no Answer, but sate some time in a Muse: then brake of that Discourse, and fell upon another Subject. . . . And when afterwards I went to wait on him . . . he shewed me his Second Poem, called *Paradise Regained;* and in a pleasant Tone said to me, *This is owing to you: for you put it into my Head, by the Question you put to me in Chalfont; which before I had not thought of.*" Scholars have tended to regard this account as naive, but it has the ring of truth.

REDEMPTION AND *PARADISE REGAINED*

Regina M. Schwartz

WHAT DOES MILTON MEAN by the re-gaining of Paradise? The question is simple enough, but the answer is anything but simple. In his epic so titled, Milton deliberately sets out to speak of the restoration of Paradise. The subject is announced, proleptically, at the beginning of *Paradise Lost:* "til one greater man restore us and regain the blissful seat," and then it is announced explicitly as the subject of *Paradise Regained* at its own opening: "I who erewhile the happy garden sung, / By one man's disobedience lost, now sing / Recovered Paradise to all mankind" (1.1–3). And it is reiterated at the epic's close: "now thou hast avenged / Supplanted Adam, and by vanquishing / Temptation, hast regained lost Paradise" (4.606–8).[1] These testimonials to Milton's ostensible subject matter are ample enough without the famous apocryphal witness Thomas Ellwood offers in his autobiography:

> After some common Discourses had passed between us, he called for a Manuscript of his which being brought he delivered to me, bidding me take it home with me, and read it at my Leisure: and when I had so done, return it to him, with my Judgment thereupon.
>
> When I came home, and had set my self to read it, I found it was the Excellent Poem, which he entituled *Paradise Lost*. . . . He asked me how I like it, and what I thought of it . . . and after some further Discourse about it, I pleasantly said to him, "Thou has said much here of *Paradise Lost;* but what hast thou to say of Paradise found? He made me no Answer, but sate some time in a Muse: then brake of[f] that Discourse. . . .
>
> And when afterwards I went to wait on him [in London] . . . he shewed me his Second Poem, called *Paradise Regained;* and in a pleasant Tone said to me, This is owing to you: for you put it into my Head, by the question you put to me at Chalfont; which before I had not thought of.[2]

But what does Milton mean by the restoration of Paradise, the repair of the ruin of our first parents, the regaining of bliss, the redemption of man, even by salvation? What is Milton's understanding of salvation in the context of theological positions on the subject? The Nicene Creed confessed that it was "for the sake of us men and for the purpose of our salvation" that Christ "came down and was made flesh, was made man, suffered, was raised on the

third day, ascended into the heavens and will come to judge living and dead."
But neither this nor any later dogmas describe how these events, historical and heavenly, achieve salvation. Furthermore the components of this
confession—the life and teachings, the suffering and death, the Resurrection
and exaltation—received different emphases at different times. In the early
church, it was the life and teachings that offered an example, so much so that
the apostolic fathers have been critiqued summarily: "The most astonishing
feature was the failure to grasp the significance of the death of Christ."[3] The
apologists, eager to depict Christ as the fulfillment of the hopes of all the
nations, not just the Jews, even depicted him as answering the hopes of
Greek philosophy.[4] By the Reformation, the emphasis had shifted decisively
to the suffering of Christ. And so, the theological solutions Milton could
invoke have turned to the Incarnation, Passion, Resurrection, or the Second
Coming of Christ; with differing emphases, any or all of these have signaled
the redemption of man. Instead, Milton describes the foiled temptation of
Jesus by Satan in the wilderness, an episode drawn from the Gospels (Luke
4:1–13; Matt. 4:1–11; Mark 1:12–13), but one which has not, in any theological tradition, been called upon to suffice as the definition of the redemption
of mankind.

No such problem attends defining man's Fall. Milton tells us immediately in no uncertain terms what the loss of Paradise means: "death and all
our woe," and he has a divine messenger paint a devastating visual and verbal
portrait of the lineaments of that human misery in the final books of *Paradise
Lost*. He is engaged obsessively in defining the cause: Why is mankind lost?
Because man disobeyed God. Why? Because he succumbed to the temptation by Satan. And why did Satan tempt man? Out of envy and revenge. And
why was he envious? Because the elevation of the Son injured his pride, and
so on. From one perspective, *Paradise Lost* is a sustained rational inquiry into
the cause and meaning of the Fall of man. But in contrast to all of this clarity
of explanation of the loss of Paradise, what it means for man to be restored to
Paradise, to be redeemed, and why man is redeemed are far more mysterious. This is no accident. For Milton, salvation is a mystery, the mystery of a
divine goodness unmerited by man, and he is careful to maintain that mystery
as such.

I

Contrary to the Milton criticism that takes its lead from Calton who first
claimed in the 1752 edition that the temptations concerned the question of
the divine identity of Jesus, relying on patristic exegesis, the temptations of
Paradise Regained are not designed to prove the divine nature of Jesus.[5] That

nature is never in doubt in Milton's brief epic, as Ashraf H. A. Rushdy has argued recently and as Irene Samuel had urged before him.⁶ "The idea of an 'identity contest' has achieved that rare place in critical debate where it is both premise and conclusion, both the question asked and the answer given" (Rushdy, 193). Rushdy shows why it is the wrong question and the wrong answer and goes on to demonstrate how this conviction leads to deeply distorted readings of the poem. Making the final temptation on the pinnacle the decisive scene in which Jesus does or does not manifest his divinity in a kind of apotheosis, scholars have attached themselves to one of five options, as Rushdy astutely discerns: (1) when Jesus stands on the pinnacle he is divine, that is, he is God; (2) he reveals, only at the pinnacle scene, that he is divine but not God the Father; (3) Jesus achieves "some degree" of divinity in the pinnacle scene; (4) he is both God and man in the final scene; and (5) Jesus is a "mere man," hence in need of divine help to stand on the pinnacle. Instead, argues Rushdy, Jesus is consistent: in his final temptation as in his earlier ones, Jesus does not invoke his divinity to bolster his case or resort to miracle. As he so eloquently (and economically) puts it: "Milton gives us a Jesus who is, from the baptism, evidently divine, and who expresses that divinity in meritorious obedience to God" (204). Surely he is right, and to corroborate his conclusion that the poem does not include progressive or sudden revelations of the divine nature of Jesus, we need only note that at the outset of the epic, the narrator identifies Jesus as the Son of God, so we are never in doubt:

> nor was long
> His witness [John the Baptist's] unconfirmed: on him baptized
> Heaven opened, and in likeness of a dove
> The Spirit descended, while the Father's voice
> From Heav'n pronounced him his beloved Son.   (1.28–32)

Milton specifies that Satan bore witness to that baptismal announcement

> That heard the Adversary, who roving still
> . . . .
> About the world . . . th'exalted man, to whom
> Such high attest was giv'n, a while surveyed
> With wonder.   (1.33–38)

So Satan is never in doubt. And Jesus is also never in doubt about his divine nature and his office as Savior:

> My Father's voice,
> Audibly heard from Heav'n, pronounced me his,
> Me his beloved Son, in whom alone

> He was well-pleased; by which I knew the time
> Now full, that I no more should live obscure,
> But openly begin, as best becomes
> The authority which I derived from Heaven.   (1.283–89)

Why would Milton include so many repeated references to the announcement of Jesus' divinity if he intended it to be revealed only at the end,
at the final temptation? Or, as Irene Samuel has asked polemically,

What would [Milton] have said to readings of *Paradise Regained* that make its meaning turn on sudden secret mysterious revelations from on high to the protagonist, not
one of which is narrated in the gospels—his main source—and not one of which is so
much as indicated by a single word in his poem. . . . What would he say to the subtle
exegetes who have supplied an *anagnorisis,* and with it a theophany, and from that a
whole action leading to the discovery of Christ's identity—all out of what he did *not*
write into his poem?[7]

Milton is willing to include a description of divine revelation at the baptism of
Jesus, where his source is scriptural. "But," insists Samuel, "on the supposed
revelation by which, according to recent commentary, his protagonist comes
to know his own divinity Milton is as silent as scripture" (118–19). These
impatient Miltonists could find common cause with Luther, who ridiculed
the scholastics who worried over the nature of Christ mercilessly, labeling
their inquiry as "sophistic": "What difference does that make to me?" he
continued. "That he is man and God by nature, that he has for his own self;
but that he has exercised his office and poured out his love, becoming my
Savior and Redeemer—that happens for my consolation and benefit."[8]

What interests Luther also interests Milton—that Jesus is Savior and
Redeemer—but the reason that so many Miltonists have for so long been
blindsided by the identity debate is not hard to discern, for the doctrines on
the natures of Christ have been well articulated in Christian theology since
Nicea, while doctrines of salvation have not been. As one historian of theology notes astutely,

The very absence of explicit dogmatic and extensive polemical treatment of the meaning of salvation makes it necessary as well as hazardous to find some other scheme for
organizing the doctrinal material on this subject. . . . For example, . . . since the
doctrine of the person of Christ did become a dogma even though the doctrine of the
work of Christ did not, the history of doctrine could examine the major alternative
theories about the person of Christ with a view toward making explicit the definition
of salvation at work in each.[9]

The vital connection between the person of Christ and work of Christ has not
always been apparent to the Miltonists who have engaged in debates about

the person of Jesus to the neglect of salvation. But in *Paradise Regained,*
Milton portrays Jesus as centrally preoccupied with how to begin his saving
work:

> Meanwhile the Son of God,
>
> . . . .
>
> Musing and much revolving in his breast,
> How best the mighty work he might begin
> Of Saviour to mankind, and which way first
> Publish his Godlike office now mature,
> One day forth walked alone, the Spirit leading.
>
> (1.183–89)

For Milton, the mighty work of Jesus alone can achieve salvation for mankind; neither the works of the church nor even the faith of men have any
consequence without the mighty and lonely saving work of Jesus.

II

But if the temptations of Jesus need no longer be mined to discern and
debate the person of Jesus, what other purpose are they serving? Ironically
enough, we need look no further than the title, *Paradise Regained,* to find our
answer. The temptations Satan offers to Jesus are the temptations of redemption. Seeing that Jesus is ruminating over the best way to begin his mighty
work, Satan offers him solutions. In each of his temptations, Satan is giving
Jesus a way to understand redemption: each of them is plausible, each has
had its historical heyday, each has been regarded as a saving activity in either
pagan or Christian contexts (or both), and many of these understandings of
redemption even have a savior attached to them. Each has scriptural precedent and each can also be found in the Christian tradition. Furthermore,
each of these understandings of redemption was available to Milton when he
composed *Paradise Regained* in Restoration England. But none will satisfy
Jesus. In his quest for how to fulfill his role as Savior—ruminating on "how
best the mighty work he might begin"—he is radically alone, without contemporary or historical precedent. Satan's offers are the offers of history, and they
are of no help to him. And yet, having no example before him, Jesus must,
nonetheless, become the example himself. *Paradise Regained* offers a vexing
account of salvation: Jesus refuses all the examples before him of saving acts
and saviors, and others are to be saved only insofar as they imitate Jesus'
example, the example of refusal.

While the persistence with which Miltonists have focused their attention on the question of the identity of Jesus has led them away from this

pressing question of what it means to regain Paradise, that problem is indeed the constant focus of conversation between Satan and Jesus in the wilderness. The first temptation offers, logically enough, the most obvious understanding of redeeming: saving is feeding. Extended explicitly as the solution to saving, this first offer sets the terms for the others:

> But if thou be the Son of God, command
> That out of these hard stones be made thee bread;
> *So shalt thou save thyself and us relieve*
> *With food,* whereof we wretched seldom taste.
>
> (1.342–45; my emphasis)

Satan is neither bizarre nor original to understand salvation as feeding; he is scriptural. Not only did Joseph save his brothers, the tribes of Israel, by feeding them, and Boaz sustain Ruth, and hence the Davidic line, with grain, but also the ancient Israelites understood feeding as saving when they begged for food in the wilderness. For the hungry, salvation is food. Then too, Yhwh also understood salvation that way when he rained food from the heavens, miraculously, enough to feed everyone. And he alludes repeatedly to the Promised Land, the earthly paradise, as the land where milk and honey flow. In the New Testament, Jesus multiplies loaves and fishes miraculously to feed his flock, and before his suffering begins he asks to be remembered by eating the bread that symbolizes his broken body. That act is ritualized to become the saving work of the Eucharist.

But Milton's Jesus turns down the temptation of thinking salvation as feeding: "thinkst thou such force [saving force] in bread?" Is Jesus daring to reject the option, so often offered in the Scripture, of miraculous feeding? Is casting aspersions on the Roman doctrine of transubstantiation—which Milton believed to claim that the bread, the element itself, could have saving force, and not just the faith of the communicant—so important that he would deny Scripture? Or do the biblical precedents on feeding demand some interpreting, and according to what principle? Elsewhere I have argued for the hermeneutic of charity: that for Milton, the Scripture does not say anything that would run counter to charity.[10] Here, his preoccupation is different. Precisely because his interlocutor is unworthy—he likes not the giver—charity is misplaced. Here, the hermeneutic principle is as fiercely focused as Milton's theme and plot are on one concern: obedience. Hence, Jesus interprets the manna story, not to signal salvation through bread, but to demonstrate that salvation depends solely on obedience to God. He follows the spirit of Exodus, chapter 16, where God rains bread from the heavens but asks the receivers to count on that sustenance and rise to the challenge of living with the assumption that each will have his needs met. In the wilderness, the Israelites beg for food, are indeed given manna, but fail to follow their Giver's will: " 'That,' said Moses to them, 'is the bread Yahweh gives you to eat. This is Yahweh's command: Everyone must gather enough of it for his needs.' . . . When they measured in an omer of what they had gathered, the man who had gathered more had not too much, the man who had gathered less had not too little. Each found he had gathered what he needed" (Exod. 16:15–18). Distrusting providence, they reject both the will of God and the divine economy of fair distribution: they hoard the manna. "Moses said to them, 'No one must keep any of it for tomorrow.' But some would not listen and kept part of it for the following day, and it bred maggots and smelt foul; and Moses was angry with them" (Exod. 16:19–20).[11] Later, when the murmuring Israelites complain of manna, distrusting providence again, Yhwh answers their demand for meat with a plague of quail:

Again the Israelites started wailing and said, "If only we had meat to eat! We remember the fish we had in Egypt at no cost, also the cucumbers, melons, leeks, onions and garlic. But now . . . never see anything but this manna." . . . The Lord said to Moses, "Tell the people, 'Now the Lord will give you meat, and you will eat it. You will not eat it for just one day, or two days, or five, ten or twenty days, but for a whole month—until it comes out of your nostrils and you loathe it—because you have rejected the Lord who is among you, and have wailed before him, "Why did we ever leave Egypt?" ' " (11:4–6, 18–20)

These are the scriptural texts Jesus alludes to in order to illustrate, not the saving power of bread or meat, but obedience (1.351). Refusing to "distrust," Jesus hungers only to do his father's will (2.259). "My meat is to do the will of him that sent me" (John 4:34).

Satan does not discern this hermeneutic right away and returns to the manna story to suggest, in his envious reading, that after all, God took care of the others in the wilderness, feeding the ancient Israelites and even Elijah—but does not take care of Jesus. Uninfected by this envy, Jesus responds with his own principle of obedience: if God has not fed him, then he must not need feeding (PR 2.318). The satanic principle of envy has no persuasive power at all. When Satan renews his efforts to tempt Jesus with food, he sets a banquet table before him, punctuating his temptation of the banquet three times with the repetition, "sit and eat." The phrase is from Exodus, chapter 24, where the elders sit and eat in a covenant with God. Like the offer of bread, this is a scriptural allusion with redemptive overtones: Yhwh is saving the Israelites from bondage and delivering them through his covenant to an earthly paradise. "Sit and eat" has another allusion, to Thomas Tallis's hymn in the Book of Common Prayer, one of the sources of George Herbert's "Love III," the Eucharistic lyric that concludes "so I did sit and eat." Here the saving is apocalyptic; the banquet obviously alludes to the heavenly banquet. But Jesus also rejects this apocalyptic "answer" to salvation. Rejecting the giver, he must reject the gift: "thereafter as I like the giver" (2.321–22). Anticipating recent gift theory, Milton understood that both the giver and the receiver are part and parcel of what constitutes "the gift." When they are false, the gift is false: "thy pompous delicacies I contemn /And count they specious gifts no gifts but guiles"(2.390–91).[12] He plumbs the doctrine of things indifferent, showing Satan his error, for according to that doctrine it is not all meats that are now allowed contra the Levitical prohibitions; the meats that had been reserved for idolatry are still forbidden, and Satan is just such an idol, making these idolatrous foods unclean even under the doctrine of things indifferent. The entire banquet scene is an exemplum on the succinct verse from 1 Corinthians: "Ye cannot drink the cup of the Lord and the cup of devils: ye cannot be partakers of the Lord's table and the table of devils" (10:28).

Even as Satan pretends to have received this message, he insinuates a new temptation: "I see what I can do or offer is suspect" (2.399). Jesus had refused his offer, not what he does. Again, his hunger is to do the will of God, hence "with my hunger what hast thou to do?" Preying upon that "do," Satan now turns to action, to deeds:

> And all thy heart is set on high designs,
> High actions; but wherewith to be achieved?
> Great acts require great means of enterprise;
>
> . . . .
>
> Therefore, if at great things thou wouldst arrive,
> Get riches first, get wealth, and treasure heap. (2.410–27)

Satan's offer of wealth is functional: according to him, wealth could grant Jesus the throne of Judah. Again, Satan is reading the Bible—"The Lord God shall give him the throne of his father David: And he shall reign over the house of Jacob forever; and of his kingdom there shall be no end" (Luke 1:32–33; Isa. 9:6–7, 16; Ezek. 34:23–24; Amos 9:11)—and again, he is reading it perversely. He dares to cite as an example Antipater and his son Herod who became "king of the Jews" according to Josephus when he promised Mark Antony funds and then abused his power, becoming slaughterer both of the innocents and of the Innocent. And once again, Satan tries to incite envy without success, reminding Jesus of all the younger men who have achieved more than he has: Alexander, Scipio, and Pompey were already triumphant in their ostensibly saving missions at an early age, and this knowledge made the great Caesar himself weep at his own tardiness. Throughout, Satan once again offers another version of salvation, deliverance from servitude: "This offer sets before thee to deliver" (3.380).

With his allusions, Milton is surely glancing at Charles I, whose scandalous heavy levying of taxes were accompanied by rife abuses, who sold the crown jewels to fund his war against Parliament, and whose wicked son Charles II accepted the crown when Cromwell had been virtuous enough to refuse it, and who proceeded to slaughter many an innocent (in Milton's eyes) dissenter from the crown and church. Jesus responds that "to give a kingdom hath been thought / Greater and nobler done, and to lay down / Far more magnanimous, than to assume" (2.481–83). Jesus rejects the golden crown as really a "wreath of thorns" (ironically)—the burdens a king must bear—neither of which he is willing to assume. The frontispiece of many editions of *Eikon Basilike* portrays Charles I receiving the crown of thorns in exchange for his crown of gold, and that crown of thorns became of the symbol of his imitation of Christ. Milton inveighs against this blasphemy in his *Eikonoklastes:* "Many would be all one with our Saviour, whom our Saviour will not know. They who govern ill those Kingdoms which they had a right to, have to our Saviours Crown of Thornes no right at all."[13] Milton distinguishes between the thorns of a king's own making (including Charles's) and the redemptive crown of thorns of the Savior in *Eikonoklastes* in no uncertain terms: "Thornes they may find anow, of thir own gathering, and thir own twisting: for Thornes and Snares, saith Solomon, are in the way of the forward; but weare them as our Saviour wore them is not giv'n to them that suffer by thir own demerits" (YP 3:417–18). Like the illustrator of *Eikon Basilike,* Satan will confuse one crown with another; Jesus will not. Just as he refused the sacramental option of redemption, the Eucharist, and the theological one of the Apocalypse, so he will reject the temporal solution of empire. Momentarily, it seems like he is willing to embrace another concept of kingship, not the kingdom on earth but within, where the king rules over his own lawless passions, "as every wise and virtuous man could attain" (2.466–68), but this Platonic defense quickly gives way to Jesus' consistent hermeneutic of obedience. What, after all, is true kingship? "To know and knowing worship God aright" (2.475). Luther's influential explanation of the Apostles' Creed specifies that salvation is not achieved through silver and gold, but through the suffering and death of Christ:

I believe that Jesus Christ, true God, begotten of the Father from eternity, and also true man, born of the Virgin Mary, is my Lord, who has redeemed me, a lost and condemned creature, delivered me and freed me from all sins, from death, and from the power of the devil, not with silver and gold but with his holy and precious blood and with his innocent sufferings and death, in order that I may be his, live under him in his kingdom and serve him in everlasting righteousness, innocence, and blessedness, even as he is risen from the dead and lives and reigns to all eternity.[14]

The emphasis on the suffering of Christ was reiterated by Calvin, especially (and notably, given that Milton modeled his epic on the temptations of Job) Calvin's *Commentary on Job,* where he argues that God afflicts, rather than rewards, those he loves, swayed by the argument of Eliphaz: "It is the heavenly Father's will thus to exercise them so as to put his own children to a definite test. Beginning with Christ, his first born, he follows this plan with all his children. . . . Why should we exempt ourselves, therefore, from the condition to which Christ our Head had to submit, especially since he submitted to it for our sake to show us an example of patience in himself?"[15] While Jesus will refuse the silver and the gold (which are, according to the Psalmist, not Satan's to offer for they belong to God), in Milton's poem he will not proffer his holy and precious blood—not here, not yet.

Satan is justifiably confounded, for his arsenal has included time-honored means to redeem. When he recovers speech, he turns to glory. He is rebuffed once again with the (by now) familiar answer of obedience: "Shall I seek glory then, as vain men seek / Oft not deserved? I seek not mine, but his / Who sent me, and thereby witness whence I am" (3.105–7). Satan presses Jesus that if he would only assume the throne of David, he could save the ten northern enthralled tribes of Israel and he could secure that throne by an alliance with one of ancient Israel's enemies: either Roman or Parthian. Satan recommends Parthia and offers it. In this anti-monarchical poem, the republican poet has Satan implicitly suggest that the readiest way to save England is to gain and secure the throne and to enter an alliance with one of England's enemies: Scotland or France—fine suggestions from the devil. In response to Satan's urging of "deliverance of thy brethren, . . . from servitude thou shalt restore / To their inheritance" (3.374–75), Jesus is uncharacteristically cynical: he asks if these idolaters (Israelites/Englishmen) really deserve saving. But then he imagines mercy even for them, but not now, not yet, not until the Father says it is time. Returning to his own hermeneutic principle of obedience, he understands the promise of the throne of David to be achieved "in his due time."

When Satan recovers from his next bout of speechlessness, from being "perplexed and troubled at his bad success" and so bereft of a reply, he renews the "vain battery" that ends "in froth or bubbles" (4.20) with another offer of the kingdoms of the earth—this time, Rome. And while Satan explicitly describes the luxuries of classical Rome, implicitly the later Roman church is involved; the Idol offers Idolatry itself. And, like the idolatrous tribes of ancient Israel, these men are not worth saving either, replies Jesus: "What wise and valiant man would seek to free / These thus degenerate, by themselves enslaved, / Or could of inward slaves make outward free?"

(4.143–45). We have here a warning that Jesus may not extend his salvation to the degenerate (Catholics?), the inwardly enslaved, but isn't that all of fallen mankind? Is he distinguishing between the virtuous and the degenerate, the saved and the reprobate? No, Milton retains the Arminianism that offers grace freely to all: "Know therefore when my season comes to sit / On David's throne, it shall be like a tree / Spreading and overshadowing all the earth" (4.147–46). Jesus alludes to Jotham's fable (Judg. 9:7–15) where the trees went out to anoint a king for themselves, and after the olive, the fig, and the vine have turned down their offer, they turn to a thornbush. Only a thornbush of a man is willing to accept the offer of kingship, the fable suggests, with its ironic offer to shield its followers in its "shade": "The thornbush said to the trees, 'If you really want to anoint me king over you, come and take refuge in my shade; but if not then let fire come out of the thornbush and consume the cedars of Lebanon!' " (Judg. 9:15). Here is also Jesus' most explicit (although hardly explicit) allusion to the cross, as a tree that overshadows (and typologically shadows) redemption for all the earth and, by allusion to the thornbush, his own crown of thorns and redemption through the Passion. But there is no lingering at the cross, for Jesus abruptly shifts the metaphor of his redemption to a stone that dashes all monarchies to pieces, thereby invoking the tradition of salvation as conquest and victory. Here his allusion is to Daniel 2:31–45 where the monarchies of the world are crushed for all time: "the God of heaven will set up a kingdom that will never be destroyed, nor will it be left to another people. It will crush all those kingdoms and bring them to an end, but it will itself endure forever" (Dan. 2:44).[16] This allusion to the final victory over the monarchies thrusts the saving work of Jesus into the apocalyptic future. When will he act? When will he save?

During the sustained dialogue between Satan and Jesus, the mighty saving work is pulled in two different temporal directions: Satan urges haste, while the disciples, Mary, and Jesus himself speak of waiting, of "prolonging their expectation." Satan intones repeatedly, if you are the savior, then save, save now, save in this way. Punning on *full, fullness,* and *fulfilling,* Satan insists, with his various temptations of salvation, that the prophecies be fulfilled now: "Now at full age, fullness of time, thy season / When prophecies of thee are best fulfilled" (4.380–81). Appealing to duty, zeal, glory, fame, and all the while, biblical prophecy, Satan demands that the deliverer begin to deliver:

> If kingdom move thee not, let move thee zeal,
> And duty; zeal and duty are not slow;
>
> . . . .
>
> Zeal of they father's house, duty to free
> Thy country from her heathen servitude;

> So shalt thou best fulfill, best verify
> The Prophets old, who sung thy endless reign,
> The happier reign the sooner it begins;
> Reign then; what canst thou better do the while?   (3.171–80)

And Satan has finally asked the Savior an amazing question: "What have you better to do than begin the mighty work of salvation?".

At first, Andrew and Simeon belie a similar impatience, asking poignantly:

> For whither is he gone, what accident
> Hath rapt him from us? Will he now retire
> After appearance, and again prolong
> Our expectation?   (2.39–42)

In their plea resonates the cry of so many historical victims, from ancient Israel to Milton and his fellow sufferers through the death camps of the twentieth century, "God of Israel / Send thy Messiah forth, the time is come" (2.43–44). But then the disciples school themselves in patience and make hope the antidote to their despair:

> But let us wait
>
> .   .   .   .   .   .
>   and all our fears
> Lay on his Providence; he will not fail
> Nor will withdraw him now, nor will recall
> Mock us with his blest sight, then snatch him hence;
> Soon we shall see our hope, our joy return.   (2.49–57)

Mary, with knowledge that he is absent for some obscure great purpose, "awaited the fulfilling" (2.108). Even as Jesus is engaged in the work of redemption then, refusing the temptations of the devil as the first man and woman did not, his disciples and mother perceive only an absence, a disappearance, a redemptive activity that has not yet begun. But they are in the space prior to redemption—awaiting the fulfilling—even as it is upon them, for Milton has transvalued the wilderness from the place prior to redemption to the place of redemption. Jesus is in the very process of performing his mighty work with his refusals. In the Hebrew Bible, the wilderness is the temporal and physical space before salvation, the place where the ancient Israelites are not yet ready to inherit their promised land, where their faith in God is tested and tried to qualify them for their redemption. In the New Testament scenes of temptation—Luke, chapter 4, and Matthew, chapter 4— that space has the same significance, the space prior to Christ's saving work, and in the Anglican liturgy the Gospel account of the temptation in the wilderness is celebrated at Lent when Jesus' forty days in the wilderness are imitated with abstinence, prior to and preparatory for the Passion and Resurrection. But Milton's version is contradictory: redemption is both "about to begin" after the temptation, and already achieved in the very process of renunciation: "Now thou hast avenged / Supplanted Adam, and by vanquishing / Temptation, hast regained lost Paradise" (4.606–8). How does this work?

III

Recourse to the context of earlier Christian thought on salvation may be of help. Theologically, salvation has meant satisfaction, reparation, punishment, suffering—with its debt to both Roman public law where satisfaction meant punishment and private law where it meant paying back or satisfying justice. Under the doctrine of satisfaction, man's sin must be paid for and Christ will assume this debt through his suffering and death. But Milton understands this willingness on Christ's part as a radical passivity. It is achieved only by refusing to take another role in salvation: feeding the hungry, acquiring a nation, securing an empire, gaining all wisdom. Christ can do nothing. He must suffer everything. And the portrait of his passivity deepens when we understand that he cannot even choose what he suffers. His Father has appointed his persecutors, has permitted their violence, and has designed the saving work of his Son to be their victim. Jesus waits, obeys another's will, another's time, and in that waiting, in that obedience, he paradoxically acts, fulfilling his destiny as the obedient suffering servant.

From Irenaeus on, the suffering, passion, and exaltation of Christ have been understood as the work of redemption, not to the exclusion of his lifework, but certainly receiving greater emphasis. For Irenaeus, Christ not only recapitulated each stage of human life, but the obedience of his Passion brought salvation by undoing the sin of the tree of disobedience on the tree of the cross.[17] Tertullian added the notion of satisfaction, elaborated by Hilary who saw the death of Christ as "paying satisfaction" for the sins of mankind and by Anselm's doctrine of Atonement in which Christ, as God-man, had assumed human nature of his own free will so that he could voluntarily pay the satisfaction owed by humanity and make that salvation available to them. With Maximus, the concept of Christ the victor was elaborated: in his death, Christ overthrew the dominion of Satan. "By his suffering, Christ destroyed death and error, corruptibility and ignorance, and he endowed believers with incorruption."[18] This victory over sin and death was signaled by the Resurrection, not just confirmation that an atonement achieved by the Crucifixion had taken place, but part of an atonement that included both the Crucifixion and the Resurrection. To the imagery of sacrifice, satisfaction, and crucifixion was added, especially in the liturgy of the Eastern church, the imagery of battle and victory for salvation. Needless to say, understanding salvation as achieved through the suffering of Christ was given renewed emphasis during the Reformation by Luther's elaborate theology of the cross. The "wondrous duel" between Christ and the enemies who enthralled mankind issued in the victory over sin and death at the cross where God was revealed while remaining hidden. The only access to God is through his suffering, for speculative reasoning cannot discern him.[19] On the redemptive suffering of Christ, Calvin concurred, as well as on the hiddenness of divine justice; indeed, the temptation of Job and David, for Calvin, is that they will believe that God has abandoned them along with human history, so hidden is his justice.[20]

Where does Milton locate himself among these options? Seeing the Savior as victor? As offering, ransom, sacrifice? As paying the satisfaction? Enduring the suffering of the cross? The exaltation of the Resurrection?[21] Not in *Paradise Regained*. In *Paradise Regained*, Milton has greatly simplified the long, intricate story of redemption in the history of Christianity with the attendant complications presented by changing Christologies, and he has pared it down to what he believes is the essence: obedience. In this, he could find fit company in Irenaeus: "He [Christ] fought and was victorious; for he was man doing battle for the fathers, and by his obedience utterly abolishing disobedience. For he bound the strong man, liberated the weak, and by destroying sin endowed his creation with salvation."[22] If we needed a patristic explanation for Milton's choice to portray redemption as the obedience of Jesus (and we do not), we could not invent a more perfect one.

Irenaeus's doctrine of recapitulation is particularly resonant for Milton. Writing in the second century against the Gnostics, Irenaeus was especially eager to counter their dualism, to demonstrate that Satan does not share the governance of the cosmos. Satan does not own the kingdoms of the earth, leaving the heavenly kingdoms to another power: "As therefore the devil lied at the beginning, so he did also in the end, when he said: 'All these are delivered unto me, and to whomsoever I will I give them'" (Matt. 4:9). Only God distributes the kingdoms of the world. "This also the Lord confirmed when he did not do what he was attempted to by the devil."[23] "For Irenaeus the imitation of Christ by the Christian was part of God's cosmic plan of salvation which began with Christ's imitation of the Christian, or, more precisely, with Christ's imitation of Adam. . . . After his incarnation he passed through every stage of human growth, hallowing each and redeeming each by being made for them an example of piety, righteousness, and submission. . . .

The disobedience of the first Adam was undone though the complete obedience of the second Adam; so that many should be justified and attain salvation."[24] "So the Word was made flesh, in order that sin, destroyed by means of that same flesh through which it had gained the mastery and taken hold and lorded it, should no longer be in us; and therefore our Lord took up the same first formation for an incarnation, that so he might join battle on behalf of this forefathers, and overcome through Adam what had stricken us through Adam."[25] This understanding of recapitulation is far richer than the notion of imitation we have inherited from classical philosophy, for it holds within it the key to salvation. Because Christ recapitulated Adam's temptations, he saves, and because Christians recapitulate Christ's, they are saved. For a blind poet who believed he was denied the light of nature in order to better see the light of God, Irenaeus's understanding of salvation was especially apt: "to follow the Savior is to participate in salvation, and to follow the light is to perceive the light."[26] Nevertheless, one historian of theology summarizes, upon reviewing the whole tradition, that "while the relation of Jesus Christ to God and the relation of the human and the divine within his person became the subject for doctrinal controversy and doctrinal definition, the saving work of Christ remained dogmatically undefined."[27] And I will argue that beyond his affinities for the logic of recapitulation in Irenaeus that allows the saving work of Christ to be focused at the temptations, in Milton's epic devoted to salvation, the concept of salvation itself ultimately remains radically undefined. And this is, in part, because of Milton's lifelong distrust of "the concept" itself, one that emerges so strongly in Satan's temptation of knowledge.

When Satan shifts from the option (if only momentarily) of salvation as ruling, whether from Jerusalem or Rome, he suggests the philosopher's solution to redemption: wisdom. His description of an imperialism of knowledge goes "beyond" Scripture to include the learning of the Gentiles. Taking Jesus from Rome to Athens, Satan offers him another solution to the problem of salvation; he can conduct his "mighty work" with the instruments of classical learning, reason, and persuasion. Given that Milton's dialogue between Satan and Christ is proceeding on these terms—relying, as it does, on scriptural and classical learning, proceeding by reason and persuasion—Milton's Satan is now striking close to Milton's home. Milton cannot really be attacking learning, Miltonists have not hesitated to apologize. But his Jesus is rejecting learning as tantamount to salvation. As Irene Samuel discerned long ago, to grant limits to learning is nothing new:[28] in *Paradise Lost,* one angel cautions the curious Adam to "be lowly wise" in his paradise and another gives his parting advice to the exiled couple to cling only to the wisdom "that to obey is best" (12.561):

Th'Angel last repli'd:
This having learnt, thou hast attained'd the sum
Of wisdom; hope no higher, though all the Stars
Thou knew'st by name, and all th'ethereal Powers
All secrets of the deep, all Nature's works,
Or works of God in Heav'n, Air, Earth, or Sea.   (12.575–79)

"To obey is best": the first Adam's last words in *Paradise Lost* succinctly contain the proscription the second Adam embraces in *Paradise Regained*. Still, the temptation of learning causes scholars unease for good reason. It is easy enough to grasp that Milton regards monarchy and empire as idolatrous solutions to the problem of saving mankind. History, his own experience of monarchy, and the incessant scriptural and even classical cautions against embracing power without virtue corroborate the inadequacy of the solution of power. But making wisdom the offer of the devil, regarding poetry and philosophy, arts and ideas, as idolatrous solutions to the problem of salvation is surely more difficult.

In his reappropriation of the apophatic tradition from Pseudo-Dionysius, the philosopher Jean-Luc Marion has exposed the idolatry of embracing concepts of God; indeed, in his critique of Western metaphysics, he has exposed the idolatry of "the concept" itself. In a sense, this is the worst of idolatries, for it is the slyest: renouncing the external achievements of worldly power, philosophers have long claimed the superiority of defining the good (Plato), virtue (Aristotle), and how to live the good life (the Stoics). But in the end, these are the rational idols of metaphysics. Like Satan's options for redemption, they must be refused in order for the incomprehensibility of God to be "thought" and the ineffability of God to be "expressed." Food, power, learning: all of these are categories of the "being" that has so strangled both metaphysics and theology, and it is precisely Milton's effort to move beyond these that makes the stubborn scholarly focus on "identity," another category of being, so misguided. Instead of reinscribing the idolatry of being, in effect, we need to unsay what has been said.

IV

This "unsaying" is precisely the procedure of the dialogue between Satan and Jesus. As Northrop Frye notes, it is a dialogue like none other:

None of the ordinary literary categories apply to it; its poetic predecessors are nothing like it, and it has left no descendants . . . its closest affinities are with the debate and with the dialectical colloquy of Plato and Boethius, to which most of the Book of Job also belongs. But these forms usually either incorporate one argument into another dialectically or build up two different cases rhetorically; Milton's feat of constructing a double argument on the same words, each highly plausible and yet as different as light from darkness, is, so far as I know, unique in English Literature.[29]

In it, Jesus does far more than contradict Satan's evidence or quarrel with his reasoning; he pulls the ground out from under each of Satan's presuppositions, rendering him literally speechless but also bereft of further options. When Jesus completes his repudiations, Satan has nowhere else to take his reasoning: his idols have been silenced, as they were by the Incarnation in Milton's youthful Nativity ode. Having silenced these idolatrous concepts of salvation, Jesus does not propose a new one; he does not say that now that he has rejected the satanic options for redemption, he will offer divine ones.[30] While his adversary falls silent, Jesus stands silent, silent because he has submitted himself to the mystery of divine will, to the mystery of divine grace, to the mystery of redemption.[31]

   Throughout, Jesus has distinguished between the false gift falsely offered, demanding, as it does something impious in return, the worship of the devil, and the true gift of redemption, no "thing" that is offered with no expectation of return. In the sixth century thinker known as Pseudo-Dionysius, the post-Heideggerian thinker Marion perceives both a "negative" language, a way not to say or predicate God, and an unthinkable goodness that language cannot describe. The poet who implored that the celestial light shine inward to reveal things invisible to mortal sight would surely have resonated to the *Mystical Theology,* where Pseudo-Dionysius writes,

If only we lacked sight and knowledge so as to see, so as to know, unseeing and unknowing, that which lies beyond all vision and knowledge. For this would be really to see and really to know: to raise the Transcendent in a transcending way, namely through the denial of all beings. We would be like sculptors who set out to carve a statue. They remove every obstacle to the pure view of the hidden image, and simply by this act of clearing aside [*aphaeresis,* literally, denial] they show up the beauty which is hidden.[32]

In *Paradise Regained,* it is Satan who offers what we can know and what we can think about redemption. When that is denied, when he is refuted, we have entered a realm beyond knowing and beyond speech. "The fact is that the more we take flight upward, the more our words are confined to the ideas we are capable of forming; so that now as we plunge into that darkness which is beyond intellect, we shall find ourselves not simply running short of words but actually speechless and unknowing. . . . The more [my argument] climbs, the more language falters, and when it has passed up and beyond the ascent, it will turn silent completely, since it will finally be at one with him who is indescribable" (1033C, 139). To know God would be to join God. The Neoplatonism of the narrator of *Paradise Lost* echoes that of Pseudo-Dionysius: all proceeds from the All and up to him returns. It is instructive to juxtapose the building denials of *Mystical Theology* in the context of the denials of Jesus to Satan and to hear in them the renunciation of vast traditions of speaking about God, about goodness, and yes, about redemption:

> It cannot be spoken of and it cannot be grasped by understanding. It is not number or order, greatness or smallness, equality or inequality, similarity or dissimilarity. It is not immovable, moving or at rest. It has no power, it is not power, nor is it light. It does not live nor is it life. It is not a substance, nor is it eternity or time . . . it is neither knowledge nor truth. It is not kinship, it is not wisdom. It is neither one nor oneness, divinity nor goodness . . . it is not sonship or fatherhood and it is nothing known to us or to any other being. It falls neither within the predicate of nonbeing nor of being. . . . Darkness and light, error and truth—it is none of these (1048A, 1048B, 141).

Finally, *Mystical Theology* concludes with a negation of the negations: "It is beyond assertion and denial."[33]

How do we reconcile Milton the epic poet, the loquacious prose writer, the man who speaks so eloquently and frequently of God, even here in *Paradise Regained*, with this speechlessness? In Pseudo-Dionysius the *via negativa* is never separated from the *via affirmativa;* apophatic or negative theology is never isolated from kataphatic or positive theology, so we would violate him to tear the negative way out of the context of divine naming, a naming that proliferates endlessly, for all of creation can name God. And so it is "when all talk about God has been exhausted that the rest is silence." Another way this has been helpfully phrased is that "the *via negativa* is not the way simply of saying nothing about God, but the encounter with the failure of what we must say about God to represent God adequately."[34] In short, Milton *earns* the silence that concludes *Paradise Regained* only after all of Satan's rich verbal representations of salvation are proven to be inadequate. Satan and Jesus talk their way to silence.

When Satan resorts to his last option for salvation, it is, of course, to a miracle. In fact, he turns to Christianity's final solution to salvation, the Resurrection. The defeat of death by Christ is as miraculous as Satan's offer: jump from the pinnacle, defeat death, defy nature, for it was prophesied in Scripture (Ps. 9:11–12) that

> He will give command
> Concerning thee to his angels, in their hands
> They shall uplift thee, lest at any time
> Thou chance to dash thy foot against a stone.   (4.556–59)

In this extraordinary test, Jesus says no to the miraculous triumph over death. This is almost but not quite the "mighty work" of redeeming: indeed, Jesus must die and be lifted up. But he will not select the time or the conditions of his defeating death, nor accept those conditions from the devil, and he will not test his Father's will to resurrect him. Quoting Deuteronomy 6:16, "Do not put the Lord God to the test," he refuses to satisfy Satan's curiosity:

> Of gaining David's throne no man knows when,
> For both the when and how is nowhere told,
> Thou shalt be what thou art ordained, no doubt;
> For angels have proclaimed it, but concealing
> The time and the means.   (4.471–75)

Here, as ever, he only hungers to do his Father's will. Instead of performing a miracle in order to redeem mankind, Jesus will submit to his Father. He "stands fast"—the central lines in *Paradise Lost,* the final warning in Deuteronomy, and the ringing admonition given to Adam, to obey. The first Adam's failure to stand is undone by the second Adam's success: "now thou hast avenged / Supplanted Adam, and by vanquishing Temptation, hast regained lost Paradise" (4.606–8). Foiled in his efforts to take hold of redemption, to grasp its moment and to define its means, Satan falls; unable to comprehend the obeisance of redemption and unable to invent it, to control it, and to name it in his own terms, he is unable to achieve it and falls again, silenced and doubly lost.

In giving the temptations such prominence of place that Milton employs that Gospel narrative, rather than the narrative of the Passion for his version of regaining Paradise, Milton has done indeed something radical. He has made our redemption depend on the drama of refusal of options for redemption rather than the more familiar drama of acceptance of his self-sacrifice. Milton is well aware that the first foreshadows the second typologically, as shadow and fulfillment, and relies on his reader's awareness of the way the temptations in the wilderness presage the temptation in Gethsemane to let this cup pass. Still, he makes the focus of a poem about "salvation" the temptations and we would do well to restore the sense of surprise that such a move induces. For Milton, redemption is Jesus saying no. We know he will say yes to his death, but not yet, and not here. Here, he will return private to his mother's house, after having ventured out to make himself public. Private renunciation of the wrong options, more than the public activity of preaching and miracle working, more, perhaps, than even the suffering of Jesus, regains Paradise for mankind. And Milton expresses this, not coincidentally, at the end of his own public career, transvaluing what may look like political impotence during the restoration of a monarchy he fought to destroy into something far more heroic: refusal.[35] Milton offers no active mission for his Savior, no positive definition of salvation. Only negations. If in this, Milton is heir to

the tradition of negative or apophatic theology that gained such currency
from Pseudo-Dionysius through Maximus the Confessor, Bernard of Clair-
vaux, and Nicholas of Cusa, Milton may have also felt, having been defeated
in his struggle for a republic, that no earthly solution to salvation was within
reach.[36]

No nation, no empire, no wealth, and no wisdom could redeem man.
But this did not give way to hopelessness. Despite—or because of—his blind-
ness, isolation, poverty, and defeat, he wrote of redemption and when he did,
he understood it as refusal to succumb to the temptations that so many others
have. In refusal, his example is no less than Jesus, the stakes are no less than
redemption. Irenaeus's description of salvation becomes movingly apt for the
blind poet: "to follow the Savior is to participate in salvation, and to follow the
light is to perceive the light."

When we leave behind the tired controversies over the person of Christ
and refocus our attention on the question of *Paradise Regained,* we do more
than attend to Milton's chief concern in his epic and thereby adhere more
faithfully to his poetry. We allow one of the most contentious debates in the
history of Western religious thought—one that split the Western church from
the East, that allowed many a pious person to be accused of heresy, and
required many a so-called heretic to endure grotesque physical violence and
appalling murder—to rest in peace. Furthermore, while the problem of the
divinity of Jesus is now, hopefully, a historical curiosity, the problem of redemption is not. The problem of redemption is the problem of justice, and I
hope we have not lost sight of that. At the end of a career devoted fully to
forging justice in any way he could, articulating visions of a just republic, a
just marriage, a just church, never at a loss for words, Milton found himself at
a complete loss to define justice. In the end, like his Jesus, he no longer had a
historical precedent to offer: from ancient Israel, Greece, Rome, the early
church, and certainly not from the history of England. There was no paradise
on earth; worse still, there was no way that this most imaginative of political
and religious thinkers, who had bequeathed to posterity his exquisite vision
of an earthly paradise in his major epic, could now imagine one. Ultimately
this is why *Paradise Regained* is about renunciation—not because of Milton's
theological forebears, whom he only marshaled (as always) to lend credence
to his own vision—and this is why the work ends in silence.

According to Thomas Ellwood's account, when he suggested to Milton
that while he had written of Paradise lost but not of its being regained, Milton
initially fell silent. Later, he gave Ellwood *Paradise Regained.* I would suggest
that these two responses, Milton's initial instinctive silence before the subject
of redemption and the manuscript of the epic, were, after all, one. In his
epic, he portrays Satan at a loss after the failures of his offers, and before

his last desperate attempt he summarizes the options for saving that Jesus has denied:

> Since neither wealth, no honour, arms nor arts,
> Kingdom nor Empire pleases thee, nor aught
> By me proposed in life contemplative,
> Or active, tended on by glory, or fame,
> What dost thou in this World?   (4.368–72)

There is no answer.

Finally, this inability to imagine and articulate the restoration of justice is also, I believe, why he appended *Samson Agonistes* to *Paradise Regained,* wanting them to be read synoptically. For the impossibility of imagining, describing, or achieving justice gives way to two responses. One is hopeful, hope streaming from that poet who claims to see inwardly because he is blind. Here, the inability to see and the inability to speak signal complete capitulation to the will of an unknowable unsayable God. Redemption is only achieved, Paradise regained when we give up seeking it, says the poet who always sought it, and instead throw ourselves upon the mystery of that final goodness. Fully aware that I invert the direction of imitation that Milton himself would make, I want to note with historical sensibility that, like Milton, the public career of Christ was devoted to preaching (in its broadest sense) and like Milton, what Christ spoke of insistently and consistently was justice. Some ears opened, some were hardened; Milton surely derived his strength and his hope from his example.

But another response to the impossibility of achieving paradise on earth has more tragic tones, more mournful than hopeful: while Milton could not imaginatively fathom the suffering and death of his God, he could put the less perfect Samson in the place where his Savior's sufferings would go—after the temptations of Jesus—to show him enduring the same Job-like trials with less calm than the perfect man and to write his agony with complete identification when he dare not compare his paltry suffering to the supreme pain of Jesus who bore all human suffering. Poised between the examples of Jesus and Samson, Milton looks toward his future with hope and dread—with undying hope that somehow, somewhere, justice will prevail, the hope that is the wellspring of apocalypticism, and the excruciating pain that justice has failed, and that we have failed to make it, whether because of the guile or the might of the various Satans/Philistines or because of our own weakness—like the first man and woman leaving Paradise, like Everyman, poised between hope and dread.

Northwestern University

NOTES

1. All quotations from *Paradise Regained* are taken from *John Milton: Complete Poems and Major Prose,* ed. Merritt Y. Hughes (Indianapolis, 1957); hereafter cited by book and line number in the text.

2. *The History of the Life of Thomas Ellwood . . . Written by his Own Hand* (London, 1714), 133–34.

3. Thomas Torrance, *The Doctrine of Grace in the Apostolic Fathers.* (Reprint, Grand Rapids, Mich., 1959), 137.

4. Jaroslav Pelikan, *The Christian Tradition,* vol. 1 (Chicago, 1971), 143.

5. "Here is what we may call after Aristotle the anagnorisis, or the discovery. Christ declares himself to be the God and Lord of the Tempter; and to prove it, stands upon the pinnacle. This was evidently the poet's meaning." Rev. Calton in John Milton, *Paradise Regained,* ed. Thomas Newton (London 1752), 4:561 n. 182. Also A. S. P. Woodhouse, "Theme and Pattern in *Paradise Regained,*" UTQ 25 (1955–56): 181. This tradition continues through even the relatively recent work on *Paradise Regained* by Barbara K. Lewalski, *Milton's Brief Epic: The Genre, Meaning, and Art of "Paradise Regained"* (Providence, R.I., 1966), where she writes, "the tower episode functions both as a temptation and as an ultimate test of identity . . . the discovery of Christ's mission and his nature are drawn together and resolved in the single gesture of Christ's calm stance on the tower" (304–5); see also 315–19.

6. Ashraf H. A. Rushdy, "Standing Alone on the Pinnacle: Milton in 1752," in *Milton Studies* 26, ed. James D. Simmonds (Pittsburgh, 1990), 193–218; Irene Samuel, "The Regaining of Paradise," in *The Prison and the Pinnacle,* ed. Balachandra Rajan (Toronto, 1973), 111–34.

7. Samuel, "The Regaining of Paradise," 118–19.

8. Martin Luther, *D. Martin Luthers Werke* (Weimer, 1883), 10-I-1:147.

9. Pelikan, *The Christian Tradition,* 1:142; my emphasis.

10. Schwartz, "Milton and the Hermeneutic of Charity," in *The Blackwell Companion to John Milton,* ed. Thomas Corns (Oxford, 2001).

11. For further discussion of interpreting the Bible according to principles of scarcity and plenty, see Schwartz, *The Curse of Cain: The Violent Legacy of Monotheism* (Chicago, 1997), esp. chap. 1.

12. Jean-Luc Marion and Jacques Derrida debate gift theory in *God, the Gift, and Postmodernism,* ed. John Caputo (Bloomington, Ind., 1999). For Marion, when the phenomenon of the absolute gift is "understood unconditionally, without any a priori and according to its pure givenness alone, any theological identification of the gift or its giver would become impossible. . . . Characterized by its remaining unforeseeable, nonpresentable and nonrepeatable for the intentional subject of consciousness, such a givenness would indicate the radical possibility 'of the impossible itself.'" See Marion, "Metaphysics and Phenomenology: A Relief for Theology," *Critical Inquiry,* 20, no.4 (1994), 572; Thomas Carlson, *Indiscretion: Finitude and the Naming of God* (Chicago, 1999), 192.

13. John Milton, *Eikonoklastes,* in *The Complete Prose Works of John Milton,* 8 vols., ed. Don Wolfe et al. (New Haven, 1953–82), 3:417, hereafter designated YP and cited parenthetically by volume and page number in the text.

14. Luther, *Small Catechism, Die Bekenntnisschriften der evangelisch-lutherischen Kirche,* 2d ed. (Gottingen, 1952), 511.

15. Jean Calvin, *Institutio Christianae religionis,* in *Ioannis Calvini opera selecta,* vols. 3–5, ed. Peter Barth and Wilhelm Niesel (Munich, 1926–36), 3:8.1.

16. See the discussion of Milton in the context of radical religion in David Loewenstein, *Representing Revolution in Milton and His Contemporaries* (Cambridge, 2001), 242–68. On the

Restoration context, see Laura L. Knoppers, *Historicizing Milton: Spectacle, Power, and Poetry in Restoration England* (Athens, Ga., 1994), chap. 1.

17. Irenaeus, *Against Heresies,* in *Sancti Irenaei . . . Adversus Haereses,* 2 vols., ed. W. W. Harvey (Cambridge, 1857), 2:368.

18. Pelikan, *The Christian Tradition,* 1:150.

19. Martin Luther, *A Commentary on St. Paul's Epistle to the Galatians*, ed. Philip S. Watson (Westwood, Conn.: Fleming H. Revell, 1953), 3:136.

20. Susan Schriener, *Where Can Wisdom Be Found?* (Chicago, 1994), 104.

21. All of these functions of salvation, so alien to *Paradise Regained,* are detailed in *De doctrina Christiana,* leaving us to ask how he could have written that section and *Paradise Regained.* The authorship of this theological treatise is a vexed problem and scholars at least agree that it is a deeply heterogeneous text, not the record of a single or even a handful of amenuenses. Without commenting on the whole of the theological treatise's authorship, I cannot discern that the discussion of regaining Paradise in *De doctrina Christiana* could have been written by the same author of *Paradise Regained,* for everything about the presuppositions of what constitute the regaining of Paradise are precisely the ones the author of *Paradise Regained* does not embrace.

22. Irenaeus, *Against Heresies*, 2:100; my emphasis.

23. Ibid., 5.24.

24. Pelikan, *The Christian Tradition,* 1:144.

25. Irenaeus, *Proof of the Apostolic Preaching (Demonstratio apostolicae praedicationis),* in *Ancient Christian Writers,* ed. Joseph P. Smith (Westminster, Md., 1946–1952), 16:68.

26. Irenaeus, *Against Heresies,* 2:184. Describing the example of Christ as moral rectitude worthy of imitation impoverishes the exalted sense of imitation offered in the tradition, so it is odd that in the *Variorum* edition, MacKellar argues that Milton never intended *Paradise Lost* or *Paradise Regained* to be theological poems, but only "moral poems" and this, for him, explains why he does not take up the (theological) question of the cross. See *A Variorum Commentary on the Poems of John Milton,* vol. 4, *Paradise Regained,* ed. Walter MacKellar (London, 1975), 19. Given his awareness of the rich discourse in theology on the notion of example, MacKellar is indeed odd to reduce the poem to this kind of secular moralism. Milton's fellow travelers are from the early church: Irenaus, Augustine, Maximus, Bernard, and from the Reformation, Luther, Bucer, Calvin, Ames, Joseph Hall, Lancelot Andrewes. All of these theologians understand the temptation of Christ by Satan as offering Christ's obedience as an example, a role that is affirmed in the liturgy of Lent in the Book of Common Prayer.

27. Pelikan, *The Christian Tradition,* I:141.

28. Irene Samuel, "Milton on Learning and Wisdom," *PMLA* 64 (1949): 708–23. See also my discussion of knowledge in *Paradise Lost* in *Remembering and Repeating: On Milton's Theology and Poetics* (Chicago, 1990), chap. 3.

29. Northrup Frye, "The Typology of *Paradise Regained,*" *Modern Philology* 53 (1956): 235.

30. Barbara Lewalski has organized the second part of her study of *Paradise Regained,* on Christ's identity and his work, around the positive roles for Savior of prophet, king, and priest, gleaned from Milton's discussion of redemption in *De doctrina Christiana.*

31. Milton's apophaticism, his desire to allow mystery to remain mystery, emerges in his discourse on the Incarnation: "Since then this mystery is so great, we are admonished by that very consideration not to assert any thing respecting it, rashly or presumptuously . . . not to add anything . . . of our own . . . what is mysterious would be suffered to remain inviolate," and he concludes, on the mystery of the God/man question: "it behooves us to cease from devising subtle explanations, and to be contented with remaining wisely ignorant." If he echoes Raphael's

advice to Adam in *Paradise Lost* to "be lowly wise," he also echoes Nicholas of Cusa's "on learned ignorance." See *The Works of John Milton*, 18 vols., ed. Frank Allen Patterson et al. (New York, 1931–38), 15:273.

32. *Mystical Theology*, 1025A, in *Pseudo-Dionysius: The Complete Works*, trans. Colm Luibheid (New York, 1987), 138. Hereafter cited in the text by original line number.

33. Ken Simpson, "Lingering Voices, Telling Silences," in *Milton Studies* 35, ed. Albert C. Labriola (Pittsburgh, 1997), 193–218, has also read *Paradise Regained* with apophatic lenses: "Christ is charged to represent the unrepresentable while transcending representation himself since his identity as 'God-man' is a mystery of faith" (180). Simpson's insightful essay on silence in *Paradise Regained* traces it back to Pseudo-Dionysius and the apophatic tradition. Focusing rigorously and convincingly on literal silence, he does not link "unsaying" to the renunciations of Jesus. Everything Satan says is unsaid by Christ; renunciation characterizes the entire poem. But Simpson wants to distinguish between the silencing of Satan and the silence of Jesus: "The silencing of Satan and the silence of Jesus on the pinnacle are two completely different events: the first reveals the emptiness of words not linked to the Word; the second reveals the saving power of the Word as well as the inability of words to present God's presence" (180). I see them as completely implicated in one another. Jesus must unsay Satan's words to arrive at his own silence.

34. Denys Turner, *Eros and Allegory: Medieval Exegesis of the Song of Songs* (Kalamazoo, Mich., 1995), 54.

35. Louis Martz, to whom this essay and this volume is dedicated, understood *Paradise Regained* as a poem of renunciation in his magisterial *Milton: Poet of Exile* (New Haven, 1980), 247–71.

36. Irene Samuel, "Milton on Learning and Wisdom," has charged her reading of *Paradise Regained* with an optimism that sounds more like the youthful Milton who would spread his mighty wings than the weary, soul-battered poet of the Restoration: "everything said [by Jesus] has established that man as man is wholly adequate to be, say, think, do all that man must to recover Eden, his full human heritage." With complete confidence in the efficacy of reasoned argument—"saying is itself a doing" (131)—she concludes that Milton "creates a highly Socratic Saviour to enact through dialogue the adequacy of 'mere man' to the regaining of the fully human Paradise" (134). Samuel has perhaps produced the most powerful secular reading of *Paradise Regained:* it is a moral poem, its protagonist is a man, like all men, not higher than all men, and its lessons are offered as "reasoned arguments," not as mysteries. "Milton's [protagonist] is willing to go on talking, even to the Devil, confident that out of right talk can come a vision of 'something better' which man will then 'strive to bring into existence.' What this persuasive secular argument misses is that there is no reasoned argument on how to regain Paradise, there is no argument to be made at all. It is only possible because of a mystery, and that mystery is completely unsayable. So that Milton's protagonist can indeed talk and talk and go on talking, but he reduces the words of his opponent, indeed, the reasoned arguments of his opponent, to nothingness.

MILTON'S *THEANTHROPOS:* THE BODY OF CHRIST IN *PARADISE REGAINED*

John Rumrich

A TTEMPTING TO BECOME a fit audience for the erudition and baroque formal complexity of Milton's major poems, we sometimes forget how very simple they are at heart. The large questions addressed by *Paradise Lost*—for example, "Why do we have to die?"—are ones that a child might pose. Milton replies copiously, with all the narrative invention and theological sophistication that his culture's flourishing literary and religious resources permitted. But the question itself remains productively resistant, as impervious to his highly rational narrative as it is to myth. The crucial question behind *Paradise Regained* is likewise simple, likewise productive of answers, and likewise finally unanswerable: if God or a god became human and mortal, what would such a hybrid be like? One need not be particularly religious or theologically informed to find the question imaginatively thrilling or ethically instructive, even now. Nor is it a question limited to the Christian tradition and can as easily be found in a pop song as in Milton's brief epic: "What if God was one of us?"

The enigma that makes this question intellectually stimulating concerns the logic of identity and, as most riddles do, flirts with paradox. God cannot be "one of us" because absolute and infinite God does not and by definition can not die. This existential constancy represents the chief classical distinction between the gods, who are identified as "the undying" or "immortals," and human beings, who in *The Iliad* are often characterized as food for birds, fish, or dogs. The paradigmatic syllogism of classical logic insists on mortality as the common ground of human identity: "All men are mortal; Socrates is a man; Socrates is mortal." If one were to conclude this syllogism by proposing instead that Socrates is immortal, one would violate Aristotle's three fundamental and interdependent laws of valid reasoning: the law of identity (A=A), the law of noncontradiction (nothing is at the same time both A and -A), and the law of the excluded middle (everything is either A or -A; there is no middle ground between them). Mortality is as definitive of human identity (A) as immortality is of divine identity (-A). Socrates, a man, must die. Zeus, a god, cannot die. There is no middle term. Similarly, in Hebrew scripture, the

God of Abraham is also the God of Isaac, and of Jacob. Each patriarch lives and dies in his turn, but the same Yahweh persists, manifesting himself to succeeding generations as they flutter toward death.

The contradiction implicit in the idea of an immortal god becoming a mortal human being did not stop the Greeks and Romans from featuring god-men in their stories. According to Greek myths concerning Achilles, for example, prophecy had declared that Thetis's son would surpass his father—a prediction that immediately repelled her once eager, immortal suitors. The gods therefore arranged to wed Thetis to Peleus, Achilles's eventual father, for precisely the reason that her offspring would then be mortal. Perseus, Theseus, and Aeneas are similarly mortal offspring of divine-human matches. But Milton scholars have long recognized Hercules as the mythological hybrid most pertinent for *Paradise Regained,* not only because he is invoked at the climax of the poem but also because of Jesus' willingness to undertake Herculean labors. Not surprisingly, the term for the Christian redeemer that an admiring Milton explicitly endorses is Hellenistic in provenance: "the Greeks express this concept very neatly by the single word *theanthropos,*" which literally translated is "godman."[1]

The generation of a hybrid Messiah from a union between God and a woman is a notion unprecedented in the Hebrew tradition and anathema to it insofar as that tradition bases all law and prophecy on the absolute oneness and transcendence of Yahweh.[2] Milton's fidelity to this the first principle of Hebrew law anchors his presentation of the Son as a secondary, created divinity: "it would have been a waste of time for God to thunder forth *[intonoare]* so repeatedly that first commandment which said that he was the one and only God, if it could nevertheless be maintained that another God existed as well" (YP 6:212). That the logic of salvation demanded the sacrifice of God himself on behalf of humanity, Milton flatly denies: "let us get rid of those arguments which are produced to prove that the person who was made flesh must necessarily be the supreme God" (YP 6:425). Just as Milton insists that the Son must be essentially distinct from and inferior to "the supreme God," so also, by the same theological principle, "the supreme God" cannot become one of us. Milton was true to his Hebrew roots in matters touching the dignity of the one true God.

The imaginative inspiration for Milton's heretical doctrine of the Incarnation lies instead in the long and varied pagan tradition of divine-human union, especially those stories that start with Zeus impregnating a mortal woman. Though in *Paradise Regained* Mary's account of her Son's conception tracks scriptural Nativity narratives, her speech to her son clashes with the biblical characterization of Mary as mild and reticent:

By matchless Deeds express thy matchless Sire.
For know, thou art no son of mortal man,
Though men esteem thee low of Parentage,
Thy Father is the Eternal King, who rules
All Heaven and Earth, Angels and Sons of men.   (PR 1.233–37)

This speech is the stuff of heroic tales and romance; the biblical Mary could never utter it. Yet when Milton imagines biblical characters speaking, he often resorts to precedents from pagan heroic traditions. It is Zeus who anticipates significant portions of God's speeches in Book Three of *Paradise Lost* (96–116; compare *Odyssey* 1.32).[3] And if Milton had written a narrative account of the Crucifixion, he would, I believe, have had the Father agonize in a manner not unlike Zeus lamenting Sarpedon, weeping "tears of blood . . . for the sake of his beloved son."[4]

The imaginative cast of Milton's epic presentation is, in short, redolent of pagan myth and legend. Yet his doctrinal articulation of the Incarnation scrupulously addresses the Christian theological tradition and takes shape in relation to it. The primacy of Milton's imaginative powers and his deep indebtedness to Greek myth may nevertheless explain why Milton's account of the Incarnation departs strikingly from all previous theological arguments, orthodox and unorthodox, concerning the union of divine and human at the heart of Christianity.

The orthodox view of the Incarnation followed and therefore had to conform to the precedent doctrine of the Trinity. According to the politically charged construction of the triune godhead at Nicea in 325 C.E., the Son was fully, truly God: absolute, eternal, immutable, equal in his deity to the Father and to the Holy Spirit. After Nicea, "the Christian concept of God" became "essentially that of the Trinity" so that anti-Trinitarian heresy, especially Arianism, was regarded as the "archetypal heresy."[5] The Toleration Act of 1689, which for the first time in England officially sanctioned all other Protestant sects, excluded anti-Trinitarians from toleration because rejection of the Trinity was construed as rejection of the Christian God. Milton, however, unequivocally rejects this foundational orthodoxy in his *Christian Doctrine* and, as many past readers have recognized, patently contradicts it in his epic depiction of the deity.[6] From Milton's heretical point of view, the church only compounded the errors of Nicea when at the Council of Chalcedon in 451 C.E. it proceeded to claim that one person of this unalterable, eternal, triune deity could be fused with a mutable human being, without involving the other participants in the Trinity: "if [the essence of the Son] were the same [as the essence of the Father], the Son could not have coalesced in one person with man, unless the Father had also been included in the same union—unless, in fact, man had become one person with the Father as well as with the Son, which is impossible" (YP 6:425). For Milton, the logical contradictions inherent in the Nicene doctrine of the Trinity irretrievably compromised the credibility of the doctrine of the Incarnation set forth a century later.

Despite Milton's low opinion of them, early Christian theologians typically did not invoke mystery or demand belief in unmitigated absurdity, but instead labored to set out a rationally plausible account of orthodox doctrine. Despite the early church's seeming disregard for basic principles of logic, Christianity has been fairly described as "a philosophical religion," one that "attaches value to being philosophically respectable."[7] The philosophically face-saving move—at Nicea as well as at Chalcedon—was to posit a distinction between person (or subsistence) and essence. At Nicea, it thus was claimed that the second person of the Trinity is truly omniscient, omnipotent, omnipresent God and that he is nevertheless distinct from the other two persons, also ruled to be truly divine. That is, all three are all equally God in essence but distinct from each other as persons. At Chalcedon, the church followed this lead. It held that the second person only—not the essence of the godhead—was subject to incarnation. Orthodox doctrine further maintained that the eternally begotten Son is truly human, just as he is truly God, but that "the human nature of Christ as such does not constitute a human person"; "there is but one person in the Mediator, the unchangeable Logos."[8] The Redeemer possesses human consciousness and will—considered essential to the human soul—but not human individuality. It would be as if the Platonic idea of humanity were to be instantiated in the flesh without the consequence of human particularity that instantiation ordinarily entails. The orthodox doctrine of the Incarnation thus suggests that generic human nature, particularly human consciousness and will, becomes, to speak anachronistically, an analog device for relaying or translating the second person of the Trinity to our world.

Nor is anachronism entirely foreign to the theology. Milton quotes Zanchius's claim that at the Incarnation the Logos assumes human nature retroactively, "in such a way that the nature never subsisted by itself, independent of the Logos, but has always subsisted, both at first and ever since, in the Logos alone." That is, by assuming human nature at the Incarnation, the second person of the Trinity assumed it eternally, as indeed he would have had to do if he were to retain divine immutability. Milton observes that nothing in Scripture justifies Zanchius's claim and derisively remarks that he depends "on his own authority, and does so as confidently as if he had been present in Mary's womb" (YP 6:422). Milton's Christology could avoid such shifts because from his perspective the Logos is not "unchangeable," nor does the Son in Milton's view share in any of the essential attributes of true deity: "In the beginning he was the Word. He was God with God, and although he was not supreme, he was the firstborn of all creation" (YP 6:419).

God's Word and Mary's mortal son thus combine in one person. And indeed, Milton acknowledges in *Christian Doctrine* that the mystery he refuses to allow in his Arian construction of the deity—the mystery of distinct persons equally participating in a single essence—occurs at the Incarnation (YP 6:420). He recognizes the inconsistency, but absolves himself by observing that, unlike the mystery of the Trinity, the Incarnation rests on an explicit scriptural foundation. He therefore rejects the judgment of reason. In short, as an Arian, he denies that the Father and the Son can both be, in essence, one God, and yet remain two distinct persons. But in writing about the incarnate Christ, he accepts that two distinct persons—the secondary deity of the begotten Son and Mary's son Jesus—can join to make one Redeemer, a single essence: "There is, then, in Christ a mutual hypostatic union of two natures, or, in other words, of two essences, of two substances and consequently of two persons" (YP 6:424).

Barbara Lewalski tells us that such a position, while uniquely Milton's, comes closest to two precedent heresies. The first is Nestorianism, which held that "two persons co-existed in Christ in a union of juxtaposition." The resultant human-divine split in the psyche of the Redeemer, however, is clearly foreign to Milton's conception of a unified if hybrid Jesus. The second precedent heresy is Monophysitism and more particularly Monotheletism (from the Greek for "one will," or, more loosely, "single-minded"), which, unlike Nestorianism, insisted on the unified nature and will of the Redeemer, but made human consciousness and will so subordinate in that unity as to be superfluous, arguing that "there was in the incarnate Christ only one redemptive energy and only one will, that of the Logos, which directed the human activities as well as the divine."9 In contrast, Milton's version of Christ possesses fully operational divine and human faculties: "he could, with the same intellect, both *increase in wisdom,* Luke ii. 52, . . . and *know everything,* John xxi. 17, that is, after the Father had instructed him, as he himself acknowledges" (YP 6:425). In other words, although Milton insists that it is "the same intellect," he acknowledges that it is both distinctly human and distinctly divine and refuses to speculate how this violation of the rules of thought can be explained—"for the Bible says nothing of these things" (YP 6:425).

Despite the logical objections, Milton thus insisted on full human-divine partnership in the Redeemer—two persons and therefore two essences in a nonetheless single entity. *Here let the logicians sleep!* Orthodox doctrine, by comparison, permitted only a generic human consciousness to the incarnate Son, denying human individuality to the Redeemer so as to protect the divinity of the second person of the Trinity. Milton refused to countenance the notion of generic humanity, or of an individual embodying human nature without at the same time being a human person. He deemed the orthodox distinction between person and essence a sophistical evasion:

What an absurd idea, that someone should take human nature upon himself without taking manhood as well! For human nature, that is, the form of man contained in flesh, must, at the very moment when it comes into existence, bring a man into existence too, and a whole man, with no part of his essence or his subsistence (if that word signifies anything) or his personality missing. As a matter of fact, subsistence does not really mean anything except substantial existence, and personality is merely a word which has been wrenched from its proper meaning to help patch up the holes in the arguments of theologians. Obviously the Logos became what it assumed, and if it assumed human nature, but not manhood, then it became an example of human nature, not a man. But, of course, the two things are really inseparable. (YP 6:422)

"The form of man contained in flesh"—this is Milton's definition of human nature. It does not exist without the presence of both the human form and human flesh. When both are present, an individual instance of human nature—a person or essence—is also present.

　　Milton's denial that the Word could assume a generic human nature might be explained by reference to the nominalist policy of metaphysical nonproliferation, most notably Occam's razor. The more local and telling explanation for Milton's peculiar theology of the Incarnation, however, lies in his monism and Ramist logic. Orthodoxy's resort to the metaphysical device of a generic human form depends on the conventional Aristotelian analysis of phenomena into form as the generic principle and matter as the principle of individuation: "they are different in virtue of their matter (for that is different), but the same in form."[10] We know Fido to be a dog by virtue of his canine form. But he is Fido, not Spot, by virtue of his specific matter. Milton, however, transposes these analytic principles: "matter constitutes the common essence, and form the proper"; "form is the source of all difference" (YP 8:234). Though rarely noticed, this reversal, in combination with his materialist monism, is the theoretical ground for much of what is unorthodox in Milton's thought and works.[11] For Milton, Fido and Spot are dogs because canine matter constitutes them both; it is by virtue of their "singular forms" that they are distinctively Fido or Spot (YP 8:233). Milton's reversal of the ordinary Aristotelian analytic means that the child formed in Mary's womb must be, because he is indeed formed, an individual human person. Thanks largely to his mother, then, human matter in an individual human form constitutes the *anthropos* of this paradoxically singular, dual being. What constitutes the *theos* of the *theanthropos* remains to be seen.

Like his form, the Son's state of knowledge is also individualized in *Paradise Regained*. The historically localized, human contingency of the Son's knowledge appears as *Paradise Regained* opens. In a passage that, as many commentators have observed, echoes the harsher self-doubting of the ruined hero Samson, Milton represents Jesus as confronting swarming uncertainties:

> O what a multitude of thoughts at once
> Awakn'd in me swarm, while I consider
> What from within I feel my self, and hear
> What from without comes often to my ears,
> Ill sorting with my present state compar'd.
>
> (1.196–200; compare SA 19–22)

The sting of Samson's thoughts owes to his catastrophic failure to live up to the promise of his origins. The Son by contrast is stymied not by the disjunction between what he should have done and what he did do, but between the exalted perceptions of himself—both his own and others'—and his still humble state. By studying Scripture in much the same way a good Christian humanist would, the Son has gradually become convinced that he is the prophesied Messiah, but beyond that conviction, he is full of doubt. He is unaware of any past glory, and his state of knowledge is relatively impoverished until and unless God enlightens him: "he could, with the same intellect, both *increase in wisdom* . . . and *know everything* . . . , that is, after the Father had instructed him."

The Son's mutability, and thus his ability to perform God's will in distinct manifestations is set out in theoretical terms in Milton's theological treatise and represented with particular force in his epic poetry. The account of Satan's rebellion in *Paradise Lost,* for example, depicts the Son as being begotten as the head of the angels, an exaltation that provokes Satan's disobedience, as William B. Hunter reluctantly acknowledges: "that Milton has the Father beget the Son by elevating him above Satan may imply to some degree the Arian view that the Son was created inferior and then raised to a superior position by divine fiat."[12] In *Christian Doctrine,* Milton writes that "the Son existed in the beginning, under the title of the Word or Logos," and goes on to distinguish between the role of the Son as the "image . . . by which the God becomes visible," and the role of the Word as the "word by which God is audible" (YP 6:206, 297). The distinction between "Word" and "Son" registers crucially in the narrative of the Son's exaltation in *Paradise Lost*. Satan refuses to submit to the Son as God's "image now proclaim'd," a claim of novelty substantiated by God's own declaration that "this day" he has begotten his Son, whom the angels "now behold" (5.784, 603, 605). When

Abdiel justifies the ways of God to the rebellious angels, however, he asserts that the Son previously existed as God's "Word," by whom the Father "made / All things" (5.836–37). The begetting of the Son in *Paradise Lost* evidently represents a new development in the Word's existence, a development that has been persuasively glossed as his manifestation as an angel, a *theangellos,* so to speak. Certainly that is how Abdiel understands God's announcement: "since he the Head / One of our number thus reduc't becomes" (5.842–43).[13] The Father creates heaven and the angels by his Word but brings them into closer union with himself by his Son. Although in both functions the secondary divinity serves as the created agency by which the Father accomplishes his intention, Milton persistently observes the difference in title to discriminate between the Word's and the Son's distinct roles (for example, 7.208–9).[14]

Paradise Regained similarly presents the being of the Son as mutable, and to a remarkable degree. In heaven he became one of the angelic number; on earth he is explicitly "th' exalted man" (*PR* 1.36). A witness to both exaltations, Satan recognizes the similarity between the events in heaven and on earth. Yet he does not identify the two exalted Sons as the same entity, just as in debate with Abdiel he seems genuinely unaware that God's abruptly begotten Son, the newly proclaimed head of the angels, is the same entity as the Word. In neither case is there reason to judge Satan as being especially obtuse, or devious, because he publicly fails to recognize the Son as also being the Word, or the human Messiah as also being the head of the angels. The abrupt disjunctions in the role and constitution of the secondary deity legitimately place his identity into question. Jesus is not now the same being as the Son in heaven or as the creative Word. This time he has become *theanthropos* instead of *theangellos.* The problem of his identity is a genuine one, for Satan and for himself.

The Son's identity crisis is more pronounced on earth than in heaven. With God's performative utterance to the assembled angels in Book Five of *Paradise Lost,* the Son appears full-blown, instantly embodying, or heading rather, the simultaneity and sameness of angelic being. The gap between his status as the Word and as the head of the angels tends to go unnoticed presumably because in either role he is, like the angels, entirely his Father's production. As the Word and as the Son in heaven, he is an exclusively patrilineal entity, so that his character seems unusually coherent and single-minded, in an obsequiously filial way. The psyche of Jesus is also singular, a blithely paradoxical Milton claims, yet dual—both fully human and fully divine. "There is nothing to stop the properties of each from remaining individually distinct," he insists; "it is quite certain that this is so." Having acceded to this apparent absurdity, he acknowledges, "we do not know how it is so," and seems satisfied to stop there: "it is best for us to be ignorant of things which God wishes to remain secret" (YP 6:424). Milton rests content because the problem of two-in-one fusion is not subject to rational solution. As one logician has recently asked, "can we really understand what it is to attribute two minds, or two ranges of consciousness, to one person?"[15]

If Milton *were* to allow himself to speculate about a phenomenon as mysterious and off-limits as the Incarnation, however, he would inquire not into Christ's psyche, as the scholastic philosophers do, but into the problematic physical form of the *theanthropos:*

If it were legitimate to be definite and dogmatic about mysteries of this kind, why should we not play the philosopher and start asking questions about the external form common to these two natures? Because if the divine nature and the human nature coalesced in one person, that is to say, as my opponents themselves admit, in a rational being numerically one, then they must have coalesced in one external form as well. As a result the divine form, if it were not previously identical with the human, must have been either destroyed or blended with the human, both of which seem absurd. Or else the human form, if it did not precisely resemble the divine, must have been either destroyed or blended with the divine. Or else Christ must have had two forms. (YP 6:424)

The prospect of an inquiry into the physical composition of the *theanthropos* may strike us as silly, and, surely, part of Milton's intention in this passage is to burlesque scholastic inquisitiveness. Yet the body of Christ plainly fascinates Milton, as it did many in the primitive church, especially those whose beliefs were so dualistic that they proclaimed Christ's human appearance a sham.

Even in his salad days as an idealistic young Neoplatonist, Milton never doubted the physicality of the Redeemer. This poet after all composed verses on Christ's circumcision. The persistent reluctance he exhibits over representing the Crucifixion likely owed more to the bodily bias of his powerful imagination than to moral squeamishness about the fairness of an innocent Son's blood sacrifice. Physically, crucifixion was, according to Cicero, the cruelest of deaths—too cruel to be inflicted on a Roman citizen—and Milton would have known about that very public cruelty in more detail than most of us would willingly stomach.[16] As many readers have observed, his poetry regularly returns with horror to mythic scenes of dismemberment at the hands of a violent crowd. Like any citizen of seventeenth-century London, furthermore, he could hardly have avoided familiarity with the common judicial spectacle of cruel, slow death and the human body in excruciating pain. Given the extent of his knowledge and the bodily disposition of his imagination, we should not think it odd that he never found the public execution of Jesus to be a congenial subject for poetry. It would be frightening if he had.

When Milton introduces the question of the incarnate Christ's body, he raises a theological problem that these days goes relatively unnoticed. Many theologians prior to Milton had pondered the human foibles of the body of Christ and the doctrinal ramifications of his bodily suffering. Aquinas's discussion of the "bodily defects" inherent in human nature seems particularly pertinent as he distinguishes between defects common to all, such as "susceptibility to hunger, thirst, and death" and those "that result from particular occasions," for example, "fatal falls from high places."[17] On the other hand, although much ink was spilled in attempting to explain the duality of Christ's single psyche, scholastic philosophers did not ask how that singular duality extended to his "external form." Presumably they did not consider it an issue because, for orthodoxy, God is a bodiless spirit, and any material being that the Incarnate Word might possess would derive entirely from his mother.

Milton, a monist and materialist, insists on the contrary that God does have a body, or at least "bodily force in his own substance; for no one can give something he has not got" (YP 6:309). God, furthermore, dwells in Christ "bodily" according to Colossians 2:9, a verse that Milton quotes four times in *Christian Doctrine,* once to argue that God must possess a body to allow him to contribute "bodily" to his Son's body (YP 6:310). One must tread cautiously here, however. The Greek term used for "bodily" in Colossians, *sômatikôs,* ranges fairly widely in meaning, and Milton's readings of this verse are tentative and vary (compare YP 6:137, 273, 419).[18] Still, I want to suggest that, in Milton's poetic imagination, God's incarnate Son, in addition to his hybrid psyche, possesses a hybrid body. This duality would stretch to his external form, which even so would not in Milton's opinion appear any different than an ordinary human being's. Milton thinks it proper to imagine "not only [God's] mind but also his external appearance" as closely resembling humanity's because "God attributes to himself again and again a human shape and form" (YP 6:135–36). As a theologian Milton realizes that there can be no certainty on this point. No creature, except for the Son in heaven, knows what God looks like. Still, given his premises, Milton is being logical, not silly, when he expresses a curiosity notoriously common to Renaissance paternity: did Mary's baby look like his father?

In *Paradise Lost* Milton hardly ventures to describe specifically what the Son as head of the angels looks like, though Raphael represents him as having legs and arms, or at least a "puissant thigh" and a "right arm" (6.714, 835). There is no mention of wings, and the Son's repeated resort to a chariot driven by a four-by-four angelic transmission suggests that he did not sprout them upon being begotten head of the angels. Mostly, and with strong scriptural authority, we hear about the Son's face which, like angels' faces generally in Milton's epic, and to a lesser degree Adam and Eve's faces, registers

attitude and affect with allegorical force and consequence: "in his face /
Divine compassion visibly appeerd, / Love without end, and without measure Grace"; or, "into terrour chang'd / His count'nance too severe to be
beheld / And full of wrauth bent on his Enemies" (3.140–42; 6.824–26).
The Son's face also is the port by which he absorbs and incorporates the
fullness of the Father's potent light (6.720–22). Compared to the "conspicuous count'nance" he bears in heaven—where "without cloud / Made visible,
th' Almighty Father shines"—the human face of Jesus is quite dim, betraying
only "glimpses of his Fathers glory" (*PL* 3.385–86; *PR* 1.93).

In *Paradise Regained* Satan is perplexed by Christ's thoroughly human
external form and barely shining morning face. Otherwise he would recognize him before he does:

> His first-begot we know, and sore have felt,
> When his fierce thunder drove us to the deep;
> Who this is we must learn, for man he seems
> In all his lineaments.   (1.89–92)

In Giles Fletcher's *Christs Victorie on Earth* (1610), Jesus bears a more striking and efficacious physical resemblance to God.[19] Predatory beasts "when
they saw their Lords bright cognizance / Shine in his face, soone did they
disadvaunce, / And some unto him kneele, and some about him daunce"
(3.6–8). Milton similarly allows that "wild beasts . . . at his sight grew mild,"
but that mildness does not extend beyond the absence of violence (1.310).
Unlike Fletcher's dancing beasts, Milton's "lion and fierce tiger glared aloof"
(1.313). The worshipful predators of Fletcher's poem befriend lambs and
goats when they see the Son because he "shines bright as God": "from him
breake / Such beames, as mortall eyes are all too weake / Such sight to see"
(6.3, 6–8). Not surprisingly, then, Fletcher's tempter easily recognizes his
target: "Certes the Sonne of heav'n [I] now behold"; "The old Serpent knewe
our Saviour well" (18.8; 30.2).

Various critics maintain that Milton's Satan likewise perceives the truth
of Christ's heavenly identity and only feigns uncertainty. They draw this
conclusion from the Son's early query of Satan: "Why dost thou then suggest
to me distrust, / Knowing who I am, as I know who thou art?" (1.355–56).
Commenting on these lines and citing Fletcher's precedent, John Leonard
claims that Satan and the Son mutually and fully recognize each other.[20] If,
however, either of the adversaries at the beginning of *Paradise Regained*
recognizes Christ's identity as the "Sonne of heav'n," the dramatic impetus of
Milton's narrative would be spoiled. The Son's lines are spoken categorically.
He and Satan both know he is the prophesied Messiah and "Son of God," but
neither knows what precisely that will turn out to mean. And both Christ and

Satan know that Satan is the tempter and his adversary, a fallen angel. Satan, sounding something like Raphael at his worst, notes the Son's superiority to Adam, especially "against the charm of beauty's powerful glance" (*PL* 8.533; see *PR* 2.196–200). But his standard for manliness is human and historical, with Alexander and Scipio as previous exemplars of such virtue. Given the human if heroic precedent for the Son's virtue, Satan will resort to "manlier objects" to tempt him, a resolution that sorts well with the Son's own youthful aspirations: "victorious deeds / Flamed in my heart, heroic acts"—deeds and acts like those accomplished by Alexander and Scipio (1.215–16).

I have suggested that the problem of the Son's identity is more pronounced in *Paradise Regained* than in *Paradise Lost* in part because the Son begotten as head of the angels is entirely his Father's production. There is no Mary among the angels. But when the Word begotten as the Son in heaven proceeds at last to combine with a human person, a woman's womb lends him human form and substance. None of the humbling physical details of human birth and development appear in *Paradise Regained,* of course, yet memories of the Nativity and childhood of Jesus play a prominent part in the brief epic. Milton could have easily elided the Son's maturation by making his poem correlate better with the narrative of the Son's more abrupt begetting in *Paradise Lost*. He could have disregarded the Nativity altogether, for example, as the gospels of John and Mark do, and paid no notice to events prior to the Baptism. Even Matthew and Luke, who begin their gospels with the Nativity, do not refer to it in their relation of the temptation nor do they inventory Jesus' youthful aspirations. But Milton, as the human Son approaches the critical stage of his life, chooses to stress the birth and development of "this man born and now up-grown" (1.140). Fletcher by contrast never alludes to the Nativity and excludes Mary from his poem. But that is put the wrong way. Fletcher does not omit her; Milton inserts her where she does not belong.

During his internal monologue early in Book One, Christ runs through his childhood, his devoted study of Scripture, and his heroic ambitions (201–26). Then his mother's words occupy his mind:

> These growing thoughts my mother soon perceiving
> By words at times cast forth inly rejoiced,
> And said to me apart, high are thy thoughts
> O Son, but nourish them and let them soar
> To what heighth sacred virtue and true worth
> Can raise them, though above example high;
> By matchless deeds express thy matchless Sire.
> For know, thou art no son of mortal man,
> Though men esteem thee low of parentage,

> Thy Father is the Eternal King, who rules
> All Heaven and earth, angels and sons of men.
> A messenger from God foretold thy birth
> Conceived in me a virgin; he foretold
> Thou shouldst be great and sit in David's throne,
> And of thy kingdom there should be no end.   (1.227–41)

Mary continues speaking in her Son's mind, relating the miraculous events surrounding his birth (242–58). In total, she accounts for nearly a third of her son's autobiographical meditation and speaks at greater length on her own behalf in Book Two (60–108), making her the character, aside from Christ and Satan, with the most lines in the poem. She seems to have been the medium for much of Jesus' self-consciousness, especially his grand ambition.

Yet Milton scholars commonly overlook or understate the key part Mary plays in *Paradise Regained* and in the constitution of Christ's humanity, not only physically as we have seen, but also psychologically. Roy Flannagan's commentary on the passage quoted above suggests, unaccountably, that Milton gives short shrift to Mary: "Milton downplays the role of Mary in the life of Jesus . . . giving her here only a short speech as quoted by Jesus." As "indirect discourse" the passage further slights Mary's presence in the text, Flannagan writes, because what she says is contained within her son's thoughts and is not graphically distinguished from them.[21] The opposite conclusion makes far more sense, however. Her seamless fit into Jesus' most consequential meditations indicates that she has intimately influenced his developing sense of identity. There is no gap separating them. She is evidently the single most influential person in his psyche.

Mary thus critically shapes her son's self-exploration in Book One. In Book Two, after lamenting his absence, she and her son are juxtaposed in a pivotal narrative transition:

> Thus Mary pondering oft, and oft to mind
> Recalling what remarkably had passed
> Since first her salutation heard, with thoughts
> Meekly composed awaited the fulfilling:
> The while her son tracking the desert wild
> Sole but with holiest meditations fed,
> Into himself descended, and at once
> All his great work to come before him set;
> How to begin, how to accomplish best
> His end of being on earth, and mission high.   (2.105–14)

There is a definite meditative echo between Mary and her son. The holy thoughts that nourish him, the self into which he descends, and his conviction regarding his "mission high" are largely a maternal inheritance. William Kerrigan has noted how structurally this moment reverses the temptation in *Paradise Lost*, with Mary, the second Eve, waiting behind while second Adam, Jesus, exposes himself to temptation. This reversal implies a general rectification of our first parents' relations: through divine artifice, Adam gave birth to Eve, who has the problematic dual status of being both Adam's daughter and his spouse; Jesus, also a product of divine intervention, is, unlike Eve, born of a woman, not joined in wedlock with his virgin parent, and, in the end, having successfully resisted temptation, will return home to his mother. As Kerrigan observes, the two great similes with which the temptations and the poem culminate concern mythical sons, Antaeus and Oedipus, storied for their relations to their mother.[22] They also concern mysteries, or riddles, that a hero must solve in order to continue on his way. And that, I would claim, is very much the crossroads at which Jesus finds himself.

Milton in *Paradise Regained* presents Christ as being, like Oedipus, under deep cover, from Satan, of course, but also from himself. The understanding of the Messiah that both Christ and Satan possess derives partly from scriptural prophecies and partly from knowledge of the early events of Christ's life:

> Of the Messiah I have heard foretold
> By all the Prophets; of thy birth at length
> Announced by Gabriel with the first I knew,
> And of the angelic song in Bethlehem field,
> On thy birth-night, that sung thee Saviour born.   (4.502–6)

These lines, spoken by Satan near the end of the poem, are followed by his account of his surveillance of Jesus' youth (507–13). The speech as a whole recapitulates what we learned from the Son himself near the beginning of the poem (1.229–63). Satan shares the knowledge that Christ has been "Declared the Son of God" and perceives in him "more than human gifts from Heaven," but nonetheless persistently speaks of him as a man, "by his mother's side at least" and to the bitter end seeks clarity as to just what Christ's divine heritage might be (1.385; 2.137, 136).

In sum, Satan's knowledge of Christ's identity, like Christ's own, is neither definitive nor predictive. The title "Son of God," as Satan rightly observes, "bears no single sense" (4.517). "All men are Sons of God," and Christ has not yet demonstrated anything like superhuman filiation: "To the utmost of mere man both wise and good, / Not more" (4.535–36). "Mere" in this passage retains its old meaning of "entirely" or "purely." The Father himself refers to his Son as a man: "this man born and now upgrown"; "I can produce a man / Of female seed" (1.140, 150–51). The Son is being exercised in the desert so "that all the angels and ethereal powers, / They now, and men hereafter may discern, / From what consummate virtue I have chose / This perfect man, by merit called my Son" (4.163–66). The question animating *Paradise Regained* concerns the nature of the "consummate virtue" that entitles "this man" to be called Son of God "by merit."

Because of its ambiguity and grandiose ontological displacement, the title Son of God is potentially misleading. It seems to reinforce the Son's youthful inclination toward "victorious deeds" and "heroic acts," or, in Mary's phrase, "matchless deeds" (1.215–16, 233). Such language is not the sort usually applied to Christian heroism. The Son may well expect to ascend to David's throne as a victorious freedom fighter, but as Satan points out, "the when and how is nowhere told" (4.472). The Parthian, Roman, and Athenian temptations sort well with the youthful Christ's threefold desire "to rescue Israel from the Roman yoke," "to subdue and quell o'er all the earth / Brute violence and proud tyrannic pow'r," and "by winning words to conquer willing hearts, / And make persuasion do the work of fear" (1.217–19, 222–23). They are temptations that conform to his own ambitions, to his mother's nurture of them, to scriptural accounts of the Messiah, and to the apostles' hopes. None of these lofty goals exceeds human capacity or ambition, nor do any of them call for a kind of virtue beyond the reach of classical or scriptural literature: throw Socrates and David or Scipio and Job into a blender and—voilà. Milton's Christ does not at the beginning of *Paradise Regained* contemplate liberating humanity from the tyranny of sin and death, after all, but from the oppression of human tyrants. The young Redeemer does not seem especially concerned with human sinfulness or the sorrow of mortality. At the historical moment represented in this narrative, what Nietzsche described as Christianity's transvaluation of the classical ideal has not yet occurred. One might argue that the moral position of which Nietzsche wrote is the reversal gradually defined by Satan and the Son during the course of *Paradise Regained*.

At its heart *Paradise Regained* is a dialectical detective story: none of the scriptural and biographical knowledge possessed by Christ and Satan indicates how this Son of God is meant to achieve a destiny beyond human nature and human expectation. God himself sums up the situation best when he talks to Gabriel at the beginning of the epic action and says, with his customary precision, that the Son "shall first lay down the rudiments / Of his great warfare" (1.157–58). What Satan and Christ accomplish together in *Paradise Regained* is a "rudimentary" understanding of what is to come: "I send him forth / To conquer Sin and Death the two grand foes / By humiliation and strong sufferance" (1.158–60). The dialectical process of the temptations might be described as the doubling of a negative, little by little: that is, the Son incrementally negates the Fall, which was a sudden and total negation. When he successfully tempted Adam and Eve, Satan accomplished the perversion of our entire world. If we were to express his achievement in logical equations, where A equals the perfection of the unfallen world, we would write the Fall as the transition from A to -A. Christ's mission, to continue with this logic, is to negate the negation: -A. But as William Kerrigan has observed, A and -A, though equal in the eyes of logicians, indicate very different kinds of experience, with the negation of the Fall being the duty of true wayfaring Christians.[23] Satan cumulatively offers Christ something like the keys to his kingdom, and Christ refuses, item by item. It is a long, relatively slow process, nothing like biting into an apple. Yet the suddenness and the totality of the Fall also meet their match in *Paradise Regained*—at the pinnacle of the temple—and that is where Christ's more than human heritage appears.

At this point, God's portion in Christ's body becomes evident, even as the mystery of the Son's superhuman virtue is resolved. As a consequence of Satan's scornful demand, Christ shows his "progeny" by standing on a spire where a human being's body, vulnerable as Aquinas observed, to "fatal falls from high places," cannot stand (4.554). In the course of tempting him, Satan has offered Christ various means to accomplish the heroic destiny he contemplated as a youth, and Christ has rejected them all. Having rejected them, he is left in a position in a fallen world very much like that of Satan in Paradise or in heaven: there is no place for him, "none left but by submission" (*PL* 4.81). Satan in steadfastly refusing to submit to God eternally refuses to "stand": he is *still* fallen, the irretrievably apostate (literally, "from standing") angel. The corresponding, consummate virtue displayed by Christ is that of refusing not to stand, and so forsaking any means under the apostate's dominion to achieve his end. Since that dominion for all practical intents and purposes includes all the world, the Son effectively denies the entire world without denying his intention to liberate it. That is his merit. At the point where Mary's Son as a meritorious human being has no place left in the world to make a stand, and yet nonetheless *would* stand, Christ, in whom the fullness of God dwells bodily, does stand, miraculously, signaling the arrival of a new order in the apostate's world. The paradoxical fusion that is the *theanthropos* is thus made manifest in the standing body of Jesus, Son of God and Mary.

University of Texas, Austin

NOTES

1. John Milton, *Christian Doctrine*, in *The Complete Prose Works of John Milton*, 8 vols., ed. Don M. Wolfe et al. (New Haven, 1953–82), hereafter designated YP and cited parenthetically in the text.

2. Hebrew scripture and various commentaries do relate stories of hybrid beings, however, with the best known being the nephilim (see Gen. 6).

3. Milton quotes Zeus's theodical remarks from Book One of the *Odyssey* while discussing predestination in *Christian Doctrine* (YP 6:202). I follow Milton's citation in the text.

4. Homer, *The Iliad*, trans. Richmond Lattimore (Chicago, 1951), 16.459–60. Divine fore-knowledge of the Resurrection would presumably have mitigated any Zeuslike weeping on God's part, but the tenor of the unfinished *Passion* suggests that the impulse to bewail the Son's death would nonetheless have been registered.

5. Maurice Wiles, *Archetypal Heresy* (Oxford, 1996), 63; Keith Ward, *The Concept of God* (Oxford, 1974), 180–81.

6. I have written at length elsewhere on Milton's anti-Trinitarianism and the significance of critical controversies surrounding his rejection of orthodox Trinitarian dogma. See "Milton's Arianism: Why It Matters," in *Milton and Heresy*, ed. Stephen B. Dobranski and John P. Rumrich (Cambridge, 1998), 75–92; *Milton Unbound* (Cambridge, 1996), 36–49. These studies depend on Michael E. Bauman's *Milton's Arianism* (Frankfurt, 1987), the single most lucid and reliable account of Milton's Christology.

7. William Charlton, *Philosophy and Christian Belief* (London, 1988), i.

8. L. Berkhof, *Systematic Theology* (Grand Rapids, Mich., 1941), 322.

9. Barbara K. Lewalski, *Milton's Brief Epic* (Providence, R.I., 1966), 151.

10. References to Aristotle follow *The Basic Works of Aristotle*, ed. Richard P. McKeon (New York, 1941). Quotation is from *Metaphysics* 7.8.1034a7. Form and matter are for Aristotle two of the four causes of phenomena, the other two being the efficient and final causes. For an account of matter and form in Aristotle, and of Aquinas's complication of these principles, see Etienne Gilson, *Being and Some Philosophers* (Toronto, 1952), 154–89.

11. Milton criticism has mostly overlooked Milton's consequential reversal of the Aristotelian categories of form and matter. For fuller treatment, see my *Matter of Glory: A New Preface to "Paradise Lost"* (Pittsburgh, 1987). On the reversal's pertinence to Milton's doctrine of the Incarnation, see Kenneth Borris, "Milton's Heterodoxy of the Incarnation," in *Living Texts: Interpreting Milton*, ed. Kristin A. Pruitt and Charles Durham (Selinsgrove, Pa., 2000), 264–82.

12. William B. Hunter, "The War in Heaven: The Exaltation of the Son," in William B. Hunter, C. A. Patrides, and J. H. Adamson, *Bright Essence* (Salt Lake City, Utah, 1971), 118. Hunter admits that "the Arian position does nicely fit with the motivation of Satan's rebellion," but he characteristically rejects any such explanation because he does "not believe that Milton was an Arian" (118).

13. "Abdiel appears to regard the Messiah's kingship over the angels as a kind of incarnation, involving the setting aside of divinity," observes Alastair Fowler, ed., *Paradise Lost* (London: Longman, 1971), 5.842–45 n. See also Albert C. Labriola, " 'Thy Humiliation Shall Exalt': The Christology of *Paradise Lost*," in *Milton Studies* 15, ed. James D. Simmonds (Pittsburgh, 1981), 29–42.

14. On the distinction between Word and Son, see Rumrich, *Matter of Glory*, 162–64.

15. Thomas V. Morris, *The Logic of God Incarnate* (Ithaca, N.Y., 1986), 104.

16. The "extreme and ultimate punishment of slaves" [servutitis extremum summumque supplicium], crucifixion had for Cicero the distinction of being the "cruelest and most disgusting penalty" [crudelissimum taeterrimumque supplicium]. Marcus Tullius Cicero, *Against Verres*, in *The Verrine Orations*, 2 vols., trans. L. H. G. Greenwood (Cambridge, Mass., 1953), 2:169, 165.

17. My representation of Aquinas depends on Marilyn McCord Adams, *What Sort of Human Nature? Medieval Philosophy and the Systematics of Christology* (Milwaukee, 1999), 61.

18. Michael Bauman, *A Scripture Index to John Milton's "De doctrina christiana"* (Binghamton, N.Y., 1989), 139.

19. Giles Fletcher, *Christs Victorie on Earth,* in *The English Spenserians,* ed. William B. Hunter Jr. (Salt Lake City, 1977), 49–90. Parenthetical citations are from this edition, by stanza and line.

20. *John Milton: The Complete Poems,* ed. John Leonard (London, 1998), 882. Leonard is not the first to rely excessively on Fletcher's poem in reading Milton's. See Northrop Frye, "Revolt in the Desert," in *Five Essays on Milton's Epics* (London, 1966), 126–53.

21. Roy Flannagan, ed., *The Riverside Milton* (Boston, 1998), 728 n. 82.

22. William Kerrigan, *The Sacred Complex* (Cambridge, 1983), 89–92; John Shawcross, *Paradise Regained: Worthy t'have not remain'd so long unsung* (Pittsburgh, Duquesne University Press, 1988, 63–68.

23. William Kerrigan, *The Prophetic Milton* (Charlottesville, Va., 1976), 180–83.

SATAN AND THE PAPACY IN
PARADISE REGAINED

Laura Lunger Knoppers

T RAVELING IN ROME IN 1644, John Evelyn toured Saint Peter's, "that most stupendious & incomparable Basilicam," and noticed
"amongst all the Chappells one most glorious, having for Altar-piece a Ma-
dona bearing a Cristo mortuo in White marble, on her knees, the worke of
Mich: Angelo."[1] In Michelangelo's *Pieta*, Mary—youthful, lovely, and serene
though sorrowful—holds the lifeless but graceful body of Christ, marked on
the hands, side, and feet with the wounds of the Crucifixion. With one hand,
Mary frames Christ's wounded side; with the other, palm upward, she offers
her dead son to the worshipper in a gesture recalling the elevation of the host
at the Eucharist. The observer comes face-to-face with the reality of suffering for the human Christ and his grieving mother; yet, as altarpiece, the *Pieta*
is poised at the moment of transformation, as the body and blood of Christ
are literally renewed in the sacrifice of the mass.[2]

If John Milton, visiting Rome five years earlier in 1638–1639, viewed
the Michelangelo *Pieta* in Saint Peter's, he left no record. Indeed, one looks
in vain for Milton's impression of any sculpture, painting, or work of architecture observed during his time in Italy.[3] Some influential Milton scholars
have assumed that the artistic masterpieces that Milton saw during his grand
tour must have had a distinct and profound impact on his visual and poetic
imagination.[4] Yet, as Michael O'Connell has recently observed, the art that
Milton—and Evelyn—viewed was not culturally neutral, but part of the sacramental complex of Catholic worship and belief.[5] As altarpiece, the Michelangelo *Pieta* pointed to mysteries of life and death, spirituality and materiality in
the mass, which Milton and his contemporaries regarded as idolatrous. Indeed, a wide array of Renaissance and baroque artwork—the wall frescoes of
the Sistine Chapel, Michelangelo's ceiling, the Raphael tapestries, the new
Saint Peter's, the Julius tomb, and the Vatican *stanze*—variously celebrated
and forwarded the temporal and ecclesiastical power of the papacy.[6] I want to
argue, then, that art and learning of papal Rome did have a distinct impact on
Milton's late poetry, albeit in a different sense than previously understood.
Much of the alleged asceticism of *Paradise Regained* is the Son's renunciation of the culture of papal Rome: the wealth, power, learning, military might,

and arts that reached an apogee in the Renaissance and were reclaimed for the Counter-Reformation in Milton's own time. But the Son rejects false (papal) appropriations of the visual arts, architecture, classical learning, and the heroic, only to reappropriate the arts and learning in service of a radical Protestant inwardness and spiritual discipline.

The papacy reached its golden age under Julius II (1503–1513) and, especially, Leo X (1513–1521).[7] A patron of Michelangelo, Raphael, and Bramante, Julius II commissioned plans for the new Saint Peter's Basilica, to be funded by the sale of indulgences. Julius also had vast military and imperial ambitions and directed much of his energies toward restoring and enlarging the papal states. Leo X was acclaimed as bringing a time of peace after the warmongering Julius. A highly cultured Renaissance prince, born Giovanni de Medici, Leo presided over a rich florescence of art and learning; among the artists he patronized were Raphael, Michelangelo, and Leonardo da Vinci. But in his support of indulgences and his flagrant sale of ecclesiastical offices to support his own opulent lifestyle and lavish church-building programs, Leo embodied, for Martin Luther and the reformers who came to oppose him, the worst excesses of the Catholic Church.

Within a broader Reformation tradition of anti-Catholic polemic, *Paradise Regained* directs an attack on papal Rome.[8] While considerable attention has been given to *Paradise Regained* in a Restoration context, analysis of the work in relation to the papacy helps to explain some of the still puzzling features of the poem, including the choice of the temptation in the wilderness, the "coldness" of its hero Jesus, the inclusion of the lavish banquet, the depiction of Rome, and the harsh rejection of learning.[9] Milton's choice of topic in *Paradise Regained* eschews both the Crucifixion and the Virgin Mary upon which so much attention had been lavished in Catholic art. The poem reflects a broad and uncompromising "Protestant" vision of inwardness and self-discipline in contrast to the material splendors of the papacy.[10] The false models of the church, in particular the temptations to wealth, glory, learning, and temporal power that Satan offers, reflect Milton's lifetime opposition to the corrupting conjunction of spiritual and temporal power evinced in the papacy. *Paradise Regained,* then, continues the anti-Catholic impetus that recent scholars have explored in *Comus, Lycidas, Paradise Lost,* and in Milton's prose.[11]

Exploring the anti-Catholic resonance of the temptations and the alignment of Satan with the papacy in *Paradise Regained* adds a new dimension to recent studies showing how the poem—seemingly quietist and pacifist—in fact polemically engages its political and religious Restoration context.[12] Popery—long a concern of Milton's and of many of his contemporaries—was perhaps an obvious target in 1671, with the looming threat of an absolutist and Catholic France under Louis XIV and Charles II's perceived pro-French and pro-Catholic sympathies.[13] Although the secret provisions in the 1670 Treaty of Dover, in which Charles had agreed to profess Catholicism and impose it upon England in return for French subsidies, were not yet known, suspicions ran high.[14] Two years after the publication of *Paradise Regained,* Milton's final prose work, *Of True Religion,* addressed the specific religious/ political situation in England, arguing in part that in not tolerating their fellow Protestants the prelates were themselves behaving like papists.[15] Adumbrating the concerns of this last prose tract, *Paradise Regained* evokes both popery and prelacy in their shared abuses of temporal and ecclesiastical power to impinge upon the conscience of the true believer.

Yet I would also argue that the critique of Catholicism in *Paradise Regained* is deeper and broader than a topical response to the immediate political situation in England. Aligned with Reformation polemic, Milton targets the history of the Roman Catholic Church and points his attack in part at the golden age of the papacy, marked by the rebirth of art and learning. The painting, sculpture, and architecture of Renaissance Rome, along with the rediscovery of Greek and Latin learning, helped to shape and promulgate the imperial and ecclesiastical mission of the papacy. The poverty and humility of the Son of God in the wilderness and his rejection of satanic offers of wealth, power, glory, and learning boldly redefine spirituality as the inner discipline of hearing and obeying the word of God.

The seeming avoidance of the Crucifixion and the treatment of Mary as fully human and struggling for patience make *Paradise Regained* a sharp contrast to Catholic art. Travelers to Italy in Milton's time routinely noticed the Madonna altarpieces, the *Pietas,* and the numerous depictions of Mary as mother of the infant Christ.[16] In addition to the Michelangelo *Pieta* in Saint Peter's, John Evelyn observes at Santa Maria della Vitoria "the high Altar . . . infinitely frequented for an Image of the Vergine." Of Santa Maria Maggiore, he writes "Here they affirme that the B: Virgine appearing, shewed where it should be built, 300 yeares since."[17]

Like other travelers to Rome, Evelyn also notes the relics—and their accompanying miracles—associated with Mary and with Christ. Hence, at the Cathedral of Saint John de Laterana, relics include "a robe of the B: virgins which she gave to Christ, and the towell with which he dried the Disciples feete: the reed, sponge, some of the blood & water of his precious side: some of the Virgins haire, the Table on which the Passover was celebrated, the rods of Aron & Moses, and many such bagatells" (275). In a chapel dedicated to Saint Helena, Evelyn views with equal skepticism "a world of Reliques, expos'd at our request, with a Phial of our B: Saviours blood, two thornes of the Crowne, three Chips of the real Crosse, one of the Nailes, wanting a point, St. Thomas's doubting finger, and a fragment of the Title, being part of a thin board, some of Judas's pieces of silver, and innumerable more, if one had faith to believe it" (380). The relics of Rome—the robe or hair of the blessed Virgin, the Veronica or handkerchief showing the imprint of Christ's face at the time of his Passion, chips of the cross, thorns of the crown, and, above all, drops or vials of Christ's blood—gave tangible contact with the humanity and suffering of Christ.

In sharp contrast, the more radical and iconoclastic Milton seems to avoid the Crucifixion and any focus on the body of Christ. The Son in *Paradise Regained* knows that his "way must lie / Through many a hard assay even to the death" (1.263–64), and Satan himself foresees that ahead of the Son lie "scorns, reproaches, injuries, / Violence and stripes, and lastly cruel death" (4.387–88).[18] But the poem itself depicts temptation and testing, martyrdom as witness to the truth rather than physical suffering. In a redefinition of martyrdom countering both the Catholic relics and the more recent English example of martyrdom with Charles I, Milton's Son of God waits, abstains, resists, declines, perseveres: he seems intent on doing nothing.[19] Similarly, Mary, mother of Jesus, is presented not as intercessor or miracle worker but as a humble, historical figure who waits with patience for news of her Son, aligned with the "plain Fishermen" (2.27) who likewise lament the loss of their Lord.

The language used by and about Satan in *Paradise Regained* recalls the language in which Milton—from his earliest antiprelatical tracts to his final prose work, *Of True Religion*—critiqued and attacked the pope and popery as fraudulent, carnal, and idolatrous. The brief epic opens with a "gloomy Consistory" (1.42) in midair, a "Council" (1.40) in which Satan consults his troops, reminiscent of the papal conclave in which the new pope is elected. Satan's initial disguise as "an aged man in Rural weeds" (1.314) evokes Spenser's Archimago as a figure of Catholic deception. Christ himself is described in the opening of *Paradise Regained* as "this glorious Eremite" (1.8)—perhaps a true eremite or friar in comparison to the false Satan. Satan's "vain importunity" (4.24), "ostentation vain" (3.387), and "vain batt'ry" (4.20) recall the explicitly antipapal Limbo of Vanity in *Paradise Lost,* in which are blown about "Cowls, Hoods and Habits with thir wearers tost / And flutter'd into Rags, then Reliques, Beads, / Indulgences, Dispenses, Pardons, Bulls, / The sport of Winds" (3.490–93).

Most strikingly, Milton employs with Satan language of pretense, fraud, and usurpation that is elsewhere part of his anti-Catholic arsenal. Satan in *Paradise Regained* is, above all, a fraud: he lies, feigns, dissembles, changes shape, and claims miracles. As such, he recalls the "shifts and evasions" and the "wiles and fallacies" of papists as depicted in *Of True Religion* (YP 8.432–33). As the title of that tract indicates, Milton highlights, above all, the *true* worship and service of God in contrast to the pretenses of popery. As *Paradise Regained* opens, Satan, recreating the world in his own image, labels John the Baptist an imposter who "pretends to wash off sin" (1.73) and prepare the way for Christ's kingdom. But Satan himself is the great pretender. His weapons in the battle with the Son are "not force, but well couch't fraud, well woven snares" (1.97); he seeks "temptation and all guile on him to try" (1.123). Satan brings with him "a chosen band / Of Spirits likest to himself in guile" (2.236–37). The narrator describes Satan's "gray dissimulation" (1.498) and "the persuasive Rhetoric / That sleek't his tongue" (4.4–5). As such, Satan is linked with what Milton and his contemporaries saw as the deceit and pretense of the Roman Catholic Church.

The relics of Rome were one obvious example, for Protestant Englishmen, of popish fraud. Francis Mortoft, traveling in Rome in 1659, observes in the Church of Saint Sebastian a stone "on which, they say, remaines the representation of the print of our Saviour Christ's foote, which he left when he appeared to St. Peter."[20] After recounting the alleged dialogue between Christ and Peter and the genesis of the miraculous footprint, Mortoft adds tellingly: "whether this is true I know not, onely it must be taken as a narration of the Papists, who wil not spare sometymes to tel bouncers, especially if it may advance their Romish Church" (95). Mortoft elsewhere implies that other claims put forward for relics are equally "bouncers." He describes, for instance, the statue of Saint Helena, "holding 3 great nailes in her hand to represent that three of the nailes that naild our Saviour to the Crosse are kept in a place just over the statue, but I leave it to the pleasure of whoe will to beleeve"; nonetheless, he notes the widespread credulity of the people, so that "whether they be the true nailes or noe, they are shewed, with a great piece of the Crosse also on the Easter weeke to thousands of People that for that purpose comes to see them" (82).

The first temptation in *Paradise Regained* employs the fraud and false dependence on materiality associated by Milton and his contemporaries with Rome and the Catholic Church. Satan's words—"But if thou be the Son of God, Command / That out of these hard stones be made thee bread; / So shalt thou save thyself and us relieve / With Food, whereof we wretched seldom taste" (1.342–45)—tempt the Son to perform a miracle to save himself by material means, rather than trusting in God. In response, the Son rebuffs the temptation of "distrust," but he also exposes Satan as a liar and establishes his own role as true oracle. His ploy rejected, Satan endures an additional reproof: "Deservedly thou griev'st, compos'd of lies / From the beginning, and in lies wilt end" (1.407–8). Indeed the Son goes on to charge that "lying is thy sustenance, thy food. / Yet thou pretend'st to truth" (1.429–30).

While Satan's ensuing reference to the "Hypocrite or Atheous Priest" (1.487) may have an immediate referent in the Restoration church, the anti-Catholic language also places the current situation in England in the context of a long history of alleged papal abuses. The specific point at issue here—Satan's claim to speak oracular truth—may in itself aim at the oracular infallibility of Rome; more broadly, "pretense" is one crucial element of Milton's explicit prose attacks on popery, linked with fraud, usurpation, and carnality. Hence, Milton refers in *Animadversions* (1641) to "our pretended Father the Pope" (YP 1:728) and writes in *Of True Religion* (1673) that "of all known Sects or pretended Religions at this day in Christendom, Popery is the only or the greatest Heresie" (YP 8:421). In *Paradise Regained,* Christ's role as "living Oracle" (1.460) and the spirit of truth dwelling "In pious Hearts, an inward Oracle / To all truth requisite for men to know" (1.463–64) replaces the external corrupt church with the true, spiritual, and invisible church not aligned with temporal power.

If the first temptation in *Paradise Regained* is based on the false claim to truth, the second and longest temptation of the kingdoms evokes the dangerous commingling of temporal and ecclesiastical power that for Milton characterized the papacy. For Milton, popery was always marked not simply in doctrinal or ecclesiastical terms, but as a political threat. Hence, Milton explains in *Of True Religion* that most dangerous is the papal pretense to temporal power: "Ecclesiastical is ever pretended to Political. The Pope by this mixt faculty, pretends rights to Kingdoms and States, and especially to this of England, Thrones and Unthrones Kings, and absolves the people from their obedience to them" (YP 8:429). For Milton, this dangerous conjunction of temporal and spiritual power leads to corruption and carnality, as he writes in *Of Reformation* (1641): "But when through *Constantines* lavish Superstition they forsook their *first love,* and set themselvs up two Gods instead, *Mammon* and their Belly, then taking advantage of the spiritual power which they had on mens consciences, they began to cast a longing eye to get the body also, and bodily things into their command . . . and supporting their inward rottenes by a carnal, and outward strength" (YP 1:576–77).

Appearing in the second temptation of *Paradise Regained* as "one in City, or Court, or Palace bred" (2.300), Satan offers the Son luxury, wealth, military power, learning, and arts characteristic of the papacy. Having apparently rejected Belial's advice to "set women in his eye and in his walk" (2.153), Satan nonetheless begins the kingdoms temptation with a sensual offering: an elaborate banquet in the wilderness. The culinary delights of the banquet are designed to appeal to the fasting Son:

> A Table richly spread, in regal mode,
> With dishes pil'd, and meats of noblest sort
> And savor, Beasts of chase, or Fowl of game,
> In pastry built, or from the spit, or boil'd,
> Grisamber steam'd; all Fish from Sea or Shore,
> Freshet, or purling Brook, of shell or fin,
> And exquisitest name, for which was drain'd
> *Pontus* and *Lucrine* Bay, and *Afric* Coast.   (2.340–47)

The stately sideboard and lavish display contrast with the simple temptation of the fruit in *Paradise Lost,* which the narrator explicitly recalls: "Alas how simple, to these Cates compar'd, / Was the crude Apple that diverted *Eve!*" (2.348–49). Intensifying the appeal to the senses, the culinary display is accompanied by "Harmonious airs" (2.362) and heightened by evocative odors, including "wine / That fragrant smell diffus'd" (2.350–51) and winds bringing "*Arabian* odors" (2.364) and "*Flora's* earliest smells" (2.365).

Set in "regal mode," the table may recall Milton's animus in *The Readie and Easie Way* (1659) against the "sumptuous courts" and "vast expence and luxurie" of monarchy, including the "eating and drinking of excessive dainties" in the court of Louis XIV (YP 7:425–26). But the "stately sideboard" and the lavish display also recall the purported corruption and carnality of the papacy—intertwined with temporal power. Satan's pastoral grove with its sensuous banquet might well have recalled a papal history of luxurious feasting such as that under Leo X, well recorded by his admirers and detractors alike.[21] English histories of the papacy reiterated the accusations of carnality against Leo. John Bale includes in his *Pageant of Popes* the charges that Leo, "addicting him selfe to nicenesse, and takinge ease did pamper his fleshe in diverse vanities and carnal pleasures: At banqueting he delighted greatly in wine and musike: but had no care of preaching the Gospell."[22] A *Looking-Glasse for Papists* (1621) similarly asserts that Leo X "gave himself to pleasures, and lusts of the flesh: he had singers, and Musitians at his Table."[23]

Detailed accounts of Leo's banquets—such as those given upon his accession to the papal throne and on the occasion of Roman citizenship being granted to his brother and nephew—survive.[24] A contemporary account of the courses at one such banquet lists peacocks, a calf, a boar, a deer, and an eagle with a rabbit in its talons, served *rivestiti* or "redressed" in their own skins so that they appeared almost alive, and such other delicacies as kids stuffed with roast birds, testicles of roosters, gilded calves' heads with lemons in their mouths, and big pastry balls that contained live rabbits. The banquets also featured lavish wine, music, and entertainment by buffoons. Skits and plays that followed included young men playing both nymphs and male characters.[25]

While Satan had earlier argued—against Belial— that the Son would be impervious to "beauty and her lures" (2.194), carnality nonetheless returns in a distinctly antipapal guise in the youths and maidens, as well as the lavish food and drinks, of the banquet. The banquet also appeals to sexual intemperance, as it features "tall stripling youths rich clad, of fairer hue / Than *Ganymede* or *Hylas*" (2.352–53) as well as "Nymphs of *Diana's* train, and *Naiades*" (2.355) and "Ladies of th' *Hesperides*" (2.357). As Claude Summers writes, "Ganymede, the beautiful Trojan boy abducted by Jupiter and made cupbearer to the gods and Hylas, the young companion beloved of Hercules, were in the Renaissance not only archetypes of male adolescent beauty but also bywords for male homosexuality."[26] Summers adduces these youths as evidence of Milton's "sophisticated recognition of the range of fully human sexual possibilities," while Gregory Bredbeck has similarly argued that Milton has deliberately added a new and original homoerotic component to the exegetical tradition of the temptation in order to interrogate the strong masculinist stance and the language of patriarchy adopted by Belial and Satan.[27] Yet it is more likely that the stripling lads are part of a stereotypical if oblique attack on alleged homosexuality and sodomy in the Roman Catholic Church.

Again, specific instances could be adduced from the history of the Renaissance papacy. Among the "carnalities" he was said to enjoy, Pope Leo was alleged to favor banquets and entertainments that featured young boys. Antipapal writings seized upon an obscure passage in Leo's biographer, Paolo Giovio, to charge the pope with sexual intemperance and pederasty. Such accusations were reiterated in seventeenth-century England. Hence, *Two Treatises: The First, of the Lives of the Popes* (London, 1600), states that "Leo had also an evill report, because it appeared that he affected unhonestly some of his chamberlains. . . . It is not Luther his enemie, that saith this against him: but his friend, an Italian, and Bishop, Paulus Iovius."[28] Accordingly, in *Paradise Regained,* the Son's sharp rebuke—"Thy pompous Delicacies I contemn, / And count thy specious gifts no gifts but guiles" (2.390–91)—not only evinces temperance as a model for the individual Christian but recalls the church to its earlier purity in the aftermath of papal corruption.

Satan's ensuing offers of wealth, glory, and empire, based on Alexander the Great, Julius Caesar, Scipio Africanus, and Pompey, similarly have antipapal resonance. Under the Renaissance papacy, and in particular Julius II as the "warrior pope," triumph, glory, and imperial dominion replaced martyrdom and holiness as subjects for praise and worthy ideals. The Roman pontiffs seized upon the legacy of the Caesars to bolster their own imperial ambitions: the ambitious and warmongering Julius II found suitable forms in imperial Rome for expression of his military and triumphal aims. Julius identified himself as the second Julius Caesar, while his successor, Leo X, was lauded as an Augustus fully ushering in a golden age of peace and prosperity, art and learning.[29] Classicized triumphal motifs were applied to Christ himself in such works as Marcus Hieronymus Vida's *Christiad,* commissioned by Pope Leo.[30] In Milton's own time, the Rome of Pope Urban VIII (1623–1644) boasted of producing a second Roman renaissance modeled on the golden age of Julius and Leo X.[31]

Hence, in response to Satan's offers of wealth, the Son points to self-rule and spiritual kingship which sharply contrast with the luxury and power-mongering of the Renaissance papacy. Rejecting the model of the Caesars, the Son argues that military conquerors "rob and spoil, burn, slaughter, and enslave / Peaceable Nations" (3.75–76). While Satan offers glory and empire, the Son sees his kingdom as invisible and spiritual. Further, to the offer of Parthian military power—by conquest or by league—as the means to gain the throne of Israel and deliver the ten lost tribes, the Son again reiterates the spiritual nature of his kingdom and refuses to free the self-enslaved and idolatrous. The true church does not need "fleshly arm, / And fragile arms" (3.387–88). In the Son's rejections of military power, *Paradise Regained* defines the true church as not allied with worldly wealth or state power.

Satan's offer of the wealth, dominion, glory, and opulence of Rome incorporates all of the earlier worldly temptations and most centrally evokes the splendor of the papacy. Rebuffed in his offer of Parthian military power, Satan turns to "great and glorious *Rome,* Queen of the Earth / So far renown'd, and with the spoils enricht / Of Nations" (4.45–47). Satan's description recalls the traditional Protestant linkage of Rome with the Roman Catholic Church and the whore of Babylon, who in Revelation, chapter 17, sits resplendent upon a scarlet, seven-headed beast with ten horns and in Revelation, chapter 18, "saith in her heart, I sit a queen and am no widow and shal see no sorrow" (Rev. 18:7).[32]

Satan's depiction of the "Imperial City" recalls the spectacle and stately magnificence of not only classical but also papal Rome:

> With Towers and Temples proudly elevate
> On seven small Hills, with Palaces adorn'd
> Porches and Theaters, Baths, Aqueducts,
> Statues and Trophies, and Triumphal Arcs,
> Gardens and Groves.   (4.34–38)

The Rome depicted in the poem, with its conflux of "Praetors, Proconsuls to thir Provinces, / Hasting or on return, in robes of State; / Lictors and rods, the ensigns of thir power" (4.63–65), recalls the frequent arrivals and departures of legations to papal Rome as a hub of international politics during the late Renaissance.

The "Houses of Gods" (4.56) that Satan reveals with his "Airy Microscope" (4.57) and Rome's "ample Territory, wealth, and power, / Civility of Manners, Arts, and Arms, / And long Renown" (4.82–84) point toward the spectacle that reached new heights in Julius's classicized triumphs and Leo's coronation and the festivities conferring citizenship on Leo's brother, Giuliano, and nephew, Lorenzo De Medici.[33] Rome's imperial palace, with its "compass huge, and high / The Structure, skill of noblest Architects, / With gilded battlements, conspicuous far / Turrets and Terraces and glittering Spires" (4.51–54), may also suggest that central sanctuary, Saint Peter's Basilica, the rebuilding of which began under Julius and Leo.[34]

While Satan urges the Son to expel the aging and much-hated Tiberius from his throne and free his vassal subjects, Jesus again refuses to free a people "deservedly made vassal" (4.133), whether enslaved to pope or monarch. The Son also points to the carnality that characterizes worldly Rome, also marking, for Milton, the Roman Catholic Church:

> Nor doth this grandeur and majestic show
> Of luxury, though call'd magnificence,
> More than of arms before, allure mine eye,
> Much less my mind; though thou should'st add to tell
> Thir sumptuous gluttonies, and gorgeous feasts
> On *Citron* tables or *Atlantic* stone.   (4.110–15)

In rejecting the luxury and carnality of Rome, the Son returns the true church to the chaste and humble poverty of its origins, underscored by his own humble origins, in Satan's words, "unknown, unfriended, low of birth, / A Carpenter thy Father known, thyself / Bred up in poverty and straits at home" (2.413–15).

The historical source of that carnality emerges in the aftermath of the temptation of Rome, as Satan suddenly, almost petulantly, reveals the "abominable terms, impious condition" of idolatry, prompting the Son's rebuke: "It is written / The first of all Commandments, Thou shalt worship / The Lord thy God, and only him shalt serve" (4.175–77). But the Son goes on to challenge Satan in language evocative of the pretended dominion of the papacy: "The Kingdoms of the world to thee were giv'n, / Permitted rather, and by thee usurp't, / Other donation none thou canst produce" (4.182–84). Elsewhere, Milton repeatedly links both usurpation and "donation" with popery. In *The Readie and Easie Way,* he writes that for a Christian man to claim his kingship is from Christ is "wors usurpation then the Pope his headship over the church" (YP 7:429). He represents the pope himself as a usurper in *Of True Religion,* writing that "Popery is a double thing to deal with, and claims a twofold Power, Ecclesiastical and Political, both usurpt, and the one supporting the other" (YP 8:429). Similarly, Milton uses the term "donation" elsewhere almost exclusively in connection with the (spurious) donation of Constantine, the first Christian emperor (c. 285–337), who built stately churches and encouraged "a Deluge of Ceremonies" (*Of Reformation*, in YP 1:556–57). Papal claims for temporal authority were based on this document, by which Emperor Constantine, miraculously cured of leprosy through baptism by Pope Sylvester, donated the City of Rome, the Western empire, and the imperial regalia to the pope. Although as early as 1440 Lorenzo Valla had shown the document to be an eighth-century forgery, Constantine was prominently featured in the art and architecture of Renaissance and baroque Rome, undergirding papal claims to imperial power.[35] For later critics, however, including Dante, Wyclif, Hus, and Martin Luther, the donation was the source of the church's corruption.

Milton too saw Constantine's gift of temporal power as setting the church on a long and sharp decline. In more than a dozen references in his prose, Milton decries the deleterious influence of the donation of Constantine on the church. In *The Likeliest Means to Remove Hirelings* (1659), for instance, Milton writes that "the church fell off and turnd whore sitting on that beast in the Revelations, when under Pope *Silvester* she receivd those temporal donations" (YP 7:306). Milton at times seems to acknowledge that the alleged donation endowing Pope Sylvester and his successors with supremacy in religion and temporal dominion over Rome was a forgery, writing in *Of Reformation:* "Mark Sir how the Pope came by *S. Peters* Patrymony, as he feigns it, not the donation of *Constantine,* but idolatry and rebellion got it him" (YP 1:578). But most often, for polemical purposes, Milton takes the donation at face value, observing in *Eikonoklastes,* for instance, that "those [true] Churches in *Piemont* have held the same Doctrin and Government since the time that *Constantine* with his mischeivous donations poyson'd *Silvester* and the whole church" (YP 3:514).

The Son's rebuke of Satan's idolatrous terms thus takes on historically specific connotations in Restoration England. In his rejection of the dangerously commingled powers of church and state, the Son both condemns current practices and places the bishops in a papal tradition. The Son reveals that underlying this dangerous conjunction is the danger of idolatry, and he definitively rejects the offer of the kingdoms: "Get thee behind me; plain thou now appear'st / That Evil one, Satan for ever damn'd" (4.193–94).

The temptation of learning is both unique to Milton and, for many commentators, the most puzzling of the earthly temptations. Coming after the apparent end of the kingdoms temptation—Satan avows, "Therefore let pass, as they are transitory, / The Kingdoms of this world; I shall no more / Advise thee, gain them as thou canst, or not" (4.209–11)—the temptation nonetheless continues the commingling of temporal and ecclesiastical power that marks Satan's earlier offers. In turning to Athens and Plato's Academy, Satan once again evokes the learning and arts revived under Popes Julius and Leo as part of their claim to temporal and spiritual power and reclaimed again by Pope Urban in Milton's own time. Hence, he offers these arts as a means of power and glory—"Be famous then / By wisdom; as thy Empire must extend, / So let extend thy mind o'er all the world" (4.221–23). In keeping with the claim of the papacy to incorporate the best of classical learning, Satan eschews a strict biblicism:

> All knowledge is not couch't in *Moses'* Law,
> The *Pentateuch* or what the Prophets wrote;
> The *Gentiles* also know, and write, and teach
> To admiration, led by Nature's light.   (4.225–28)

The description of "*Athens,* the eye of *Greece,* Mother of Arts / And Eloquence" (4.240–41) recalls the arts and rhetoric that Milton himself had studied and admired. But those arts were also part of the intellectual and artistic revival of Renaissance Italy, nurtured by and contributing to the enhanced power of the papacy. Although in the end the revival of Latin, not Greek, mattered more to Renaissance Rome, the theme of Rome as the new Athens developed under both Julius and Leo, in particular with the acquisition of Greek manuscripts in the Vatican library.[36] Further, Satan's presentation of Plato's enchanting grove summons up the sensuous appeal of the earlier banquet scene: "See there the Olive Grove of *Academe,* / *Plato's* retirement, where the *Attic* Bird / Trills her thick-warbl'd notes the summer long" (4.244–46). The revival of ancient Greek eloquence and Ciceronian rhetoric also marked Renaissance Rome, recalled in Satan's evocation of the "famous Orators" (4.267) whose "resistless eloquence / Wielded at will that fierce Democracy" (4.268–69).

And thus while Milton himself followed the example of Cicero and used classical oratory for republican ends in his *Defenses,* the Son must reject the arts and learning of Rome as they serve temporal power and pretend to divine wisdom. As Satan pretends to truth, evoking the fraudulence of popery, so classical learning has been misappropriated as the false twin of divine wisdom: "Who therefore seeks in these / True wisdom, finds her not, or by delusion / Far worse, her false resemblance only meets, / An empty cloud" (4.318–21).

The Son's rejection of arts and rhetoric defines true faith and the true church in terms sharply opposed to the flourishing of learning and humanistic knowledge that marked the corrupt papacy. Much of what Satan offers Christ in the kingdoms temptation—wealth, power, military power, learning and the arts—was central to the exultant vision of the Renaissance papacy. To the pursuit of temporal power, territorial consolidation, and military expenditure marking the papacy, *Paradise Regained* opposes the contrasting values of humility, obedience, poverty, and chastity.

Following the kingdoms temptation, the third and final temptation of the tower in *Paradise Regained* again shows antipapal sentiment. But while Milton had earlier seemed to avoid the Crucifixion, attention to physical suffering—and the rhetoric, arts, banquet, and heroic mode earlier rejected when offered in the service of temporal power—are returned in spiritualized form to the triumphant Son. The storm preceding and Satan's placing of the Son on the tower threaten violence and foreshadow the Passion and death.[37] Satan himself now professes to read in the stars the suffering and death that the Son must endure: "Sorrows, and labors, opposition, hate, / Attends thee, scorns, reproaches, injuries, / Violence and stripes, and lastly cruel death" (4.386–88). The tower temptation suggests the violence of the scourging and Crucifixion. Having placed the Son on a precarious, perhaps impossible, perch on the pinnacle—"There stand, if thou wilt stand; to stand upright / Will ask thee skill" (4.551–52)—Satan further challenges him to show his divinity:

> if not to stand,
> Cast thyself down; safely if Son of God:
> For it is written, He will give command
> Concerning thee to his Angels, in thir hands
> They shall up lift thee, lest at any time
> Thou chance to dash thy foot against a stone.   (4.554–59)

While Satan tauntingly paraphrases the Psalms, his words also evoke the reviling of Christ upon the cross: "If thou be the Son of God, come down from the cross. . . . He saved others; himself he cannot save. If he be the King of Israel, let him now come down from the cross, and we will believe him" (Matt. 27:40–42). Hence, if much of *Paradise Regained* has seemed to avoid the suffering and the Crucifixion, the body of Christ so prominent in Catholic art and sacrament, this final scene boldly reinscribes and revises that climactic moment.

The Son's patient refusal to save himself by miracle— or to call upon God miraculously to save him—points ahead to and on one level enacts the temporary submission to satanic power evinced in the Crucifixion. But that very submission brings about revelation of divinity and victory over the forces of evil: "To whom thus Jesus. Also it is written, / Tempt not the Lord thy God; he said and stood" (4.560–61). If, at the cross, the centurions acknowledge, "Truly this was the Son of God" (Matt 27:54), Satan is likewise amazed and at the same time defeated in the only real action of the poem:

> But Satan smitten with amazement fell
> As when Earth's *Antaeus* (to compare
> Small things with greatest) in *Irassa* strove
> With *Jove's Alcides,* and oft foil'd still rose,
> Receiving from his mother Earth new strength,
> Fresh from his fall, and fiercer grapple join'd,
> Throttl'd at length in th'Air, expir'd and fell:
> So after many a foil the Tempter proud,
> Renewing fresh assaults, amidst his pride
> Fell whence he stood to see his Victor fall.   (4.562–71)

In this and the simile of the *"Theban* Monster" that follows, Milton brings back in the classical myth and learning refused in the temptations of Athens— Oedipus overthrowing the Sphinx, the story of Hercules and Antaeus—not to further the worldly, imperial church but to reveal the achievement and true identity of the obedient, disciplined Son. The comparison to Hercules assigns to the Son the heroic qualities and conquest eschewed in the temptation of Parthia, now revised as appropriate to his spiritual conquest over Satan. If the Son has earlier rejected false, worldly models of imperial conquest, he is nonetheless now praised as a conqueror in a spiritual triumph that outgoes the physical, as "Angelic Choirs / Sung Heavenly Anthems of his victory / Over temptation and the Tempter proud" (4.593–95). While the Son has rejected satanic offers of fame on earth, "where glory is false glory," like the glittering display of papal Rome, he now attains true renown in heaven.

Similarly, for the false, luxurious banquets that he has rejected, the Son is now given a heavenly banquet, with Eucharistic overtones that replace and defeat the earlier parodic banquets in the wilderness and of Rome offered by Satan. Rescued by angels from his precarious perch, the Son receives "A table of Celestial Food, Divine, / Ambrosial, Fruits fetcht from the tree of life, / And from the fount of life Ambrosial drink" (4.588–90). The "Heavenly Feast" with which the Son is refreshed at the end of *Paradise Regained* recaptures for the steadfast believer the true sacrament of Christ's sacrifice: the song of victory replaces the lavish displays of imperial power as the heavenly feast replaces papal extravagance and luxury.

While *Paradise Regained* rejects what Milton views as the beautiful, opulent, but ultimately decadent and even idolatrous culture of papal Rome, it is not in the end a wholly ascetic work. The obedient and patient Son ultimately gains—albeit in revised and spiritualized form—both renown and the riches of human culture, not to promulgate the false temporal power of the papacy, but to nurture the internal discipline that marked the true believer in an age of persecution. From an external, worldly perspective, nothing has changed for the Son. But he now has within him the faith, knowledge, and discipline by which worldly powers can ultimately be overturned. "Sung Victor, and from Heavenly Feast refresht" (4.636), the Son returns privately, quietly to "his Mother's house" (4.638). As the Son of God begins "to save mankind" (4.635), the agony—and triumph—of Michelangelo's *Pieta* lie just ahead.

The Pennsylvania State University

NOTES

An earlier version of my essay was presented in the general Milton session of the December 2000 Modern Language Association meeting, chaired by John Mulryan. I am grateful for the valuable responses I received at that session, as well as for the useful insights and suggestions of David Loewenstein and Al Labriola, the editors of this volume.

1. John Evelyn, *The Diary of John Evelyn*, ed. E. S. de Beer, 6 vols. (Oxford, 1955), 2:255, 264.

2. See Loren Partridge, *The Art of Renaissance Rome, 1400–1600* (New York, 1996), 101–4.

3. Milton does not allude to the art and architecture in his description, some years later, of his travels in *Defensio Secunda* (1654). All quotations from Milton's prose are taken from *Complete Prose Works of John Milton*, 8 vols., ed. Don. M. Wolfe et al. (New Haven, 1953–82), 4:614–19; hereafter designated as YP and cited parenthetically by volume and page number in the text.

4. Roland Frye, *Milton's Imagery and the Visual Arts: Iconographic Tradition in the Epic Poems* (Princeton, 1978), argues that the corporal forms that Milton delineates in *Paradise Lost* and *Paradise Regained* derive from the traditions of sacred art.

5. Michael O'Connell, "Milton and the Art of Italy: A Revisionist View," in *Milton in Italy: Contexts, Images, Contradictions*, ed. Mario Di Cesare (Binghamton, N.Y., 1991), 221. O'Connell goes on to argue for a "strong disapprobation" of such visual arts in *Paradise Regained* (235).

6. For a broad overview, see John T. Paoletti and Gary M. Radke, *Art in Renaissance Italy* (New York, 1997); and Partridge, *The Art of Renaissance Rome*.

7. On Julius and Leo, see Ludwig Pastor, *The History of the Popes*, trans. and ed. Ralph Francis Kerr (London, 1923), vols. 6 and 7; and on Leo X, Thomas Roscoe, *The Life and Pontificate of Leo X*, 2 vols., 5th ed. (London, 1846). For an influential contemporary life of Leo, see Paolo Giovio, *Pauli Iovii Novocomensis episcopi Nucerini de Vita Leonis Decimi Pont. Max. libri quatuor* (Florence, 1549).

8. On anti-Catholicism in seventeenth-century England, see Caroline Hibbard, *Charles I and the Popish Plot* (Chapel Hill, N.C., 1983); Anthony Milton, *Catholic and Reformed: The Roman and Protestant Churches in English Protestant Thought, 1600–1640* (Cambridge, 1995); Robin Clifton, "Fear of Popery," in *The Origins of the English Civil War*, ed. Conrad Russell (London, 1973), 144–67; John Miller, *Popery and Politics in England, 1660–1688* (Cambridge, 1973); Peter Lake, "Anti-Popery: The Structure of a Prejudice," in *Conflict in Early Stuart England: Studies in Religion and Politics, 1603–1642*, ed. Richard Cust and Ann Hughes (London, 1989); and Frances Dolan, *Whores of Babylon: Catholicism, Gender, and Seventeenth-Century Print Culture* (New York, 1999).

9. Barbara Lewalski, *Milton's Brief Epic: The Genre, Meaning, and Art of "Paradise Re-*

gained" (Providence, R.I., 1966), notes that "precedents for a brief epic on the subject of the temptation of Christ are almost nonexistent" (104). Much of the dissatisfaction centers on the character of the Son. John Carey, *Milton* (London, 1969), terms Christ a "celibate detective" (137), while for Alan Fisher, "Why Is *Paradise Regained* So Cold?" in *Milton Studies* 14, ed. James D. Simmonds (Pittsburgh, 1980), the Son is "heartless, prissy, or downright cold" (206); Northrop Frye, "The Typology of *Paradise Regained,*" in *Milton: Modern Essays in Criticism,* ed. Arthur E. Barker (New York, 1965), sees an "inhuman snob" (439). Of the particular temptations, the temptation of learning has most puzzled commentators. In early studies, Douglas Bush, *The Renaissance and English Humanism* (Toronto, 1939), termed "the violent denunciation of Greek culture" a "painful shock," going on to observe that "it is painful to watch Milton turn and rend some main roots of his being" (124–25); and George Sensabaugh, "Milton on Learning," *Studies in Philology* 43 (1946): 258–72, likewise found it "distinctly surprising" to "hear Christ, in *Paradise Regained,* belittle the whole heritage of Greece and Rome" (258), positing that "not so much the march of events as the force of theological dogma compelled Milton to speak against his earlier convictions and his deepest experience" (272). In my view, these concerns have not been fully answered in subsequent criticism. A helpful perspective is given by David Loewenstein, *Representing Revolution in Milton and His Contemporaries: Religion, Politics, and Polemics in Radical Puritanism* (Cambridge, 2001), who notes that Jesus "dramatizes that fierce Miltonic stance of polemical engagement and vehement response . . . countering rhetorical extreme with rhetorical extreme" (266).

10. On the politics of interiority and radical religious culture, albeit not in the context of Catholicism, see Loewenstein, *Representing Revolution,* 254–59.

11. Particularly instructive on Milton and Catholicism are recent studies by Achsah Guibbory, *Ceremony and Community from Herbert to Milton* (Cambridge, 1998), and John King, *Milton and Religious Controversy* (Cambridge, 2000). Both focus more on *Paradise Lost* than on Milton's later poems, but see the helpful brief comments on *Paradise Regained* in Guibbory, 219–27, and King, 189–90. Also useful is John Shawcross, " 'Connivers and the Worst of Superstitions': Milton on Popery and Toleration," *Literature and History,* 3d ser., 7, no. 2 (1990): 51–69. The most sustained treatment of *Paradise Regained* and Catholicism, however, remains the early work of Howard Schultz which, while useful, tends to overallegorize the Son as a figure for the true church versus the Catholic Antichrist. See Schultz, "Christ and Antichrist in *Paradise Regained,*" *PMLA* 43 (1952): 790–808, and his *Milton and Forbidden Knowledge* (London, 1955).

12. Christopher Hill, *Milton and the English Revolution* (New York, 1978), 413–27, views the Son as rejecting those things that led the revolutionaries astray. Andrew Milner, *John Milton and the English Revolution: A Study in the Sociology of Literature* (Totowa, N.J., 1981), 167–79, and Michael Wilding, *Dragons Teeth: Literature in the English Revolution* (Oxford, 1987), 249–53, find quietism and withdrawal in the poem. Among recent studies, David Loewenstein, "The Kingdom Within: Radical Religious Culture and the Politics of *Paradise Regained,*" *Literature and History* 3, no. 2 (1994): 63–89, sees the poem as more radically resistant, linked with the Quakers. Loewenstein places even greater emphasis on the polemical dimensions of *Paradise Regained,* including the subversiveness of the Son's obscurity and "mighty weakness," in *Representing Revolution,* 242–68. David Quint traces the poem's ongoing challenge to Stuart monarchy in "David's Census: Milton's Politics and *Paradise Regained,*" in *Re-membering Milton: Essays on the Texts and Traditions,* ed. Mary Nyquist and Margaret Ferguson (New York, 1988), 128–47. My own book, *Historicizing Milton: Spectacle, Power, and Poetry in Restoration England* (Athens, Ga., 1994), 13–41, discusses *Paradise Regained* as challenging Stuart claims to Christic martyrdom.

13. On anti-Catholicism in seventeenth-century England, see Caroline Hibbard, *Charles I*

and the Popish Plot (Chapel Hill, N.C., 1983); Anthony Milton, *Catholic and Reformed: The Roman and Protestant Churches in English Protestant Thought, 1600–1640* (Cambridge, 1995); Robin Clifton, "Fear of Popery," in *The Origins of the English Civil War,* ed. Conrad Russell (London, 1973), 144–67; John Miller, *Popery and Politics in England, 1660–1688* (Cambridge, 1973); Peter Lake, "Anti-Popery: The Structure of a Prejudice," in *Conflict in Early Stuart England: Studies in Religion and Politics, 1603–1642,* ed. Richard Cust and Ann Hughes (London, 1989); and Frances Dolan, *Whores of Babylon: Catholicism, Gender, and Seventeenth-Century Print Culture* (Ithaca, N.Y., 1999).

14. On anti-popery in the 1670s, see especially Miller, *Popery and Politics*.

15. On *Of True Religion,* see Reuben Sanchez, *Persona and Decorum in Milton's Prose* (Madison, N.J., 1997), 180–94; Raymond Tumbleson, *Catholicism in the English Protestant Imagination: Nationalism, Religion, and Literature, 1660–1745* (Cambridge, 1998), 41–68; Shawcross, "'Connivers and the Worst of Superstitions'"; and, most recently, Hong Won Suh, "Belial, Popery, and True Religion: Milton's *Of True Religion* and Antipapist Sentiment," in *Living Texts: Interpreting Milton,* ed. Kristin Pruitt and Charles Durham (Selinsgrove, Pa., 2000), 283–302.

16. In addition to Evelyn's account, see Fynes Moryson, *An Itinerary Containing His Ten Yeeres Travell,* vol. 1 (Glasgow, 1907), 258–304; *Francis Mortoft, his Book. Being His Travels through France and Italy, 1658–59,* ed. Malcolm Letts (London, 1925). See also John Raymond, *An Itinerary Contayning a Voyage Made Through Italy* (London, 1648); Richard Lassels, *The Voyage of Italy* (Paris, 1670).

17. *The Diary of John Evelyn,* 2:240, 242.

18. All quotations from *Paradise Regained* and *Paradise Lost* are taken from *John Milton: Complete Poems and Major Prose,* ed. Merritt Y. Hughes (Indianapolis, 1957).

19. On *Paradise Regained* as a rebuttal of Stuart claims of martyrdom, see Knoppers, *Historicizing Milton,* 13–41; on the poem in alliance with Quaker martyrdom, see Loewenstein, "The Kingdom Within," and *Representing Revolution,* 242–68.

20. *Francis Mortoft, his Book,* 94.

21. I am indebted to Stella Revard for suggesting a link between the banquet scene and Leo X.

22. John Bale, *The Pageant of Popes Contayning the lyves of all the Bishops of Rome, from the beginninge of them to the yeare of Grace 1555* (London, 1555), fol. 179v.

23. *A Looking-Glasse for Papists . . . with a briefe History of Popes lives* (London, 1621), 67.

24. Bonner Mitchell, *Italian Civic Pageantry in the High Renaissance: A Descriptive Bibliography* (Firenze, 1979), 117–24. Primary sources are collected in Fabrizio Cruciani, *Il Teatro del Campidoglio e le Feste Romane del 1513* (Milano, 1968); see especially the account of Paolo Palliolo (21–67), including a detailed listing of the banquet courses (39–44).

25. See the description in Bonner Mitchell, *Rome in the High Renaissance: The Age of Leo X* (Norman, Okla., 1973), 68–70, and the primary sources in Cruciani, *Il Teatro del Campidoglio*.

26. Claude J. Summers, "The (Homo)Sexual Temptation in Milton's *Paradise Regained,*" in *Reclaiming the Sacred: The Bible in Gay and Lesbian Culture,* ed. Raymond-Jean Frontain (New York, 1997), 53.

27. Ibid., 65; Gregory Bredbeck, "Milton's Ganymede: Negotiations of Homoerotic Tradition in *Paradise Regained*" *PMLA* 106 (1991): 262–76.

28. *Two Treatises: The First, of the Lives of the Popes* (London, 1600), 150; see similar charges in *A True History of the Lives of the Popes of Rome* (London, 1679), 12, and *A Satirical Account of the Lives of the Popes* (London, 1702), 177.

29. Charles L. Stinger, *The Renaissance in Rome* (Bloomington, 1985), 10–12.

30. Lewalski, *Milton's Brief Epic,* 53–67, points to Vida's *Christiad* as well as other humanist

biblical epics as part of the literary tradition of Milton's brief epic; she does not, however, explore Milton's epic as a *challenge* to the triumphal epics produced as part of an overarching papal cultural program.

31. John D'Amico, *Renaissance Humanism in Papal Rome: Humanists and Churchmen on the Eve of the Reformation* (Baltimore, 1983), 142.

32. For other commentators on this point, see Schultz, "Christ and Antichrist," 803; Barbara K. Lewalski, *The Life of John Milton* (Oxford, 2000), 519; and Lewalski, *Milton's Brief Epic,* 275–77.

33. See sources cited in Bonner Mitchell, *Italian Civic Pageantry,* esp. 15–25 (on Julius II) and 117–24 (on Leo X). Such ceremonies continued in the mid-seventeenth century. Evelyn, *The Diary of John Evelyn,* for instance, observes the people busy "in erecting temporary Triumphs & arches, with statues, and flattering Inscriptions" in preparation for a papal installation (2.228).

34. Lewalski, *The Life of John Milton,* also makes this point (519). For an important (and neglected) early linkage of Saint Peter's and Milton's Pandemonium, see Rebecca W. Smith, "The Sources of Milton's Pandemonium," *Modern Philology* 29 (1931–1932): 187–98.

35. On Constantine, see Partridge, *The Art of Renaissance Rome,* 14–15. On Constantine's arch, the various churches said to be founded by Constantine, and the relics linked with Constantine and his mother, Helena, see the travel accounts of Evelyn, *The Diary of John Evelyn; Francis Mortoft, his Book;* Lassels, *The Voyage of Italy;* and Raymond, *An Itinerary Contayning a Voyage.*

36. Stinger, *The Renaissance in Rome,* 286–87.

37. On this point regarding the third temptation, and on literary precedents, see Lewalski, *Milton's Brief Epic,* 308–15.

WILDERNESS EXERCISES: ADVERSITY, TEMPTATION, AND TRIAL IN *PARADISE REGAINED*

N. H. Keeble

I. "STEP BY STEP LED ON"

"I who erstwhile the happy garden sung."
(*Paradise Regained*, 1.1)

THE FIRST LINE OF *Paradise Regained* makes explicit the implication of its title: this is Miltonic work. The poem begins in recollection of *Paradise Lost,* and in metonymic allusion to humanity's original innocence and bliss. Thereafter, *Paradise Lost* shadows its successor as the movement between hell and heaven of its first three books is reproduced in miniature in the opening two hundred lines of *Paradise Regained*. The demonic council summoned by Satan "in mid air," "Within thick clouds and dark tenfold involved, / A gloomy consistory," at which the infernal powers commit to "their great dictator" Satan the "main enterprise" of subverting the "attested Son of God" (1.112, 113, 122, 124), is succeeded by the rejoicing of the "full frequence bright / Of angels" in heaven upon hearing that the Father is to fulfill his "purposed counsel pre-ordained" by frustrating the "stratagems of hell" through "This perfect man, by merit called my Son" (1.127, 128–29, 166, 180).[1] Heaven and hell are once again preoccupied with distant, and apparently inconsequential, human beings, the "puny habitants" of earth, this time a man "obscure, / Unmarked, unknown" (1.24–25), the Father's "new favourite."[2] And it is with explicit reference to his previous "dismal expedition" that Satan sets out for this second stage of his "exploit" to "ruin Adam" (1.101, 102).

His destination, though, is this time very different. While the opening of *Paradise Regained* announces continuity with *Paradise Lost*, it also registers a stark contrast between the "happy garden" context of Adam and Eve's prelapsarian life and the fallen world in which the Son must fulfill his mission. Shortly after his baptism by John, the Son

> One day walked forth alone, the spirit leading
> And his deep thoughts, the better to converse
> With solitude, till far from track of men,
> Thought following thought, and step by step led on,
> He entered now the bordering desert wild.   (1.189–93)

In his reverie the Son does not watch where he is going, and later, a little surprised to find just how far he has wandered, he has no idea where he is, or why he is there; but, though careless of himself, and mystified, he is confident that he has walked with divine purpose. No less than Milton's Samson led by the "guiding hand" of Providence is the Son "step by step led on"; he is "by some strong motion . . . led / Into this wilderness" (1.290–92) as Samson is inspired by "rousing motions" (*SA*, lines 1, 1383). However, if the Son does not (yet) understand "to what intent" an unknown "guide" has brought him to this place (1.336), the reader, privy to divine intentions, knows very well: the Father means "To exercise him in the wilderness" (1.156).

In this Milton is of course following his sources in which "Jesus was led up of the Spirit into the wilderness to be tempted of the devil" (Matt. 4:1; compare Luke 4:1). Mark is more forceful—"the Spirit driveth him into the wilderness" (1:12)—but none of the synoptic gospels has much more to say on the matter. Mark mentions that Jesus "was there in the wilderness . . . with the wild beasts" and Matthew and Luke both have him there for forty days, fasting, after which he is "hungred" (when in Matthew he is tempted, though throughout the forty days in Luke). Beyond this, the evangelists show no interest in the material circumstances of the temptation. In Milton's much expanded narrative, however, that "desert wild" is insistently present.[3] It is again a "desert wild" at Book Two, line 109, but also a "pathless desert" (1.296) and a "woody maze" (2.246), akin—rather unexpectedly in view of Milton's denigration of the "fabled knights" of romance in *Paradise Lost* (9.30)—to the "Forest wide" in which were tested "Knights of Logres, or of Lyones" (2.359–60). The Son, in a "wild solitude . . . / Of all things destitute" (2.304–5), is "Lost in a desert here and hunger-bit" (2.416). Indeed, after only ten lines it is the "desert" which the poem explicitly identifies as his "victorious field / Against the spiritual foe" (1.9–10). The wilderness, it seems, is not incidental but essential to the divine plan. No other locus is adequate to the action: the Father will have his Son prove himself there, and nowhere else.

The wilderness, then, matters. Within this barren place lies something of the meaning of the poem. It is the purpose of this essay to explore why (and how) in Milton's amplification of the biblical narratives the desert develops from a circumstantial detail to a resonantly significant part of the poem's design. Milton takes up with traditional assumptions and hermeneutical strategies but he deploys them to serve his own very particular and pointed cultural ends. His desert is shaped by the cultural landscape of the 1660s. The Miltonic wasteland, this essay will argue, both issues a challenge to, and offers a refuge from, the political and religious configuration of the Restoration regime.

II. LOCATING THE WILDERNESS

We may begin by asking: Where, in fact, does Satan confront the Son? Initially, as we might expect, this "desert wild" borders "Bethabara, where John baptized" and where the Son "some days / Lodged" before taking his meditative stroll (1.183–84). He walks a good way, for later the disciples, searching "nigh to Bethbara" (2.20), fail to find him, and when the Son himself looks around, he

> on every side beheld
> A pathless desert, dusk with horrid shades;
> The way he came not having marked, return
> Was difficult, by human steps untrod.   (1.295–98)

His isolation is becoming ominous, as though removed from the realm of the human. Here, lost, he wanders for forty days. By the time he meets Satan, disguised as an "aged man in rural weeds" (1.314), his predicament has grown dire: he is "far from path or road of men, who pass / In troop or caravan, for single none / Durst ever, who returned, and dropped not here / His carcase" (1.322–25). Its distance from human habitation is so emphasized (the "nighest" town or village "is far" [1.333]) that this desert is hardly any longer local and specific, though it still has a foothold in topographical fact and contemporary human experience: it is at least traversed by caravans. Shortly afterwards, however, when the Son replies to Satan's first temptation, it becomes altogether vaster and vaguer:

> Is it not written
>
> . . . .
> Man lives not by bread only, but each word
> Proceeding from the mouth of God; who fed
> Our fathers here with manna; in the mount
> Moses was forty days, nor eat nor drank,
> And forty days Elijah without food
> Wandered this barren waste, the same I now.   (1.347–54)

The Son, it seems, has wandered far into biblical history. "Here" is no longer near Bethabara; it is rather the locus of a series of significant moments in Israelite history: Moses receiving the Ten Commandments on Mount Sinai; the forty years' desert wanderings of the Israelites; the fasting of Elijah. Indeed, for the alert reader this desert had already begun to slip its geographical and temporal moorings when the disguised Satan warned the Son that none wandered in it solitary "and dropped not here / His carcase:" that "your carcase . . . shall fall in the wilderness" was the punishment pronounced by Jehovah on those rebellious Israelites who, following the Exodus, desired to return to Egypt and "murmured against Moses and against Aaron" in the wilderness of Paran (Num. 12:16; 14:2, 4, 29). The Son walks where Israel had walked to the Promised Land, in the footsteps of the prophets: as Satan later observes, "Others of some note, / As story tells, have trod *this* wilderness" (2.306–7; italics mine). The location of the temptation of Christ has become a conflation (or identification) of many wildernesses.[4]

III. TYPE AND SHADOWS

This is not because Milton's grasp of geography was weak. In both its history of Israel's covenant relationship with Jehovah and in its records of the lives of patriarchs and prophets, religious dedication and desert journeys are so interconnected in the Old Testament that wilderness landscapes, and journeys through them, become the context in which spiritual destinies are fulfilled. In the two traditions of Israel's origins, in the Abraham legends and the Exodus saga, is repeated the same pattern of a decision to leave, a journey under divine guidance, testing in the wilderness, divine approval and covenant. In Milton's own summary account, Moses "had forsaken all the greatness of *Egypt,* and chose a troublesome journey in his old age through the wilderness."[5] Subsequent biblical narratives repeatedly contrive adverse circumstances to drive those favored of God into the desert to find divine succor and spiritual illumination. Again and again the biblical story is peripatetic, nomadic, migratory, its protagonists outcasts, wanderers, exiles in barren and hostile lands. Moses fled after killing the Egyptian to live as "a stranger in the land of Madian," "a stranger in a strange land" (Acts 7:29; Exod. 2:22); Elijah "fled / Into the desert" to escape Jezebel (*PR* 2.271–72; 1 Kings 19:4–8); and David sought refuge from Saul in a succession of wilderness places (see, for example, 1 Sam. 23:14, 24, 29), where, in the words of the gloss of the old Geneva Bible on 1 Samuel 16:18, "God would exercise him in sundry sortes."[6] Epiphany awaits such desert wanderers: it is "in the church in the wilderness," "in the wilderness of Mount Sinai," that "an angel of the Lord" appears to Moses (Acts 7:30, 38); Isaiah's prophecy of one "that crieth in the wilderness" (Isa. 40:3) is realized in John's proclamation of the Lord "in the wilderness of Judaea" (Matt. 3:1).

An incentive (and authority) for the Christian tradition to seize on, and develop, the figurative suggestiveness of this repeated patterning was provided by the presentation of the Old Testament patriarchs as models of faith in the epistle to the Hebrews. Hebrews, chapter 11, turns the Old Testament story to Christian purpose through an interpretative strategy that reads desert journeys as quests for salvation and wilderness habitation as exile from heaven. Its presentation of Noah, Abraham, Moses, and other Old Testament figures as Christian exemplars seizes on migrancy and exile as the condition of their faith: they are "strangers and pilgrims on the earth" who "seek a country," "a better country, that is, an heavenly: wherefore God is not ashamed to be called their God: for he hath prepared for them a city" (Heb. 11:13–16).

On the authority of Paul (the supposed writer of Hebrews) and of Augustine (who developed this reading in *The City of God*[7]), these narrative patterns and topoi came to control the shape of the Protestant—still more, Puritan—imagination, for here was a biblically authorized model for the representation of experience.[8] Traditional patristic and medieval typological readings of the Old Testament survived the Reformation and were developed in such works as *Christ Revealed; or, The Types and Shadows of Our Saviour in the Old Testament* (1635) by the early-seventeenth-century English Puritan divine Thomas Taylor, in the massive *Tropologia: A Key to Open Scripture Metaphors* (1681) by Milton's contemporary, the English Baptist Benjamin Keach, and in *The Figures or Types of the Old Testament* (1683) by the ejected Congregational minister Samuel Mather.[9] In the 1690s they engaged the imagination of the New England minister and poet Edward Taylor in a collection of thirty-six (then unpublished) sermons, *Upon the Types of the Old Testament*.[10] Such works read the details of Old Testament narratives as "some outward or sensible thing ordained of God under the Old Testament to represent and hold forth something of Christ in the New."[11] Just this approach is adopted by *De doctrina Christiana* when it understands "the name of CHRIST" to include "Moses, and the prophets, who foretold his coming" and when it argues that the "Israelites were commanded to keep the Sabbath holy" "as a shadow or type of things to come."[12] In *Paradise Lost* it is the exegetical way of angels: Michael instructs Adam that the "imperfect" Mosaic law was given to prepare for "a better Covenant" that the Israelites might move "From shadowy types to truth"; through his dealing with the Israelites in history God is "informing them, by types / And shadows . . . / . . . by what means he shall achieve / Mankind's deliverance" (*PL* 12.300–303, 232–35). The Bible thus becomes a series of iterations and reiterations, duplications and repetitions: every wilderness story anticipates the Son's, and his epitomizes all that have preceded his forty days in the desert. To situate them all in the one location is to enact this narratological interdependence by linking type with antitype, Moses or Elijah with Christ.[13]

Wilderness narratives, however, resonated extratextually no less than intertextually. For Taylor, they offered "a notable guide through this pilgrimage of our life"; in them the reader could "see his owne case."[14] Old Testament events were read as symbolic anticipations of individual personal experience and of the general experiences of saints, sinners, and nations. Seventeenth-century circumstances contrived to make this "moral" construction of desert narratives peculiarly apt for English Protestants.[15] In biographical fact, Abraham was called "to get thee out of thy country" Haran and to journey "unto a land that I will show thee." His exodus, in obedient response, from a center of civilization and from his family, to live in the foreign and hostile land of Canaan (Gen. 12:1–10; 14:4, 10) anticipated the demands their religious commitment placed upon many Protestant exiles and later Puritans, many of whom chose exile in the Great Migration of the 1630s. The earliest such group was John Robinson's separatist church at Scrooby in Nottinghamshire which, in 1608, decided to emigrate to Amsterdam, "to go into a country they knew not . . . for their desires were set on the ways of God." In 1620 that same resolution took them, as the colonists known to history as the Pilgrim fathers, to New England. They were, Cotton Mather later wrote, "*satisfy'd*, they had as plain a command of Heaven to attempt a Removal, as ever their Father *Abraham* had for his leaving the *Caldean* Territories." William Bradford, Plymouth colony's historian and governor for most of its first thirty-five years, could reflect, in a poem published in *New England's Memorial* (1669), Nathaniel Morton's history of Plymouth based upon Bradford's own journal:

> [God] call'd me from my native place
> For to enjoy the means of grace
> In wilderness he did me guide,
> And in strange lands for me provide.[16]

That Jehovah had led his people home through the wilderness from their Egyptian captivity subsequently inspired the many "faithfull and freeborn Englishmen," as Milton called them, who sought relief from "the fury of the Bishops" in "the savage deserts of America" (*Areopagitica,* in YP 1:585) by undertaking what Samuel Darnforth called their *Errand into the Wilderness* (1670).[17]

Given their Eurocentric assumptions, we could understand Puritan emigrants to America believing that they were embarked for a wilderness, but when, in her untitled poem "As weary pilgrim," the New England poet Anne Bradstreet creates a wilderness as the context of her mortal life, beset by "dangers," "travails," "burning sun," "briars and thorns," "hungry wolves," "erring paths," and "parching thirst," it is not Massachusetts she is describing.[18] Bunyan, after all, found precisely the same topography in Bedfordshire, England. The narrator of *The Pilgrim's Progress* walks "through the wilderness of this world" until he lights "upon a certain place, where was a Denn," and it was "from the *Lions Dens,*" from the prison where "I stick between the Teeth of the Lions in the Wilderness" that he addressed the reader of his autobiographical *Grace Abounding*.[19] In seventeenth-century texts, England no less than New England can appear an uncultivated wasteland of scrub and brambles, scorched by a relentless sun, prowled by wild beasts; signposting is poor and travelers are prone to lose themselves in featureless deserts. These details do not derive from observation. They are recalling a far distant land and time in order to trace in their authors' and readers' experience the patterns of significance that the Book of Hebrews taught them to read in Old Testament story. Bunyan's representation of his experience reproduces a recognized type: like the exemplars of faith in Hebrews, chapter 11, "of whom the world was not worthy," Bunyan suffers "bonds and imprisonment"; he wanders "in deserts, and in mountains, and in dens and caves of the earth" (11:36, 38). Just so, his Nonconformist contemporary Oliver Heywood lamented, "woe is me that I am forced to dwel in meshech [Ps. 120:5], and sojourne in this weary wildernes, when shal my soul be set at liberty out of the mouldy cage."[20] To walk by faith is to perceive oneself a pilgrim providentially led like the Israelites through the desert. Consequently, one could as readily discern the wilderness in old England as in New England.

In the Pentateuch narratives the Israelites, of course, are seeking a homeland. However, in the passage in Hebrews that inspired Richard Baxter's *The Saints Everlasting Rest* (1650), the "rest" denied to the erring Israelites is identified as eternal bliss (3:7–4, 16). Abraham's preference for exile over return to Mesopotamia is similarly rendered as the hope "for a better country, that is an heavenly" (11:8–16). Just so, *De doctrina Christiana* remarks of Moses, "who was the type of the law," that he "could not lead the children of Israel into the land of Canaan, that is, into eternal rest"; this was reserved for Joshua, "that is, Jesus."[21] With eternal salvation replacing Canaan as the journey's destination, allegorical and narrative logic demands that the wilderness topography of the desert wanderings signifies the mortal experience that leads to that destiny. The work in which the Presbyterian Nonconformist Thomas Gouge, addressing London apprentices, wrote that we are to live "as a citizen of heaven, and a pilgrim on the earth" is entitled *The Young Man's Guide through the Wilderness of This World to the Heavenly Canaan*

(1670). As Bunyan put it at the conclusion of his preface to *Grace Abounding*, "The Milk and Honey is beyond this Wilderness."[22]

As journeys not for temporal possession but for an eternal kingdom the Israelites' forty years of desert wandering thus provides a figurative model for the representation of Christian experience. The Geneva Bible supplied Numbers, chapter 33, with a map showing "the way, which the Israelites went for the space of fourtie yeres from Egypt though the wilderness of Arabia, vntil they entred into the land of Canaan." Clearly marked is the wilderness of Sin (Exod. 17:1). When in 1655 Faithful Teate published *A Scripture-Map of the Wildernesse of Sin, and the Way to Canaan; or, The Sinners Way to the Saints Rest*, he explained that the wilderness he described was "the WILDERNESSE OF SIN spiritually so called." He did not "deny in the least the Historicall respect some Scriptures have," but, reading them "mystically," he understands "by the Antitype, by the Wildernesse" the state of unregeneracy: "my work is Topographical to draw out the Map of the wilderness . . . of unconversion."[23] The "waste howling wilderness" (Deut. 32:10) has become the mortal experience of sin, of postlapsarian exile, where, like the Israelites in the wilderness of Sin, God will "humble thee . . . and prove thee" (Deut. 8:2), words Milton uses of the Son's wilderness trial in *Paradise Regained* (1.11, 3.189). These are the very terms in which Michael offers Adam a typological reading of Joshua/Jesus' future victories in, and occupation of, Canaan. He

> shall quell
> The adversary serpent and bring back
> Through the world's wilderness long wandered man
> Safe to eternal paradise of rest.   (*PL* 12.311–14)[24]

This, then, is the wilderness into which the Son in *Paradise Regained* has wandered, the wilderness of sin, of temptation, of challenge—God's preferred arena for spiritual exercises ever since Adam and Eve first became exiles. By bringing to mind the first Adam, the poem's opening allusion to Eden incidentally identifies the Son as the second Adam.[25] In that office, he inhabits the fallen world: he is "Our second Adam in the wilderness," as Michael styles him when preparing the first Adam for expulsion from Paradise (*PL* 11.383).

IV. DAVID THE KING

In the circumstances of the 1660s, however, this became a politically charged wilderness. In the mid-century, it had been particularized in the experience of civil war, as it was by Milton himself when, in *Eikonoklastes*, he compared

the desolation of war to "wandring over that horrid Wilderness" and Parliament's victory to "the strong and miraculous hand of God assisting us" as it
had the Israelites in their need (YP 3:580). After the Restoration, Nonconformists, subject to material distraints, to imprisonment, to social and political exclusion and, through the Five Mile Act, to a kind of internal exile,
understandably found the wilderness figuration particularly serviceable, but
their political opponents were hardly less fond of it in their moment of
triumph. The comfortable and reassuring royalist and Episcopalian notion
that at the Restoration the divine plan was restoring right order led to representations of Charles II as a man of exemplary patience who had been tested
by trial. Concentration upon Charles's deprivations during the 1650s became
a way of according to him the victory that had eluded him militarily. Writing
in late March 1660 in reply to Milton's *Readie and Easie Way*, the author of
The Dignity of Kingship dedicated his apologia for monarchy to "Charles the
Good" since he is "the most *Illustrious* for *Vertue, Constancy* in *Religion*, and
Heroick Patience, under the most sharp *Tryals*, and extraordinary *Afflictions*,
wherein (in imitation of his true *Magnanimous Royall Father*) he hath appeared *more then Conqueror*."[26] This construction of Charles inflated his
sufferings through references to Israel's wilderness wanderings and to the
Babylonian exile. In his speech at the close of the convention Clarendon
observed that God would not have led Charles "through so many Wildernesses of Afflictions of all Kinds" and preserved him against all enemies, "but
for a Servant whom He will always preserve as the Apple of His own Eye."
Old Testament history furnished other parallels: like Moses (who, in the eyes
of royalist interpreters, was Israel's first king) Charles had taken refuge in
flight to be providentially returned from a foreign land to save his people; like
David, he was delivered from his enemies.[27] In Richard Allestree's *Sermon
Preached at Hampton-Court* on the anniversary of the Restoration in 1662
the defeat at Worcester and subsequent exile are turned into a wilderness
training ground and Charles into the elect king David:

We cannot look upon his life but as the issue of prodigious bounty, snatch'd by
immediate Providence out of the gaping jaws of tyrannous, usurping, murtherous
malice, merely to *keep* him for *our needs,* and for *this day:* One whom God had train'd
up and manag'd for us, just as he did prepare *David their King,* at *thirty* years of age to
take possession of that *Crown* which God had given him by *Samuel* about *twelve* years
before; and in those years to prepare him for *Canaan* by a *Wilderness,* to *harden* him
with discipline, that so the luxuries and the effeminacies of a Court might not *emascu-
late* and *melt* him; by constant Watches, cares and business, to make him equal for,
habituated to, careful of, and affected with the business of a Kingdome; and by
constraining him to *dwell in Mesech,* with Aliens to his Religion, to teach him to be
constant to his *own,* and to *love Sion.* And hath he not prepared *our David* so for us?[28]

Hailing the *Happy Restoration of . . . His Sacred Majesty* in *Astraea Redux* (1660), Dryden made the point more succinctly: "Thus banished David spent abroad his time, / When to be God's anointed was his crime."[29]

The wilderness, then, is a contested site: proof of Charles's entitlement to the throne (and so of the justness of the Restoration) or divinely appointed trial of faith for the persecuted (and so of the injustice of the restored regime and its satanic agents working through God's permissive will). *Paradise Regained* intervenes in this contestation. While Milton's presentation of the bearing of the Son is in a general way applicable to all believers, it is also in a number of particulars directed to discrediting the royalists' appropriation of the wilderness topos for Charles's escapades and to encouraging dissenting Protestants in the right way to survive their disempowerment.

V. THE WILDERNESS WAY

The Son's encounter with the wilderness begins in submission to the divine will. Just so commentators read those earlier types of the Messiah, notably Abraham. The observation in Hebrews that "by faith" Abraham "went out not knowing whither he went" (Heb. 11:8) was picked up in the gloss in the Geneva Bible on Genesis 12:1: "In appointing him no certeine place, he [God] proueth so muche more his faith & obedience." The point was to be a standard one in Protestant commentaries: for the Presbyterian biblical commentator Matthew Henry, for example, Abraham's removal "was designed to try his Faith and Obedience, and also to separate him, and set him apart, for God." Abraham was "tried whether *he loved God better* than he loved his *native Soil* and *dearest Friends*," and, as he was told nothing about the Promised Land, he "had no particular Securities given him, that he should be no loser by leaving his Country to follow God. *Note,* Those that *deal with God* must *deal upon trust*."[30] In *Paradise Lost* Michael draws the same inference: Abraham "straight obeys, / Not knowing to what land, yet firm believes" (*PL* 12.126–27). Just so, the Son submits unquestioningly to the "strong motion" which leads him into the wilderness even though he does not know "to what intent" he is led to this inhospitable place nor what the outcome may be (1.290–91). When Satan tries to persuade him that survival there is impossible, he responds with an affirmation of trust in divine succor: "Who brought me hither / Will bring me hence, no other guide I seek" (1.335–36). Milton follows Calvin and the Reformed tradition in interpreting Satan's first assault as a temptation not to gluttony but to distrust: God could sustain the Israelites, Moses, and Elijah in the wilderness, "Why dost thou then suggest to me distrust" (1.355)?[31]

It is a point of this trust to accept without repining or complaint that the wilderness experience is essential to growth in grace. The point of spiritual exercises is to strengthen the sinews of faith as it is of physical exercises to tone the body's muscles. To Adam Michael explains that the Israelites, making their way to Canaan "Through the wild desert, not the readiest way" (*PL* 12.216),[32] "gain by their delay / In the wide wilderness," for there they receive the Law and establish their government and "rule by laws ordained" (*PL* 12.223–26). And individuals, no less than nations, are refined and ordered by adversity. This, of course, had been a favorite Miltonic theme ever since *Areopagitica:* "our faith and knowledge thrives by exercise, as well as our limbs and complexion"; "that which purifies us is triall" (YP 2:515, 543). By 1662, however, the theme had a pointed application in the exhortations of the ejected ministers to their people not to turn aside from the experience of deprivation and (it was already foreseen) persecution which awaited them. As the Son is to be by "firm obedience fully tried" (1.4) in the desert, so, the Quaker Thomas Ellwood wrote of the imprisonments of Isaac Penington the younger in the 1660s, "The Lord had led him through many a strait and difficulty, through many temptations, tryals and exercises (by which he had tryed and proved him)." The linguistic cluster here—*led, strait, difficulty, trial, exercise, prove*—is the lexicon of the wilderness, explicitly evoked when Ellwood salutes Penington for preferring "the reproach of Christ" to "the Treasures of Egypt" and the "Preferments and Honours of the world."[33]

To refuse Satan's recommendation that he provides food for himself shows in the Son a disregard for material provision, an unworldliness, essential to the wilderness way. The gloss of the old Geneva Bible on Hebrews 11:13 was: "And therefore put not their confidence in thi[n]gs of this worlde." This unworldliness and otherworldliness are the true distinguishing marks of such a Puritan saint as John Janeway, a "Pilgrim that looked for a better Country, a City that had foundations, whose builder and maker was God. His habit, his language, his deportment, all spoke him one of another world."[34] It was to this image that the Quaker William Penn turned when, rejecting the hedonistic culture of the Restoration, he urged mortification and self-denial: "The true self-denying man is a pilgrim; but the selfish man is an inhabitant of the world: the one uses it, as men do ships, to transport themselves or tackle in a journey, that is, to get home; the other looks no further, whatever he prates, than to be fixed in fulness and ease here, and likes it so well, that if he could, he would not exchange."[35] True faith transforms the believer to the status of a migrant, an exile, an outcast. As George Fox put it, "it is the great love of God to make a wilderness of that which is pleasant to the outward eye and fleshly mind."[36] For this reason Christian and Faithful are derided at Vanity Fair as "Outlandish-men," that is, as foreigners; they do not belong.[37]

This unworldliness is writ large in Milton's much expanded version of the second temptation during which Satan offers in succession every means to worldly power and success. The Son's worldly impoverishment and inconsequence, his apparent unpreparedness to meet his trial, are much stressed. He is a man "obscure, / Unmarked, unknown" (1.24–25) who has led a "life / private, unactive" (2.80–81; compare 3.232), "unknown, unfriended, low of birth . . . / Bred up in poverty and straits at home" in Nazareth (2.413, 415). He is "Of all things destitute" (2.305), the companion of "Plain fishermen" (2.27).[38] It is this obscurity, the Son's lack of every advantage of station, accomplishment, or power, which, as he thinks, gives Satan his opportunity. "All thy heart is set on high designs, / High actions; but wherewith to be achieved?" (2.410–11) is the question to which he seeks an answer, and the question to which the body of the poem is devoted. The Son rejects as appropriate "means of enterprise" every one of Satan's proposals. Contrary to Satan's supposition that "prediction still / In all things, and all men, supposes means, / Without means used, what it predicts revokes" (3.354–56), the "ostentation vain of fleshly arm," though "Plausible to the World," is to the Son "worth naught," merely an "argument / Of human weakness rather than of strength" (3.387, 393, 401–2).

He adheres to another model of renown: to be "singularly good" (3.57) is to be singular, that is, alone, impoverished, marginal, neglected, "Outlandish," without the insignia of earthly success, fame, or glory. Popular acclaim is derided as the ill-informed prejudice of the "miscellaneous rabble" that bestows glory on "men not worthy of fame"(3.43–56), such as (we may conjecture) Charles II.[39] "True glory and renown" is the Father's "divine approbation" and the "true applause" of heaven (3.60–64). Against Satan's heroes—Herod the Great, Herod Antipas, Philip of Macedon, Scipio Africanus, Pompey, Caesar—the Son sets men who "in lowest poverty" have attained "to highest deeds" (2.437): Gideon, whose family was "poor in Manasseh" (Judg. 6:15); Jephthah, the illegitimate "son of an harlot" who, disinherited by his father, "fled from his brethren, and dwelt in the land of Tob" (Judg. 11:1–3); the shepherd David; and a list of exemplary Romans (taken largely from Augustine).[40] These all were "men so poor / Who could do mighty things, and could contemn / Riches though offered by the hand of kings" (2.447–49).

Hence, the private and secluded action of *Paradise Regained*, "in secret done" after which the Son "unobserved / Home to his mother's house private returned" (1.15; 4.638–39). It is as if nothing has happened, and, of course, from the point of view of public affairs, of the world of which in the poem Satan is the spokesman, nothing has: "Of these forty days none hath regard" (2.315). As Laura Lunger Knoppers has argued, this apparent inconsequentiality is one of the ways in which *Paradise Regained* retorts to the assertive and triumphalist pageantry through which the restored regime insisted that something momentous and of public concern had recently occurred.[41] It is part of Milton's poetic enterprise in the 1660s to deprive this claim of its authority, as he does implicitly in the very opening of *Paradise Lost* when the poem anticipates the restoration to be effected by "one greater man." Greater than whom, we may ask.[42] Charles may have had his wilderness years, but when *he* returned, the world was "all agape" (*PL* 5.357). Pepys, watching Charles's magnificent precoronation progress through London in April 1661 was quite overcome by its splendor: "So glorious was the show with gold and silver that we were not able to look at it—our eyes at last being so much overcome with it" that it is "impossible to relate the glory of . . . this day."[43] Milton's disdain for such "tedious pomp" (*PL* 5.354) is a measure of how far the Son's way with wildernesses is to be preferred to that of the man whose more enthusiastic panegyrists—such as Dryden in *Astraea Redux*—were not above detecting in this second King David the very image of the Son of God; after all, did not David typologically foreshadow Christ?[44]

A signal aspect of this repudiation of the public world, here as in *Paradise Lost,* is its rejection of martial heroism and of military force. As Michael had insisted to Adam that those heralded as "Patrons of mankind, gods, and sons of gods" for their military conquests were "Destroyers rightlier called and plagues of men" (*PL* 11.696–97), so the Son is in no doubt "They err who count it glorious to subdue / By conquest far and wide": those "titled gods, / Great benefactors of mankind" spread only desolation, "Nothing but ruin whereso'er they rove" (3.71–87). True glory may "be attained / Without ambition, war, or violence; / By deeds of peace" (3.89–91).

This pacifism brings *Paradise Regained* close to the bias of Restoration Quakerism. "My kingdom is not of this world" (John 18:36) becomes something of a refrain in Quaker publications after 1660, coupled with an insistence that "carnal weapons" are to be repudiated in pursuing the Lamb's war (Isa. 53:7).[45] "All Friends, everywhere," wrote Fox, should "keep out of plots and bustling and the arm of the flesh. . . . Ye are called to peace, therefore follow it . . . all that pretend to fight for Christ they are deceived, for his kingdom is not of this world"; and again, "Christ . . . said his kingdom was not of this world; if it was, his servants should fight, but it was not and therefore his servants do not fight." A declaration of 1661, prompted by outrage at the uprising of Thomas Venner, of which Fox was one of twelve signatories, affirmed that "All bloody principle and practices, we . . . do utterly deny, with all outward wars and strife and fightings with outward weapons, for any end or under any pretence whatsoever. This is our testimony to the whole world."[46] "Who fights for God must not Man's Weapons use": this moral Milton's Quaker friend Thomas Ellwood drew from the defenselessness of

David before Goliath. Whether or not it was Ellwood who, as he claimed, gave Milton the idea for *Paradise Regained,* the poem articulates his view of aggression.[47] Milton is there no more "sedulous by nature to indite / Wars, hitherto the only argument / Heroic deemed" than he had been in *Paradise Lost,* nor any less committed to "the better fortitude / Of patience," the victory not of retaliation but of "suffering for truth's sake" (*PL* 9.27–29, 31–32; 12.569). The static, passive action of *Paradise Regained* constitutes, he claims, a tale "of deeds / Above heroic" (1.14–15). The Son is to be "proved" by a "great duel" but "not of arms," not by aspiring to the "victorious deeds" and "heroic acts" that had inspired his youth (1.11, 174, 215–16). He is to

> Be tried in humble state, and things adverse,
> By tribulations, injuries, insults,
> Contempts, and scorns, and snares, and violence,
> Suffering, abstaining, quietly expecting
> Without distrust or doubt, that he may know
> What I can suffer, how obey? Who best
> Can suffer, best can do; best reign, who first
> Well hath obeyed.   (3.189–96)[48]

"Quietly expecting": *Paradise Regained* shares with Quakers—and, indeed, with the politically disempowered Nonconformists generally—a quietist emphasis.[49] Christians, wrote the Presbyterian Nonconformist John Howe, should "with a proportionable unconcernedness . . . look on, and behold the various alternations of political affairs." "*A Christian,*" wrote Bunyan in 1684, "*must be a harmless Man*"; we should "with quietness submit ourselves under what God shall do to us," enduring with our "own will and consent," "patient under this mighty hand of God" in meeting trial, "not with carnal weapons, but with the graces of the Spirit of God," studying "to be quiet . . . to be at peace with all men."[50] "All things are best fulfilled in their due time," says the Son (*PR* 3.182), that is, in the Restoration context, without rebellious or revolutionary military intervention.[51]

   That is a permissible inference since the wilderness of "Contempts, and scorns, and snares and violence" foreseen by the Son, like Milton's own "evil days" in *Paradise Lost* (7.24) and the "unjust tribunals" under which faithful Israelites suffer in *Samson Agonistes* (line 695), is recognizably the persecutory Restoration regime experienced by Nonconformists. These are inescapably deictic references, no less than Bunyan's marginal gloss on his wilderness "Denn": "The gaol."[52] When in *Paradise Regained* Satan, now "Quite at a loss," foresees for the Son "Sorrows, and labours, opposition, hate, / . . . scorns, reproaches, injuries, / Violence and stripes" (4.386–88), he fails to make the connection between his own bafflement as tempter and these trials.

What he takes to be signs of the Son's inadequacy are rather the marks of his election: God's chosen suffer.[53] Hence, when Satan offers the Son a way to escape this oppression, the Son, rejecting these "politic maxims" and "cumbersome luggage of war" (3.400–401), prefers what Milton elsewhere calls "the unresistable *might* of *Weaknesse*."[54] The allusion is to 1 Corinthians 1:27: "God hath chosen the weak things of the world to confound the things which are mighty." Still more relevant is 2 Corinthians 12:9, "my strength is made perfect in weakness," Milton's own personal motto.[55] The lesson which in *Paradise Lost* Adam had learned from Michael's vision of human history, that "Subverting worldly strong" is the work of "things deemed weak" (*PL* 12.567–68), is echoed in *Paradise Regained* in the Father's assertion that the Son will "conquer Sin and Death, the two grand foes, / By humiliation and strong sufferance: / His weakness shall o'ercome Satanic strength" (1.159–61).

Refusing, then, all incentives to act, the Son "will endure the time" (*PR* 4.174). For *De doctrina Christiana,* the exemplification of such Christian patience is the very point of spiritual trial: God tempts "even righteous men, in order to prove them. He does this . . . to exercise or demonstrate their faith or patience, as in the case of Abraham and Job."[56] "Patient Job" (3.95), the type of "constant perseverance" (1.147) shadows his antitype, the Son, throughout *Paradise Regained*.[57] The Son's "strong sufferance" (1.160) follows what Barbara Lewalski has called the "Jobean heroic pattern" of patient endurance.[58] His constancy and steadfastness, are, as Laura Lunger Knoppers has noted, adjectivally, adverbially, and figuratively reiterated throughout the poem: he bears himself "temperately" (2.378), "patiently" (2.432), "calmly" (3.43); he is "unmoved" (3.386), "patient" (4.420), "Unshaken" (4.421); he is "as a rock / Of adamant" (4.533–34). This rhetorical commitment to stasis is realized, finally, in the Son's miraculous immobility upon the pinnacle of the temple (4.561).[59]

Quietist and pacifist though the emphasis of *Paradise Regained* might be, such Christian patience is no passive thing. The point was commonly made in early modern Protestant writing through the Pauline image of the race for the prize or crown of salvation (1 Cor. 9:24; Gal. 5:7; Phil. 2:16; Heb. 12:1), invoked by Milton himself in his famous assertion that "I cannot praise a fugitive and cloister'd vertue, unexercis'd & unbreath'd, that slinks . . . out of the race, where that immortall garland is to be run for, not without dust and heat" (*Areopagitica,* in YP 2:515). Though movement in *Paradise Regained* is ambulatory rather than expeditious, imagery of energetic engagement, of exertion and of contest, is recurrently present in the poem's figures of the duel and of combat, an image cluster that appeals to the figure of

Hercules (for example, 1.9–10, 155–59, 174; 4.563–71).⁶⁰ In this, Milton was following the bias of contemporary representations of the temptation of Christ: Perkins and Taylor both spoke of Christ's "combat" with the devil, Matthew Henry of his "famous duel" and of him being "dieted for combat, as wrestlers use to be."⁶¹

The poem insists, too, on the need for stamina and endurance. In *The Heavenly Foot-man* (1698), a sermon treatise on 1 Corinthians 9:24, Bunyan admonishes his readers: "It is an easy matter for a Man to *Run hard for a spurt,* for a Furlong, for a Mile or two: O but to hold out for a Hundred, for a Thousand, for *Ten Thousand Miles;* that a Man that doth this, he must look to meet with Cross, Pain, and Wearisomness to the Flesh."⁶² In *The Pilgrim's Progress,* Honest, "an old man" who has "bin a Traveller in this Rode many a day," has seen pilgrims "set out as if they would drive all the World afore them. Who yet have in a few days, dyed as they in the Wilderness, and so never gat sight of the promised Land."⁶³ Herein lies the significance of Satan's warning to the Son that those who find themselves in this wilderness leave their carcasses there: "many Thousands of the Children of Israel in their Generation, fell short of *Perseverance,* when they walk'd from *Egypt* towards the Land of *Canaan.* Indeed, they went to the work at first pretty willingly, but they were very short-winded, they were quickly out of Breath, and *in their Hearts they turned back again into* Egypt."⁶⁴ This had been the charge Milton leveled against the English in *The Readie and Easie Way:* they were "chusing them a captain back for *Egypt"* (YP 7:463). No wonder, for

the *way is long,* (I speak Metaphorically) and there is many a dirty step, many a high Hill, much Work to do, a wicked Heart, World and Devil to overcome. I say, there are many steps to be taken by those that intend to be Saved, by running or walking in the steps of that Faith of our Father *Abraham.* Out of *Egypt,* thou must go, thorow the *Red Sea;* thou must run a long and tedious Journey, thorow the wast howling Wilderness, before thou come to the Land of Promise.⁶⁵

In his capacity to endure in the wilderness, to resist the temptation to return to Egypt, the Son exemplifies the spiritually athletic Protestant hero; but he also demonstrates a bearing incompatible with the emphases of Restoration royalist culture and one which, in its repudiation of political power and military force, offers consolation to those exiled by that regime. Ironically, Satan's dismissive exclamation that "The wilderness / For thee is fittest place" (4.372–73) is quite true, though not in Satan's derisive sense. Only there can the Son construct through patient endurance the inner kingdom of fortitude ("he who reigns within himself, and rules / Passions, desires, and fears, is more a king" [2.466–67]) which will raise Eden "in the waste wilderness"

(1.7), so fulfilling another of Isaiah's prophecies:[66] "The Lord shall comfort Zion: he will comfort all her waste places; and he will make her wilderness like Eden, and her desert like the garden of the Lord" (Isa. 51:3).

University of Stirling, Scotland

NOTES

1. John Milton, *Paradise Regained*, in *Milton: Complete Shorter Poems*, 2d ed., ed. John Carey (Harlow, 1997). All citations from *Paradise Regained* and *Samson Agonistes* are from this edition.

2. John Milton, *Paradise Lost*, 2.367, 9.175, in *Milton: Paradise Lost*, 2d ed., ed. Alastair Fowler (Harlow, 1998). All citations from *Paradise Lost* are from this edition.

3. Both "desert" and "wilderness" occur far more frequently in *Paradise Regained* than in the remaining body of Milton's poetry (including *Paradise Lost*) and more frequently in this single poem than in the entire corpus of his English prose. See William Ingram and Kathleen Swaim, *A Concordance to Milton's English Poetry* (Oxford, 1972), and Laurence Sterne and Harold H. Kollmeier, *A Concordance to the English Prose of John Milton* (Binghamton, N.Y., 1985), *s.vv.*

4. Noted by Elizabeth Marie Pope, *"Paradise Regained": The Tradition and the Poem* (1947; reprint, New York, 1962), 110–12, and by Barbara Lewalski, *Milton's Brief Epic: The Genre, Meaning, and Art of "Paradise Regained"* (Providence, R.I., 1966), 195–96, both quoting the passage from *Paradise Regained*, 1.347–54.

5. John Milton, *Apology against a Pamphlet*, in *The Complete Prose Works of John Milton*, 8 vols., ed. Don M. Wolfe et al. (New Haven, 1953–82), 1:950. Hereafter designated YP and cited parenthetically by volume and page number in the text.

6. *The Geneva Bible: A Facsimile of the 1560 Edition*, ed. Lloyd E. Berry (Madison, 1969), loc. cit.

7. St. Augustine, *City of God*, in *A Select Library of the Nicene and Post-Nicene Fathers*, ed. Philip Schaff, 1st ser., 14 vols. (Reprint, Grand Rapids, 1978–79), 2:287, book 15, chapter 6; see also books 15–17 generally.

8. For fuller discussion, see N. H. Keeble, " 'To be a pilgrim': Constructing the Protestant Life in Early Modern England," in *Pilgrimage: The English Experience from Becket to Bunyan*, ed. Colin Morris and Peter Roberts (Cambridge, 2002).

9. For discussion of the apparent paradox of the survival of traditional readings despite the Reformation's hermeneutical literalism, see Thomas H. Luxon, *Literal Figures: Puritan Allegory and the Reformation Crisis in Representation* (Chicago, 1995).

10. Edward Taylor, *Upon the Types of the Old Testament*, 2 vols., ed. Charles W. Mignon (Lincoln, Neb., 1989).

11. Samuel Mather, *The Figures or Types of the Old Testament* (London, 1705), 52. For discussion of the literary consequences of typology in the early modern period, see Sacvan Bercovitch, ed., *Typology and Early American Literature* (Amherst, Mass., 1972); Joseph A. Galdon, *Typology and Seventeenth-Century Literature* (The Hague, 1975); Paul J Korshin, *Typologies in England, 1650–1820* (Princeton, 1982); Mason I. Lowance, *The Language of Canaan* (Cambridge, Mass., 1980); Earl Miner, ed., *Literary Uses of Typology* (Princeton, 1977).

12. *De doctrina Christiana*, 1.1, cited in Lewalski, *Milton's Brief Epic*, 172, and 2.7, in YP

6:126, 705, 707. For discussion of typology in Milton, see Lewalski, *Milton's Brief Epic,* 164–82; Jason Philip Rosenblatt, *Torah and Law in "Paradise Lost"* (Princeton, 1994), 220–34, which calls Michael "the typologising angel" and points to the "radically typological Epistle to the Hebrews" as "the principal thematic source" for Books Eleven and Twelve of *Paradise Lost* (160, 218).

13. While, as the Elizabethan Puritan William Perkins, *The Combat betweene Christ and the Diuell Displayed* ([London], 1606), observed, there were "diuers opinions" about the location of Christ's temptation (6), Milton was following the generality of seventeenth-century commentators in setting his poem where Moses and Elijah had been tried. For examples, see Pope, *Tradition and the Poem,* 111; Lewalski, *Milton's Brief Epic,* 195–204.

14. Thomas Taylor, *David's Learning; or, The Way to True Happiness* (London, 1617), 183, 190–91, quoted by W. R. Owens in John Bunyan, *Miscellaneous Works,* 13 vols., gen. ed. Roger Sharrock (Oxford, 1976–1994), 12:xxxix.

15. This interpretative strategy represents a continuation of what the old fourfold medieval exegetical system recognized as the "moral" or "tropological" sense; succinctly stated in Thomas Aquinas, *Summa Theologica,* 3 vols. (New York, 1947), 1:7, pt. 1, question 1, article 10.

16. William Bradford, *Of Plymouth Plantation,* ed. Samuel Eliot Morrison (New York, 1952), 11; Cotton Mather, *Magnalia Christi Americana; or, The Ecclesiastical History of New England* (London, 1702), 1.6, sec. 3; Nathaniel Morton, *New England's Memorial,* in *Chronicles of the Pilgrim Fathers,* ed. Alexander Young (London, 1910), 173.

17. Taken, of course, as the title of Perry Miller's classic study *Errand into the Wilderness* (Cambridge Mass., 1956). See also G. H. Williams, *Wilderness and Paradise in Christian Thought* (New York, 1962); Christopher Hill, *The English Bible and the Seventeenth-Century Revolution* (Harmondsworth, 1994), 126–53.

18. Anne Bradstreet, *The Works,* ed. Jeannine Hensley (Cambridge, Mass., 1967), 283.

19. John Bunyan, *The Pilgrim's Progress,* ed. James Blanton Wharey, rev. ed. Roger Sharrock (Oxford, 1960), 9; John Bunyan, *Grace Abounding to the Chief of Sinners,* ed. Roger Sharrock (Oxford, 1962), 1.

20. Oliver Heywood, *His Autobiography, Diaries, Anecdote and Event Books,* 4 vols., ed. J. Horsfall Turner (Brighouse and Bingley, 1882–85), 1:150.

21. *De doctrina Christiana,* 1.26, in YP 6:519. Compare *Paradise Lost,* 12.310.

22. Bunyan, *Grace Abounding,* 4.

23. Faithful Teate, *A Scripture-Map of the Wildernesse of Sin, and the Way to Canaan* (London, 1655), pref. ep. sigs. A4ᵛ, aa1, p. 2.

24. Compare Rosenblatt, *Torah and Law,* 219–20.

25. As noted by Lewalski, *Milton's Brief Epic,* 164, which discusses the Son as the Second Adam on 222–27.

26. G. S., *The Dignity of Kingship Asserted in Answer to Mr. Milton's Ready and Easie Way to Establish a Free Commonwealth* (London, 1660), sig. A1.

27. *Journals of the House of Lord,* 11:239. See, for example, J[ames] R[amsey], *Moses Returned from Midian; or, Gods Kindnesse to a Banished King* (Edinburgh, 1660); Gilbert Sheldon, *Davids Deliverance and Thanksgiving* (London, 1660).

28. Richard Allestree, *Sermon Preached at Hampton-Court on . . . the Anniversary of His Sacred Majesty's Most Happy Return* (London, 1662), 34–35.

29. John Dryden, *Astraea Redux,* lines 79–80, in *The Poems of John Dryden,* 4 vols., ed. Paul Hammond and David Hopkins (Harlow, 1995–2001), 1:42.

30. Matthew Henry, *An Exposition of the Five Books of Moses,* 2d ed. (London, 1710), glosses on Genesis 12:1–3.

31. Milton following Calvin and the Reformed tradition is noted by Pope, *Tradition and the Poem,* 56–64.

32. David Loewenstein, *Milton and the Drama of History: Historical Vision, Iconoclasm, and the Literary Imagination* (Cambridge, 1990), 122–23, persuasively detects here an echo of the title *The Readie and Easie Way,* in which Milton admonished the English not to choose "a captain back for *Egypt*" (YP 7:463); so here, the Israelites are to endure in the desert rather than return "back to Egypt" (*PL* 12.219).

33. Isaac Penington, *The Works* (London, 1681), sig. C2, quoted by David Loewenstein, *Representing Revolution in Milton and His Contemporaries: Religion, Politics, and Polemics in Radical Puritanism* (Cambridge, 2001), 245, 247.

34. James Janeway, *Invisibles Realities, Demonstrated in the Holy Life and Triumphant Death of Mr. John Janeway* (London, 1671), 91.

35. William Penn, *No Cross, No Crown,* ed. Norman Penney (York, 1981), 40.

36. *The Journal of George Fox,* corrected reprint, ed. John L. Nickalls (London, 1975), 13.

37. Bunyan, *Pilgrim's Progress,* 90.

38. Noted by Loewenstein, *Representing Revolution,* 251–52, remarking that "these lowly pastoral figures contribute to the poem's georgic themes" discussed in Anthony Low, *The Georgic Revolution* (Princeton, 1985), 322–52.

39. This point is made in Laura Lunger Knoppers, *Historicizing Milton: Spectacle, Power, and Poetry in Restoration England* (Athens, Ga., 1994), 40.

40. Augustine, *The City of God,* in Schaff, ed., *Select Library,* 2:98–101, bk. 5, chap. 18 (as noted by John Carey, *Milton: Complete Shorter Poems,* in his note to *Paradise Regained,* 2.446).

41. Knoppers, *Historicizing Milton,* 40–41.

42. This point is developed in N. H. Keeble, "'Till one greater man / Restore us': Restoration Images in Bunyan and Milton," in *Awakening Words: John Bunyan and the Language of Community,* ed. David Gay, James G. Randall, and Arlette Zinck (Newark, Del., 2000), 44–45.

43. Robert Latham and William Matthews, eds., *The Diary of Samuel Pepys,* 11 vols. (London, 1970–83), 2:82, 83 (April 22, 1661).

44. Steven Zwicker, *Dryden's Political Poetry: The Typology of King and Nation* (Providence, R.I., 1972), 61–77.

45. On this and other Quaker parallels, see Loewenstein, *Representing Revolution,* 242–68.

46. Nickalls, ed., *The Journal of George Fox,* 357, 399, 420.

47. Thomas Ellwood, *Davideis,* ed. Walter Fischer (Heidelberg, 1936), 23, line 252; Thomas Ellwood, *The History of Thomas Ellwood,* ed. Henry Morley (London, 1885), 199–200.

48. See on this theme John M. Steadman, "The 'Suffering Servant' and Milton's Heroic Norm," *Harvard Theological Review* 54 (1961): 29–43; John R. Knott Jr., *Discourses of Martyrdom in English Literature, 1563–1694* (Cambridge, 1993), 168–69; N. H. Keeble, *The Literary Culture of Nonconformity in Later Seventeenth-Century England* (Leicester, 1987), 229–35.

49. For this quietist bias in Nonconformist writing, see Keeble, *Literary Culture,* 191–204, which is drawn on in this and the preceding paragraph. In *Deliver Us from Evil: The Radical Underground in Britain, 1660–1663* (New York, 1986) and *Enemies Under His Feet: Radicals and Nonconformists in Britain, 1664–1667* (Stanford, 1990), Richard L. Greaves documents plotting and suspected plotting to argue that Nonconformity was far more subversively active than has been appreciated.

50. John Howe, *The Blessedness of the Righteous* (London, 1673), 4; John Bunyan, *Seasonable Counsel; or, Advice to Sufferers* (1684), in *Miscellaneous Works,* 10:5, 35, 42, 72, 96, 99.

51. For discussion of the quietism of *Paradise Regained,* see the chapter by Loewenstein cited in note 32, and also Michael Fixler, *Milton and the Kingdoms of God* (Evanston, Ill., 1964), 221–71; Andrew Milner, *John Milton and the English Revolution* (Totowa, N.J., 1981), 167–79; Michael Wilding, *Dragons Teeth: Literature in the English Revolution* (Oxford, 1987), 249–53. The view that Milton was quietist but not pacifist after 1660 is argued by John Coffey in his essay

in the present volume of *Milton Studies,* "Pacifist, Quietist, or Patient Militant? John Milton and the Restoration."

52. Bunyan, *Pilgrim's Progress,* 8. Bunyan and Milton are compared in this respect in Keeble, "'Till one greater man,'" 27–50. The likenesses are contested by Thomas N. Corns, "Bunyan, Milton, and the Diversity of Radical Protestant Writing," in *John Bunyan: Reading Dissenting Writing,* ed. N. H. Keeble (Bern, forthcoming).

53. This point is made with illustrative citations in Keeble, *Literary Culture,* 187–91.

54. *Of Reformation,* in YP 1:523, quoted by Knott, *Discourses of Martyrdom,* 169. This point is further discussed in Loewenstein, *Representing Revolution,* 252–54.

55. William Riley Parker, *Milton: A Biography,* 2 vols., 2d ed., ed. Gordon Campbell (Oxford, 1992), 1:479. I am grateful to David Loewenstein for bringing this to my attention.

56. *De doctrina Christiana,* 1.8, in YP 6:33, cited by Carey, *Complete Shorter Poems,* 1:156 n.

57. Job is more frequently mentioned in the poem than any other figure; see, in addition to 1.146, 1.369, 425; 3.64–77, 95.

58. Lewalski, *Milton's Brief Epic,* 108. Milton had, of course, identified the Book of Job as a "brief model" for epic over twenty years before (YP 1:813), the starting point for Lewalski's study.

59. Knoppers, *Historicizing Milton,* 38–39, citing these and other cases. Compare Knott, *Discourse of Martyrdom,* 170; Loewenstein, *Representing Revolution,* 260–62.

60. Discussed in Pope, *Tradition and the Poem,* 115–20; Lewalski, *Milton's Brief Epic,* 227–41.

61. Perkins, *Combat betweene Christ and the Diuell;* Thomas Taylor, *An Exposition of Christ's Temptations; or, Christs Combate and Conquest* (London, 1659); Matthew Henry, *An Exposition of the New Testament,* 2 vols., 7th ed. (Edinburgh, 1769), 1:13, 14 (glosses on Matt. 4).

62. Bunyan, *Miscellaneous Works,* 5:161.

63. Bunyan, *Pilgrim's Progress,* 257.

64. Bunyan, *Miscellaneous Works,* 5:160–61. As Margaret Kean, *"Paradise Regained,"* in *A Companion to Milton,* ed. Thomas N. Corns (Oxford, 2001), 429–43, well remarks, in this wilderness "It is not the unknown that proves perilous but rather the temptation to return to the old ways" (436).

65. Bunyan, *Miscellaneous Works,* 5:150.

66. On Satan's multiplication of false Edens in this wilderness, see Kean, *"Paradise Regained,"* 440–41.

"WITH UNALTERED BROW":
MILTON AND THE SON OF GOD

Thomas N. Corns

FOR SEVERAL DECADES THE critical tradition has recognized that the poems Milton published together in 1671 invite a range of political interpretation. Though their emphasis lies elsewhere, Arnold Stein and Barbara Lewalski ponder similarities between the Son's comments to Satan and Milton's arguments in his tracts of 1659 on the issues of the relationship between individual religious belief and the role of the state.[1] Christopher Hill sees the brief epic expressing a pessimism about the possibilities of radical political action that is qualified and perhaps corrected in *Samson Agonistes,* in which the preservation of "the vulgar only" (line 1659) points to a renewed optimism of popular support for a "purged and purified leadership," though, since the vulgar in question are not the chosen Hebrews but the reprobate Philistines, some reservations may be entertained.[2] For Michael Wilding, the 1671 volume similarly opposes the companion pieces but his account inverts the relative status attributed to them by Hill. The play rehearses values transcended by the celebration of pacifism in the brief epic: "Samson is carried dead back to his father's house with ceremony. The living Christ walks alone and unobserved back to his mother's house. The masculine military values, the maternal peace: death against life."[3] Wilding's radicalism was tempered not, like Hill's, in the age of the General Strike and the Spanish civil war, but in opposition to the Vietnam War and Australia's involvement, and the Son's resistance of the satanic draft confirms the militant potential of pacifism.

Several influential studies link the poems to the experience and culture of nonconformity in the 1660s. Seminally, Neil Keeble associated the performance of both the Son and Samson with the courtroom conduct of dissenters, primarily Quakers:

What the court conducts as the interrogation of inferiors by the officers of a superior and unassailable law is rendered as a context for mastery which, like the debates of *Paradise Regained* or *Samson Agonistes,* proceeding through linguistic fencing, the deployment of proof texts and a battle of wits, reveals the true stature and superiority of the (apparently) defenceless defendant and the (usually) condemned prisoner at the bar. His or her inadequacy proves as adequate to the challenge as the material helplessness of Milton's Christ; his or her hopeless plight as hopeful as that of Milton's Samson.[4]

Steven Marx and David Loewenstein have developed further the interpretative possibilities of a Quaker context.[5] For the former, the Son articulates the quietism enjoined on the movement by George Fox after 1661; for the latter, the Son's advocacy of "the inward kingdom" retains the idiom and the vehemence that characterized the earliest days of Quakerism. Both place the issue of quietism at the center of the text, though they resolve it differently. While focusing more on political issues than religious ones, David Quint, like Loewenstein, sees a continuing commitment in the brief epic, but recognizes an area of ideological confusion or conflict:

Critics have found it easy enough to square Milton's call for individual piety and passive witness with his supposed disillusionment and retreat from the political stage. But the conventional image of Milton the defeated Commonwealth-man turning in upon himself and his spiritual resources must be supplemented, if not replaced, by an image of Milton carrying on as polemicist against the Restoration. The problem is to explain how these two, more contradictory images should co-exist: why should a still active opponent of monarchy espouse an extreme individualism—what amounts to a political renunciation.[6]

Close attention to the Nonconformist experience in the 1660s may address the issues Quint defines, and, perhaps most pertinently, a broad spectrum of Puritan opinion distanced most sects from any notion of an imminent return to direct-action militancy, particularly in the aftermath of Venner's disastrous uprising of 1661. Not only were those Fifth Monarchists, who sought to bring in Christ in triumph through acts of violent revolution, beaten and destroyed, but also the Restoration authorities, probably opportunistically, acted to repress the activities of other radical sectaries. Loewenstein hints at what Laura Knoppers very effectively develops as a major reading of the brief epic in which the Son accepts that the coming kingdom may be almost infinitely postponed: "The construction of the self-disciplined subject is a model for the dissenters of the 1660s and 1670s. It is not an escape from politics, but a new mode of opposition, which ultimately defeats Satanic force."[7]

This essay is another political reading, though my preceding review of the literature may suggest it may be redundant since most of the interpretative options seem to have eloquent and perceptive advocates already. The brief epic has been seen as replete with the sentiments of the 1650s; as militantly pacifist; as a pessimistic interlude before the reviving optimism of *Samson Agonistes;* as emphatically linked to Restoration nonconformity; as showing the quietism of late Foxian Quakerism; as showing the militancy of the undefeated or the survivalism of the defeated; and indeed elsewhere in this volume as Milton's late poetic engagement with popery.[8] What further options can there be?

I shall argue that, while other accounts define, often brilliantly, the political issues and the ideological context, they are in danger of misconstruing the nature of the text. For *Paradise Regained* is not a handbook for failed revolutionaries, but rather a speculative reconstruction of a historical episode documented in the Gospels. Milton offers, not primarily a paradigm for Puritans, but a depiction of a Son of God who shares values, assumptions, attitudes, and opinions that are, perhaps unsurprisingly, very close to Milton's own published views. It is not that the Son invites wayfaring Christians to fashion themselves in an *imitatio Christi;* rather, Milton offers a divine figure made in his own image, a daring, almost impudent, *imitatio Miltoni*. This essay considers the ways in which both the narrative voice and the words attributed to the Son reflect aspects of Milton's political prose, including those sections of his prose in which he is establishing a tendentiously constructed self-image, and passages of his minor verse.

The critical tradition that sees the poem as exploring a contrast between militarism and other, nonviolent forms of political action misses the point that Milton, since the 1640s, has sought assiduously to equate the two. Milton persistently associates the role of committed polemicist with the dangers and responsibilities of the revolutionary army in an idiom which is echoed in the brief epic by the Son. As early as *Areopagitica* Milton represented the role of the revolutionary intelligentsia as the same as that of the parliamentary army, though in a different idiom, and often with some suggestion that the former participate in the more glorious struggle:

Behold now this vast City [London]; a City of refuge, the mansion house of liberty, encompast and surrounded with his [God's] protection; the shop of warre hath not there more anvils and hammers waking, to fashion out the plates and instruments of armed Justice in defence of beleaguer'd Truth, then there be pens and heads there, sitting by their studious lamps, musing, searching, revolving new notions and idea's wherewith to present, as with their homage and their fealty the approaching Reformation: others as fast reading, trying all things, assenting to the force of reason and convincement.[9]

Through the opening years of the civil war London had been under varying levels of threat. At the most acute danger, the royalist army, in the aftermath of the Battle of Edgehill, advanced as close as Turnham Green, about halfway between the city and what is now Heathrow Airport. Moreover, royalist garrisons commanded routes northwards. Under such circumstances, it may have seemed strange that Parliament should busy itself setting up the Westminster Assembly of Divines to complete the reformation of the national church, and strange, too, that Milton, so keen an advocate of the root-and-branch policies that had precipitated the war, should now prioritize the revision of divorce legislation. Milton answers that the intellectual struggle is not a diversion from the armed struggle but its seamless continuation.

The point, made explicitly in that passage, recurs obliquely in the imagery, as in

The adversarie . . . waits the hour, when they have brancht themselves out, saith he, small anough into parties and partitions, then will be our time. Fool! he sees not the firm root, out of which we all grow, though into branches: nor will beware untill he see our small divided maniples cutting through at every angle of his ill united and unweildy brigade. (YP 2:556)

And again, the godly scholar, after "labouring the hardest labour in the deep mines of knowledge," metamorphoses into the warfaring Christian polemicist:

[He draws] forth his reasons as it were a battell raung'd, scatter'd and defeated all objections in his way, calls out his adversary into the plain, offers him the advantage of wind and sun, if he please; only that he may try the matter by dint of argument, for his opponents then sculk, to lay ambushments, to keep a narrow bridge of licencing where the challenger should passe . . . is but weaknes and cowardise in the wars of Truth. (YP 2:562)

A contemporary reader may perhaps have concluded that Milton knows about as much about warfare as he does about deep-mine collieries. There is an unmistakable bookishness about those nippy maniples and the sporting gesture of allowing the enemy to pick the best end to play. Yet the references to pitched battle carry the imagery from its ultimate sources, among the Pauline armory of God (Eph. 6:13–17), to the conflicts of armies. It recurs, tellingly, in the invocation to *Paradise Regained:*

> Thou spirit who led'st this glorious eremite
> Into the desert, his victorious field
> Against the spiritual foe, and brought'st him thence
> By proof the undoubted Son of God, inspire,
> As thou art wont, my prompted song else mute,
> And bear through highth or depth of nature's bounds
> With prosperous wing full summed to tell of deeds
> Above heroic.   (PR 1.8–15)

The Son's struggle exceeds those of a military kind, but they share important characteristics. Moreover, that conflict is conceptualized as a duel, a single combat with Satan: "Victory and triumph to the Son of God / Now ent'ring his great duel, not or arms, / But to vanquish by wisdom hellish wiles" (*PR*

2.173–75). Milton had represented his own championing of the English Revolution in similar terms. Thus, he engages with *Eikon Basilike* with a prefatory heroism:

> Kings most commonly, though strong in Legions, are but weak in Arguments; as they who ever have accustom'd from the Cradle to use thir will onely as thir right hand, thir reason alwayes as their left. Whence unexpectedly constrain'd to that kind of combat, they prove but weak and puny Adversaries. Nevertheless for their sakes who through custom, simplicitie, or want of better teaching, have not more seriously considerd Kings, then in the gaudy name of Majesty, and admire them and thir doings, as if they breath'd not the same breath with other mortal men, I shall make no scruple to take up (for it seems to be the challenge both of him and all his party) to take up this Gauntlet, though a Kings, in the behalf of Libertie, and the Common-wealth. (YP 3:337–38)

Single combat represents for Milton as for the Son a fit image for the duel with Satan or his surrogates. Indeed, once Milton has assumed the role, he represents himself as retaining it throughout his tenure as official apologist. Thus, in perhaps the most elaborated version of the topos, he writes in the *Second Defence:*

> When he [Salmasius] with insults was attacking us and our battle array, and our leaders looked first of all to me, I met him in single combat and plunged into his reviling throat this pen, the weapon of his own choice. And (unless I wish to reject outright and disparage the views and opinions of so many intelligent readers everywhere, in no way bound or indebted to me) I bore off the spoils of honor. (YP 4:556)

For Milton, evidently, the image of the battle of the books, revitalized in his prose, is an unironized representation of the continuities between his polemical endeavors and military conflict. Like the Son, he is the godly champion in the great duel, an ectype to his archetype, in ways that clearly suggest that, whatever the Son's conduct and values may be associated with, they are not, in the Miltonic value system, to be equated with passivity; his, like Milton's, is an uncloistered virtue.

Milton, from the 1640s and arguably earlier, intermittently offers auto-biographical interludes plainly intended to shape the perceptions and responses of his contemporary audience. The image he constructs of himself is a complex one.[10] Some elements remain stable, while others are represented as changing in ideologically significant ways. It would be an implausible application of philosophical skepticism to assert that there is no connection between Milton's account and the events that happened to him and his own conduct. However, biographers have learned to recognize that these narratives must be interpreted with an awareness of the polemical exigencies that may have shaped them.

Among the recurrent elements is Milton's assertion of his childhood dedication to study. Thus, in the autobiographical digression in *The Reason of Church-Government,* he discloses his early studiousness: "I had from my first yeeres by the ceaseless diligence and care of my father, whom God recompence, bin exercis'd to the tongues, and some sciences, as my age would suffer" (YP 1:808–9). In his *Second Defence of the English People,* near the end of his career as government apologist, he still recalls, "My father destined me in early childhood for the study of literature, for which I had so keen an appetite that from my twelfth year scarcely ever did I leave my studies for my bed before the hour of midnight" (YP 4:612). Jesus, though not evidently prompted by his earthly father, had a similar commitment to a scholarly work ethic:

> When I was yet a child, no childish play
> To me was pleasing, all my mind was set
> Serious to learn and know, and thence to do
> What might be public good; myself I thought
> Born to that end, born to promote all truth,
> All righteous things: therefore above my years,
> The Law of God I read, and found it sweet,
> Made it my whole delight, and in it grew
> To such perfection, that ere yet my age
> Had measured twice six years, at our great feat
> I went into the Temple, there to hear
> The teachers of our Law, and to propose
> What might improve my knowledge or their own.   (*PR* 1.201–13)

John Carey rightly notes that Milton has added to the story in Luke 2:46–50 the detail that Jesus teaches the doctors rather than listens to them and both asks questions and gives answers. But he has added, too, the practical explanation of the achievements of an autodidact whose boyhood lifestyle curiously resembles Milton's account of his own. Luke describes his learning in miraculous terms, a point emphasized by Jesus' seemingly knowing if rather Delphic remark, "wist ye not that I must be about my Father's business" (*AV,* 2:49), a comment which the Son of *Paradise Regained* does not recall. Milton plays down the miracle and emphasizes the pedagogy. While the twelve-year-old Son and twelve-year-old Milton may have been reading different books, recognizably they are subject to the same teaching and learning strategy in the context of a similar commitment "to do . . . public good."

But as they looked up from their books, both children seem to have entertained heroic dreams of a patriotic kind, in each case abandoned on the achievement of greater maturity. Thus, the Son recalls:

> victorious deeds
> Flamed in my heart, heroic acts, one while
> To rescue Israel from the Roman yoke,
> Thence to subdue and quell o'er all the earth
> Brute violence and proud tyrannic power.   (*PR* 1.215–19)

In Milton's case the aspirations were not to perform heroic acts but to depict them. In "Mansus" he expresses the hope that he will "call back into poetry the kings of my native land and Arthur . . . or tell of the great-hearted heroes of the round table, which their fellowship made invincible, and—if only the inspiration would come—smash the Saxon phalanxes beneath the impact of the British charge" (Carey's translation, *Complete Shorter Poems*, 269–70). The aspiration is repeated in *Epitaphium Damonis* (ibid., 285), and a vague Arthurianism figures among other possible fields of epic endeavor in *The Reason of Church-Government* as he ponders "what K[ing] or Knight before the conquest might be chosen in whom to lay the pattern of a Christian Heroe" (YP 1:813–14).

Yet, like the Son, Milton grows up to reject the heroic mode (of composition, in his case, rather than action) or, more accurately, like the Son, he radically redefines heroism. The Son's deeds are "Above heroic" and "Worthy t'have not remained so long unsung" (*PR* 1.15, 17). Similarly, Milton's epic poetry is more genuinely heroic than the received and familiar celebrations of militaristic Virgilian patriotism or Arthurian chivalry. The thesis provides the very raison d'être for *Paradise Regained,* though it finds its fullest explicit statement in *Paradise Lost,* where he describes himself as:

> Not sedulous by nature to indite
> Wars, hitherto the only argument
> Heroic deemed, chief mastery to dissect
> With long and tedious havoc fabled knights
> In battles feigned; the better fortitude
> Of patience and heroic martyrdom
> Unsung.   (*PL* 9.27–33)

As in his brief epic, he describes himself as drawn to sing of a redefined heroism that has been "unsung," uncelebrated, by the larger literary tradition, thus establishing his credentials as a new kind of poet, as a writer of a specifically Christian epic that transcends the achievements of pagan precursors, as the Son establishes his status as a new kind of hero.

The action of the poem takes the form of protracted disputations, unsought for by the Son, in which Satan is routed in duelistic debate (and, as such, it shares some formal similarities with Milton's early prose, preeminently *Animadversions upon the Remonstrants Defence against Smec-tymnuus*). In part the refutation comes from the Son's actions—or rather nonactions—as he declines temptation, but by far the larger part is straight-forwardly debate as Satan, with visual aids, argues for complicity in the wealth and glory of the world and the Son demonstrates the inadequacies of those arguments and the self-sufficiency the godly possess through the spirit within them and through a familiarity with divine texts. As he does so, the controversy ranges over issues that have interested Milton for decades, and unsurprisingly the Son rests his case on theses the author has adopted elsewhere.

Thus, in his sonnets to Fairfax and to Cromwell, Milton articulates the view that military conquest, even in a righteous war, represents an uncertain achievement in comparison with the exercise of civic virtue. Putting it at its most positive, in *To the Lord General Cromwell,* written after the battles of Dunbar and Worcester, Milton warns that such victories are irrelevant with-out godly redress of religious intolerance:

> yet much remains
> To conquer still; peace hath her victories
> No less renowned than war, new foes arise
> Threatening to bind our souls with secular chains.   (9–12)

The poem gives praise for one sphere of accomplishment before immediately suggesting that the shedding of Scots blood still leaves vital areas of English spiritual life unprotected and constrained. Panegyrics usually have more to say about what their subject has done, not what he has yet to do. Moreover, military success is achieved at the expense of human suffering. Inevitably there are casualties on the victors' side and in this case the blood shed by the defeated is for the most part that of former allies who shared most of the values of English Puritanism. Milton's graphic image, of "Darwen stream with blood of Scots imbrued" (7) compels readers to focus on the gory after-math of battle.

On the Lord General Fairfax at the Siege of Colchester follows the same dialectic. The poem seems to have been written while the siege was actually underway, at a vital period for the success of the New Model Army, on which the future of Revolutionary Independency hinged.[11] Had Fairfax not sup-pressed the Kentish uprising (and had Cromwell not checked the Scots), then the second civil war would have gone the royalists' way. Yet to the commander, camped before the walls of a well-fortified stronghold, Milton sends advice that the object of his mission is far less important than the civic duty that awaits him:

O yet a nobler task awaits thy hand;
For what can war, but endless war still breed,
Till truth, and right from violence be freed,
And public faith cleared from the shameful brand
Of public fraud. In vain doth valour bleed
While avarice, and rapine share the land.   (9–14)

Of course, each poem is driven by an immediately pressing political objective. Milton would have Cromwell support a highly tolerationist and non-tithing church settlement for the early republic, just as, in the earlier poem, he is urging Fairfax and the "Army Grandees" to complete the exclusion of the Presbyterians from power in church and state. But the larger value system that lies behind those immediate imperatives is clear enough: the military enterprise is significant only insofar as it is complemented by the godly exercise of civic virtues, while in itself its destructiveness may render it futile.

The Son, working from the same principles, carries the argument a step further:

They err who count it glorious to subdue
By conquest far and wide, to overrun
Large countries, and in field great battles win,
Great cities by assault: what do these worthies,
But rob and spoil, burn, slaughter, and enslave
Peaceable nations, neighbouring, or remote.   (PR 3.71–76)

The assault on Colchester and the blood shed at Dunbar and Worcester, depicted in Milton's sonnets, may, at the time, have found justification in the political transformations they could support. But Fairfax did not persist as godly deliverer; instead, he retired to his country estates, returning to arms to help Monck usher in the restoration of monarchy, while Cromwell had delivered neither complete toleration (Quakers were often roughly treated through the 1650s) nor an unbeneficed clergy. The Son's words are written in a world in which the events of history have removed any remaining justification for a godly resort to arms, and take the argument of the sonnets to its logical conclusion.

Milton and the Son share other civic concerns. In his *Second Defence*, Milton ponders the nature of godly governance, accepting Cromwell's role as a dominant—in some respects almost monarchical—figure in contemporary English politics. This tract, we may recall, was probably written in part to support an English embassy to the queen of Sweden, so some reflection on defensible versions of kingship was timely.[12] As he builds an argument in justification of Cromwell's role, he contends: "whatever enemy lay within— vain hopes, fears, desires—he [Cromwell] had either previously destroyed within himself or had long since reduced to subjection. Commander first over himself, victor over himself, he had learned to achieve over himself the most effective triumph" (YP 4:667–68). The Son, finding himself in a world in which the republican option even on the Cromwellian model is unavailable, lectures Satan in decidedly similar terms:

> Yet he who reigns within himself, and rules
> Passions, desires, and fears, is more a king;
> Which every wise and virtuous man attains:
> And who attains not, ill aspires to rule
> Cities of men, or headstrong multitudes,
> Subject himself to anarchy within,
> Or lawless passions in him which he serves.   (*PR* 2.466–72)

The editorial tradition notes that Proverbs 16:32 underwrites the sentiment ("He that is slow to anger is better than the mighty; and he that ruleth his spirit than he that taketh a city"), and that there are echoes among Neoplatonists and in Horace.[13] Yet Milton combines this principle with another criterion for good government articulated in *The Readie and Easie Way to Establish a Free Commonwealth*. In a "free Commonwealth . . . they who are greatest, are perpetual servants and drudges to the public at thir own cost and charges, . . . live soberly in thir families, walk the streets as other men, may be spoken to freely, familiarly, friendly, without adoration" (YP, rev. ed., 7:425). Or, as the Son puts it, stripping off the republican patina of the 1660 tract and generalizing about godly governance:

>   a crown,
> Golden in show, is but a wreath of thorns,
> Brings dangers, troubles, cares, and sleepless nights
> To him who wears the regal diadem,
> When on his shoulders each man's burden lies;
> For therein stands the office of a king,
> His honour, virtue, merit, and chief praise,
> That for the public all this weight he bears.   (*PR* 2.459–65)

I am fascinated by the fact that Milton attributes the source of his theory of responsible government to Christ, citing his words to his disciples, "he that is greatest among you, let him be as the younger; and he that is chief, as he that doth serve" (Luke 22:26). Christ's words at the Last Supper read more straightforwardly as advice on the internal organization of the church in the apostolic age, but Milton, in a dogged piece of exegesis, insists that "he speaks of civil government" (YP, rev. ed., 7:424).[14] Thus, while the Son in *Paradise Regained* is made to echo Miltonic sentiments, Milton insists, somewhat tendentiously, that his own argument originates in what Christ had said.

Although there are numerous instances when Milton, as the polemical context prompts, does appeal to Providence in relation to English history, in much of his writing, the vagaries of national fortunes and governmental systems are represented in ethical, rather than providential, terms, which extend to the duties of the governed as well as the obligations of governors. Marvell, in a sentiment close to Machiavelli, declares that "the antient Rights" which bind Englishmen and their kings "do hold or break / as Men are strong or weak," thus locating the dynamics of constitutional change in power struggles between interested individuals and groups.[15] In sharp contrast, Milton at his more reflective bases both national regeneration (viewed as the overthrow of inherited and meritless monarchy) and national degeneration (variously manifest in such servile outcomes as the restoration of such monarchy or foreign conquest) on a generalized assessment of the morality of the nation.

The notion appears, as a gracefully turned humanistic compliment, in his first letter to Leonard Philaras. Philaras, though a diplomat in the service of the duke of Parma, was by birth an Athenian and evidently had written to Milton to ask him to support, in Barbara Lewalski's phrase, the "quixotic suggestion that England help free Greece from the Turks."[16] Milton could have cast a polite rebuff in many different ways, appealing to English political priorities, to military logistics, to a historical perspective pointing to the failures of earlier foreign interventions on behalf of eastern Christendom. Instead he chooses this argument:

there is another thing to be attempted, in my opinion the most important, that someone should stir and ignite the ancient courage, diligence, and endurance in the souls of the Greeks by singing of that byegone zeal. If anyone could accomplish this—which we should expect from none more than you, because of your eminent patriotism, together with greatest prudence and military skill, and finally with a powerful passion for recovering former political liberty—I am confident that neither would the Greeks fail themselves, nor any nation fail the Greeks. (YP 4:853)

Of course, Milton feeds Philaras with a gratifying sense of his cultural and political eminence. But, by implication, he is less complimentary about the Greek people, to whom he attributes, currently, a lack of those qualities that characterized the Athenian golden age. The Greeks are not free because they have fallen away from the ethical standards of their ancestors. As we shall see, this is an argument that the Son invokes as he expatiates on the futility of Israelite militancy in the absence of national regeneration.

Milton's thesis, which recurs in more belligerent form in *Eikonoklastes, The Tenure of Kings and Magistrates,* and the Latin defenses, rests once more on a substantial body of classical thought, most influentially, as Martin

Dzelzainis has argued, on Sallust's *Bellum Catilinae,* which demonstrates that "avarice and ambition were responsible for the decline of the Roman republic just as the virtues of justice and industry had been responsible for its rise."[17] Three difficulties confront the Christian version of this political philosophy. The first is a tricky aspect of the problem of evil: within societies that are degenerate, there is often to be found a godly remnant who are exposed to the viciousness of those around them. The problem fascinated Milton in the closing books of *Paradise Lost.* The second is the inevitable conclusion that God's providence engages only fitfully with the history of nations, since other dynamics at the level of human vice and virtue drive forward the process of rise and fall. Finally, all political endeavor may lead only to temporary success. A godly people may enjoy a godly republic and the benevolence of good governors who are their servants. But neither the Calvinists' dream of a Genevan theocracy nor the Fifth Monarchists' fantasy of a kingdom of the saints can finally be sustained; the godly realm lasts no longer than the godliness of its subjects, and most of them will tend to depravity.

These issues recur persistently in the Son's dismissal of Satan's offers of political power. As Satan offers personal glory, the Son recontextualizes earthly fame in a larger perspective, attributing its acquisition, for the most part, to the judgment of a degenerate multitude, and contrasting it with the achievements of those who retain a pious uprightness. Though the latter suffer on earth, they are rewarded by the only judgment that, under the view of eternity, really matters, and, as so often in *Paradise Regained,* Job is the paradigm:

> This is true glory and renown, when God,
> Looking on the earth, with approbation marks
> The just man, and divulges him through heaven
> To all his angels, who with true applause
> Recount his praises; thus he did to Job.   (*PR* 3.60–64)

The godly live endangered and often obscure, but, though God exposes them thus on earth, their achievements are noted. The argument, which is a commonplace of Christian consolation, had long interested Milton; the echoes of *Lycidas* are unmistakable: "[Fame] lives and spreads aloft by those pure eyes, / And perfect witness of all-judging Jove" (81–82).

Unprovidential history and the decay of nations figure in the interpretive framework the Son imposes on the visions and narratives presented by his tempter. When the latter explains in terms of *Realpolitik* the alternatives open to him if he is to achieve the apparently destined and providentially determined liberation of Israel, the Son dismisses their special status with a firm reminder that their sufferings are of their own making, and that Israel

118   THOMAS N. CORNS

constitutes a race "distinguishable scarce / From Gentiles, but by circumcision vain" (PR 3.424–25). Their salvation must wait its turn along with all other nations in an unspecified futurity about which the Son does not care to speculate: "To his [God's] due time and providence I leave them" (440). Such providence is global and transcendent; it does not stoop to intercede in acts of political micromanagement.

As Milton returns to a perspective established in his republican writings, it is the fate of Rome that most powerfully recurs. In that Sallustian vein identified by Dzelzainis in his republican prose, Rome figures as:

> That people victor once, now vile and base,
> Deservedly made vassal, who once just,
> Frugal, and mild, and temperate, conquered well,
> But govern ill the nations under yoke.   (PR 4.132–35)

The Son concludes with the grim corollary of Milton's argument to Philaras: "What wise and valiant man would seek to free / These thus degenerate, by themselves enslaved, / Or could of inward slaves make outward free?" (143–45). Engagement in the political process is not excluded by the Son, but the conditions—ethical, rather than social or economic—that make it worthwhile occur infrequently in the history of humankind, and where there is no moral regeneration political action is futile or unimportant. Whatever power swept the English people to "a glorious rising Commonwealth" (Readie and Easie Way, in YP, rev. ed., 7:420), the godly republic had proved unsustainable under the pressures of historical processes that lead irresistibly to degeneration; as the Son analyzes the corruption of Rome, the corruption of England is certainly foreshadowed.

The Miltonic oeuvre is profoundly and intimately shaped by many factors, including polemical exigencies imposed by the contemporary debates in which he engaged, by a sense of what could be safely written in periods of censorship and repression, and indeed quite probably in changes in his own values and beliefs. Just as I have demonstrated in this essay continuities and repetitions of Milton's prose arguments and his occasional verse in his brief epic, it would be an easy thing to demonstrate discontinuities and contradictions. What is needed urgently in Milton studies is a hermeneutics that factors out local exigencies to disclose significant developments in the recurrent cultural, religious, and ethical values that inform his work.

The critical tradition has found it extremely difficult to reconcile the Son's rejection in Book Four of classical learning and culture (286–364) with Milton's own evident debts to and enthusiasm for that culture, which extends, of course, to the adoption of the epic form for his two late narrative poems and of the Sophoclean model for the companion piece to Paradise Regained.

Yet the Son asserts the sufficiency of the Scriptures read by the godly "who receives / Light from above, from the fountain of light" (*PR* 4.289–90). In so doing, as Lewalski notes,[18] he echoes Milton's comments on the fruitless bookishness of beneficed clergy and the access to salvation open to simple people, guided if necessary by unbeneficed and minimally educated ministers:

the scriptures [are] translated into every vulgar tongue, as being held in main matters of belief and salvation, plane and easie to the poorest: and such no less then thir teachers have the spirit to guide them in all truth. . . . if men be not all thir life time under a teacher to learn Logic, natural Philosophie, Ethics or Mathematics, which are more difficult, that certainly it is not necessarie to the attainment of Christian knowledge that men should sit all thir life long at the feet of a pulpited divine. (YP, rev. ed., 7:302)

Of course, in the prose work Milton is not denigrating classically based learning; rather, he suggests, saving knowledge can be acquired very much more readily than such academic disciplines may be mastered, and without the weekly guidance of a university-trained minister. But the homology between this argument and the Son's is apparent enough, and the sheer gratuitousness of the comments Milton attributes to the Son is arresting.

Most of the speeches Milton writes for him are not shaped by any constraint or obligation posed by the Gospel narrative. Indeed, it is startling to turn back from Milton's brief epic to his sources in Matthew and Luke. There, Jesus speaks just three sentences:

It is written, Man shall not live by bread alone, but by every word that proceedeth out of the mouth of God. (Matt. 4:4; compare Luke 4:4)

It is written again, Thou shalt not tempt the Lord thy God. (Matt. 4:7; compare Luke 4:12)

Get thee hence, Satan: for it is written, Thou shalt worship the Lord thy God, and him only shalt thou serve. (Matt. 4:10; compare Luke 4:8)

Jesus' responses, which cite texts from Deuteronomy, sit curiously alongside the dialogue Milton has given him. Certainly, his words are incorporated into *Paradise Regained* (at 1.347–50, 4.560–61, and 4.175–77), and Milton attributes to him some of the brusqueness and taciturnity implied in the Gospel accounts. But, while he does not seek debate with Satan, he does not avoid it, though of course it is futile: Satan tells the Son "Man fall'n shall be restored, I never more" (*PR* 1.405), a plain statement that the latter accepts without argument.

So in what terms are the protracted disputations to be justified? Obviously, the Son has no interest in Satan's salvation, since that is no part of the Atonement, nor is it to be achieved by any other means. Moreover, no mortal hears or sees his encounter with Satan. But in its very obscurity rests its potency, for the Son enjoys there the kinds of freedom, from censorship and from prosecution, that godly Puritans lost in 1660. Within the sacred framework of the Gospel narrative, the Son may speak with an openness denied to Milton and his contemporaries; he speaks for them, and he speaks in their idiom. As he reconstructs what the Son might have said, Milton fashions him in his own image, attributing to him a childhood of study and a polemical heroism by which he once characterized himself. Again, within the protective mediation of that framework, he has the Son range, uncompromisingly, over such issues as civic virtue, the corruption of kingship, the depravity of imperial states, the soteriological sufficiency of the inner light and the biblical text, and the redundancy of a beneficed and university-educated clergy.

Milton, echoing Jeremiah, concludes *The Readie and Easie Way:* "Thus much I should perhaps have said though I were sure I should have spoken only to trees and stones; and had none to cry to, but with the Prophet, *O earth, earth, earth!* to tell the very soil it self, what her perverse inhabitants are deaf to" (YP, rev. ed., 7:462–63). In *Paradise Regained* the Son literally has none (except the damned and thus irrelevant Satan) to cry to except for the stones of the wilderness around him—and yet still he speaks "the language of . . . *the good Old Cause*" (YP, rev. ed., 7:462). It is perhaps all the godly polemicist can ever do. Sometimes those arguments may be articulated in a land and a time when a spirit of regeneration leads a free people to a transitory greatness; more often, the unregenerate prevail. But Milton's version of the Son and the words he has him speak allow that "great duel" between truth and falsehood to continue, even in so unpropitious a time and place as Restoration England. Through the figure of his last hero—at once the Son of God and a poor man in a distant land long ago—he sustains uncompromisingly the Miltonic discourse "with unaltered brow" (*PR* 1.493).

University of Wales, Bangor

NOTES

1. Arnold Stein, *Heroic Knowledge: An Interpretation of "Paradise Regained" and "Samson Agonistes"* (1957; reprint, London, 1965), 75; Barbara Kiefer Lewalski, *Milton's Brief Epic: The Genre, Meaning, and Art of "Paradise Regained"* (Providence, R.I., 1966), 283–84.

2. Christopher Hill, *The Experience of Defeat: Milton and Some Contemporaries* (London, 1984), 314–15. All references to Milton's poems are to *John Milton: Complete Shorter Poems,* 2d ed., ed. John Carey (London, 1997).

3. Michael Wilding, *Dragons Teeth: Literature in the English Revolution* (Oxford, 1987), 257.

4. N. H. Keeble, *The Literary Culture of Nonconformity in Later Seventeenth-Century England* (Leicester, 1987), 53–54; see also his "Wilderness Exercises: Adversity, Temptation, and Trial in *Paradise Regained*" in this volume.

5. Steven Marx, "The Prophet Disarmed: Milton and the Quakers," *SEL* 32 (1992): 111–32; David Loewenstein, "The Kingdom Within: Radical Religious Culture and the Politics of *Paradise Regained*," *Literature and History*, 3d ser., 3, no. 2 (1994): 63–89, which appears revised in his *Representing Revolution in Milton and His Contemporaries* (Cambridge, 2001), 242–68.

6. David Quint, "David's Census: Milton's Politics and *Paradise Regained*," in *Remembering Milton: Essays on the Texts and Traditions*, ed. Mary Nyquist and Margaret W. Ferguson (New York, 1987), 128–47; quotation is from 130.

7. Laura Lunger Knoppers, *Historicizing Milton: Spectacle, Power, and Poetry in Restoration England* (Athens, Ga., 1994), 141; see Loewenstein, "Kingdom Within," 73–74.

8. For the last interpretation, see Laura Lunger Knoppers, "Satan and the Papacy in *Paradise Regained*," in this volume.

9. *The Complete Prose Works of John Milton*, 8 vols., ed. Don M. Wolfe et al. (New Haven, 1953–82), 2:553–54. Hereafter designated YP and cited parenthetically by volume and page number in the text.

10. On the rich diversity of Milton's self-representation, see *Milton Studies* 38, *John Milton: The Author in His Works*, ed. Michael Lieb and Albert Labriola (Pittsburgh, 2000).

11. Carey, *Complete Shorter Poems*, 323, attributes its composition to between July 8 and August 17, 1648; the siege lasted from June 13 to August 27.

12. On the impact of the embassy on the argument of the *Second Defence*, see Thomas N. Corns, *John Milton: The Prose Works* (New York, 1998), 99–102.

13. "Cp. *Prov.* xvi 32 which, as [Merritt] Hughes . . . points out, Leone Ebreo cites . . . when outlining the familiar neo-Platonic case. . . . Horace, *Odes* II ii 9–12, makes a similar point" (Carey, *Complete Shorter Poems*, 462).

14. See YP, rev. ed., 7:359 n. 14; the argument from this biblical text has its first appearance in *The Tenure of Kings and Magistrates* (YP 3:216–17). On classical analogues to the notion of governors as servants, see Martin Dzelzainis, "Milton's Classical Republicanism," in *Milton and Republicanism*, ed. David Armitage, Armand Himy, and Quentin Skinner (Cambridge, 1995), 3–24, esp. 18–19.

15. Andrew Marvell, "An Horatian Ode upon Cromwel's Return from Ireland," lines 38–40, in *The Poems and Letters of Andrew Marvell*, 3d ed., ed. H. M. Margoliouth, revised by Pierre Legouis with the collaboration of E. E. Duncan-Jones (Oxford, 1971), 2:92.

16. Barbara K. Lewalski, *The Life of John Milton: A Critical Biography* (Oxford, 2000), 287.

17. Dzelzainis, "Milton's Classical Republicanism," 22.

18. Lewalski, *Milton's Brief Epic*, 283.

REPUBLICAN OCCASIONS IN *PARADISE REGAINED* AND *SAMSON AGONISTES*

David Norbrook

I

IN 1670 JOHN BEALE wrote that "Milton is abroad againe, in Prose, & in Verse, Epic, & Dramatic." Having apparently seen the advance listing of the *History of Britain* and *Samson Agonistes* in the Term Catalogue, this royalist member of the Royal Society was apprehensive of a republican revival. The following year he wrote that Marchamont Nedham, the republican journalist, "& Milton, with all their Junto, are able to doe us more mischiefe, than millions of S[tubbe] & C[asaubon?]." Beale had greeted *Paradise Lost* with a mixture of admiration and political anxiety, disliking the epic's "Plea for our Original right." He feared that this new round of publication would mark a further revival of republican discourse.[1]

Beale's sense that the publication of the later poems marked a republican speech-act has until recently not been widely shared by Miltonists. The diptychlike character of the 1671 volume has led many critics to see *Samson Agonistes* and *Paradise Regained* as offering opposed models of behavior: Samson, the vengeful exponent of the Old Law, and the Son who offers the way of self-sacrifice instead of revenge.[2] The temptations offered by Satan in *Paradise Regained* would then be temptations to worldly political power and activism. Such a reading is in line with the assumption of many historians that religious radicals after 1660 abandoned their earlier activism and turned inward. One landmark that has been frequently noted is the Quaker declaration of 1661 repudiating armed violence immediately after Venner's disastrous Fifth Monarchist rising.

More recently, however, historians have been complicating such a clear-cut distinction between the earlier and later periods. They have been finding more and more evidence of continued political organization among Dissenters and republicans, despite the many restrictions on their activities and publications, and a continuing debate about the relative merits of different forms of legal or armed resistance.[3] Laura Lunger Knoppers has proposed readings of the two poems published in 1671 as enacting resistance to Restoration ideology, albeit, in the case of *Samson,* in a "radically ambivalent" way.[4] David Loewenstein argues that "Milton's publishing the two poems together seems . . . a much more ambiguous gesture than critics often acknowledge," that there is "a profound indeterminacy about the 1671 volume in terms of its radical spiritual politics and Milton's imaginative responses. . . . By publishing *Paradise Regained* together with *Samson Agonistes,* Milton created a provocative volume that could itself function like a two-edged sword or even like a two-handed engine."[5] Loewenstein has questioned Stanley Fish's influential reading of *Samson Agonistes* as a drama of indeterminacy, noting the championing of millennial revenge among religious radicals.[6] In offering some further, more secular republican contexts for these poems, I would like to suggest that what is at issue is not indeterminacy as between inwardness and action but a choice of the right occasion for action. The poems are far from clear-cut in their message for the present, but that does not mean that they leave us suspended over a deconstructive abyss.

Beale's response to Milton's post-Restoration publications clearly recognized that they were to be seen as oppositional speech-acts. After publishing *Paradise Lost* in 1667, he brought out at least one work each year until his death, as if to demonstrate that he could not be excluded from the public sphere. Even the publication of a treatise on logic formed an oppositional speech-act in the context of Milton's other writings. As if to emphasize the links between the media of prose and verse, in 1673 his *Poems* were reissued with his treatise on education. The title page declared that it was "written above twenty Years since," postdating it to the time of the Commonwealth. Martin Dzelzainis has recently pointed out the strong polemical element in this tract. When it first appeared there was a danger that Parliament's leaders would lose their nerve and make a deal with the king, and Milton again and again emphasizes the need for education to strengthen resolution and determination both in civic affairs and in warfare. He contrasts his system with that of the Spartans where some youths were trained for war and others for political office: his ideal academy would combine civic prudence with intense preparation for military operations. In conjunction with the tracts on grammar and logic, the publications were a reminder that Milton offered a one-man program of civic humanist education. (They also make it hard to maintain that he had repudiated military action.)[7]

The works that distressed Beale in advance formed part of this program. The *History of Britain,* as Nicholas von Maltzahn has shown, was a salutary warning of the dangers of lacking a proper education in republican civility.[8] That lack was emphasized most strongly in the "Digression" that was omitted from the 1670 publication, probably under pressure from Milton's friends, for it contained a biting attack on the Presbyterian leadership of the 1640s, which no longer seemed appropriate to the new alliances of the 1670s. Milton offered a bleak analysis of the difficulties of instituting republican civility:

> Britain (to speake a truth not oft spok'n) as it is a land fruitful enough of men stout and couragious in warr, so is it naturallie not over fertil of men able to govern justlie & prudently in peace; trusting onelie on thir Mother-witt, as most doo, & consider not that civilitie, prudence, love of the public more then of money or vaine honour are to this soile in a manner outlandish; grow not here but in minds well implanted with solid & elaborate breeding; too impolitic els and too crude, if not headstrong & intractable to the industrie and vertue either of executing or understanding true civil government: Valiant indeed and prosperous to winn a field, but to know the end and reason of winning, unjudicious and unwise, in good or bad success alike unteachable. . . . Hence did thir victories prove as fruitless as thir losses dangerous, and left them still conquering under the same grievances that men suffer conquer'd.

The Britons had had "a smooth occasion giv'n them to free themselves"; they were "masters of thir own choice," but they threw it away because they lacked civil wisdom. Probably writing in the late 1640s, Milton expressed his fear that the leaders of the parliamentary cause would lose their republican *occasione*.[9]

   The word "occasion" had a wide range of meanings in early modern English, covering the general areas of causation, pretext, and contingency, with a root Latin sense of falling. Milton used a technical, logical sense of a particular subcategory of cause in his treatise on logic (YP 8:224). There was another more specific sense, linked with an iconographical tradition of seizing a personified Occasion, a female figure with a long forelock who was whirled around in the wind. Iconographically she was associated with Fortune; she was sometimes shown holding a razor to indicate the sharp knife-edge between choosing and missing the right time.[10] Machiavelli described Fortune and her companion Occasione in one of his poems, and drew on the iconography in chapter 25 of *The Prince*. In this celebrated passage, as Hanna Pitkin has shown, Machiavelli is torn between asserting the possibility that prudence can control human affairs and an admiration for a bold grasping of opportunity that responds to contingency beyond anything that can be rationally planned.[11] His language has overtones of seduction and sexual aggression, and readers of Milton may be rather surprised to find such secular republican language in a writer so concerned with godliness and Providence. Milton does indeed often use the term suspiciously. "Let us not slip th' occasion," Beelzebub urges Satan (*PL* 1.178). Satan urges the fallen angels in turn to seize the "occasion" (2.341), and when he sees Eve alone he is delighted that "Occasion . . . now smiles" (9.480).[12] The goals of these fallen angels, however, are directly inimical to the cause of God; the question of seizing occasions on God's behalf was another matter.

The discourse of seventeenth-century republican Puritanism was closely linked with civic humanism, with its ideology of civic activism and a practical wisdom based on close attention to particular circumstances. No Puritan would accept Machiavelli's purely secular notion of political calculation in a world governed by Fortune; and yet his sense of effective political agency as an impetuous yet brilliantly appropriate response to a very specific, unrepeatable set of circumstances could be adapted to a belief in a God whose Providence might work through infusing the spirit into the godly in unexpected ways. Republicans rejected the overtones of amoral sexual aggression, which in some ways were more suited to the absolutist theorists for whom Machiavelli's *Prince* offered practical counsel for overawing the populace. But the republicans' preferred Machiavellian text, the *Discourses* on Livy, did valorize what they understood as the masculine qualities of decisiveness and resistance to passion; Charles I and his courtiers were regularly denounced as effeminate. "Against political corruption, chaos, and tyranny," writes Jonathan Scott, "Machiavelli offered not just virtue (which had proved insufficient) but virtu [*sic*], realistic, relativistic, and above all, armed to the teeth."[13] Without explicitly noting the Machiavellian aspect, Mary Ann Radzinowicz gives an excellent definition of this conception of occasion: "occasion in human life being the instant at which an interchange between God and man occurs by mutual reaction, God improving the means to renew freedom and augment it and man grasping the revelation contained in God's improvisations and taking heart for a renewed effort. A contingent or flexible politics is one which sees occasions as containing possibilities for fruitful change toward a consensual social future."[14] Theories of reason of state could be combined with the Puritan doctrine of the special calling: this opened up a path to antinomianism, converting works into "works of faith" by the infusion of conscience.[15] It should be added, however, that many Puritans were anxious about keeping antinomian tendencies in their beliefs under tight control, and this led to a counteremphasis in their discourse on secular language. It was possible to want Christ's kingdom to appear on earth and still to believe that this event would be realized by means including civic prudence as well as godly zeal; to believe, indeed, that there might be such a thing as too much godly zeal, if it were not combined with wisdom. Even the most radically apocalyptic group, the Fifth Monarchists, were ready to appeal to a language of secular interest, claiming that "this good and wholesome Principle of Christs Government is so large, that it involves every honest Interest," and that their rebellion could be justified by "the Law of *Nature* and *Nations*" alone.[16] The Fifth Monarchists were unusual, however, in calling for rule by a godly elite; Milton shared with many Puritan republicans a belief that millennial expectations should not overrule institutional forms, and that ill-planned events like Venner's rising played into the hands of their political enemies. A comparison with the response of some contemporary republicans to the Restoration will illustrate the kinds of issues that Milton's poems were addressing.

An unsuccessful rising with Fifth Monarchist backing cost the life of a former member of the republican council of state, John Hutchinson. Hutchinson had repudiated his support of the regicide in 1660, and his life had been spared on the condition that he abstain from political activity, but he was accused on flimsy grounds of involvement in the Northern Rising of 1663 and died in prison. In the life of her husband composed soon afterwards, his wife Lucy combined millennial fervor with a sharp suspicion of antinomians who justified all their actions as immediate commands from God. On the one hand, Lucy Hutchinson presents her husband as responding to the defeat of his cause not with despair but with a renewed millennial hope, newly discovering "the doctrine of the Kingdome of Christ to be set up in visibillity and glory over all the nations . . . and he much admir'd at himselfe that he had so long overlook'd what seem'd to him now so plaine in the word of God, which every day gave him new glorious discoveries of the mysteries of Christ and Antichrist." He intervened on behalf of a Fifth Monarchist preacher, Thomas Palmer, when he was imprisoned, and invited him to preach at his house on his release. Shortly afterwards Palmer was a local organizer of the Fifth Monarchist rising in which John Hutchinson was implicated. The two men clearly shared a millennialist outlook; but throughout the *Memoirs* Hutchinson argues again and again that the cause of Christ has often been damaged by those who act most impulsively in his name. It was the "Munster Anabaptists," "ruling by their own arbitrary lust" and destroying property, who caused so many Protestants to go to the other extreme and identify the interest of Christ with that of secular princes, a mistake that set back the cause. Though "the interest of the people" should have been with godly reforms in church and state, so that they "had an opertunity to resume their power into their owne hands," this republican *occasione* was lost because "the different interests of religion devided them among themselves." Hutchinson combines her millennial rhetoric with the same kind of republican language Milton used in his *History;* the language of *occasione* may return on the very last page of the manuscript, which reads, "happie are you whom god giues time and oper"—breaking off in the middle of a word which may be, in Hutchinson's habitual spelling, "opertunity." In a carefully crafted text, the broken word may indicate her sense of the historical situation, poised between broken aims and future possibilities.[17]

In his later years John Hutchinson had lived in that difficult space. Though he felt bound by his commitment to abstain from political activity, his imprisonment came as something of a relief: "he thought himself oblieg'd to sitt still all [the] while this King reign'd, whatever opertunity he might have; but now he thought this usage had utterly disoblieg'd him from all ties either of honor or conscience, and that he was free to act as prudence should hereafter lead him." "Why do we sit still?" cried Jeremiah in a warning against complacency in one of John Hutchinson's favorite parts of the Bible (Jer. 8:14); sitting still provoked impatience, and yet the emphasis on "prudence" is important. In a previous situation where he considered himself living under illegitimate authority, after Cromwell's dissolution of Parliament in 1653, Hutchinson had believed he should "suffer patiently that yoake which God submitts him to till the Lord shall take it off . . . free to fall in or oppose all things as prudence should guide him, upon generall rules of conscience, which would not permitt him in any way to assist any tirant or invader of the people's rights, nor to rise up against them without a manifest call from God." This formulation begins by urging submission to God, then calls on judgment in the form of civic prudence, and ends by suggesting that such prudence may merge with a call from God that would justify taking up arms at the right moment. John Hutchinson responded to the situation after 1660 in similar terms. He believed that there would eventually be a successful rising against the Restoration regime, but he urged his son not to become entangled in a venture like the failed Fifth Monarchist plots:

Let not my sonne, how fairely soever they pretend, too rashly engage with the first, but stay to see what they make good, and engage with those who are for settlement, who will have need of men of interest to assist them; let him keep cleare from these and take heed of too rash attempts, and he will be courted if he behave himselfe piously and prudently and keepe free of all faction, making the publique interest only his.

In the meantime it was essential to wait, to be patient and prudent, even at the cost of being derided as passive and unheroic by the more hotheaded millennialists. God's purposes could not be exactly calculated, but they would work out in ways that would ultimately harmonize with such secular prudence. It is this patient virtue that Hutchinson celebrates in a poem on her husband's death in the Tower:

> To the next Staire of Cherefull Sufferance
> In patient meekenesse yet he higher Climbd
> Then holinesse his mounting Soule subblimd
> Before he to The lords will did submitt
> But now his owne was swallowd vp in It.   (40–44)

And yet the poem's conclusion presents his unmoved constancy as a form of action: "he did all Their lying boasts destroy / And like great Sampson dying Threw downe more / Then he had vanquisht all his life before" (66–68).[18] Samson's death is seen as unequivocally heroic, yet for Hutchinson her husband's fate is a very complex kind of heroism, involving an inner fortitude that nonetheless never repudiates the use of force under the right circumstances.

A similarly complex use of the Samson figure can be found in another former supporter of the Good Old Cause, Robert Overton (c.1609–1678). Overton's career illustrates the difficulty of making clear-cut distinctions in this period between mainstream Puritans and Fifth Monarchist extremists. Overton had parted company with the Hutchinsons in 1653 when Cromwell dissolved the Long Parliament in the name of godliness, and was warmly praised by Milton in the *Second Defence* the following year. But he then parted company with Milton in showing sympathy with the republican and millenarian opposition to the Protectorate and was imprisoned by Cromwell. He was arrested again in the aftermath of Venner's rising and rearrested in 1663, spending the next eight years in prison. He has gone down in history as a Fifth Monarchist, and it might be assumed that considerations of civic prudence would play a lesser part in his discourse than in the Hutchinsons'. In his prison meditations, however, he distanced himself from his alleged allies: "the 5th Monarchy Millinaryes are men of a comfortable creed, were it not for the many incongruetyes & contradictions they encounter."[19] He never supported the direct rule of the saints. Like John Hutchinson, he found himself in prison because of the impulsive actions of millenarians from whom he had in fact distanced himself, and he urges patient submission to established, Restoration authorities. And yet the language in which he urges submission can be double-edged:

Pull noe unnecessary sufferinges upon your selfe, wee see none more grounde to powder in this mill of vicissitudes then those that obstinately glory in the repute of sufferinge as state martyrs after they are dead. . . . Theirfore let nobody begg to be buried in the ruines of publick liberty, but yet hees brave whoe that way sinkes where sicophants swim, for the former shall be justified while the latter is moste deserveingely traduste by the letter. (301)

Here republicans are urged not to be like Samson and warned of the temptations of inappropriate martyrdom; yet where the choice is between sycophancy and self-destruction, the latter still remains more admirable. Overton copied out lengthy extracts from Quarles's *Historie of Samson,* which presents the destruction of the temple as a triumph. Another maxim, while reflecting his disillusion with the inconstant multitude, does not rule out the possibility of a long-term change: "Rather have patience & see the tree sufficiently shaken before youe fetch the fallen fruite since the zeale of the rable is not soe soone heated by the oppression of theire princes or rulers but may be more quickly cooled & conquered by their specious promises & plausable respects, brought forth by the breath of authority" (300). As in John Hutchinson's advice to his son, the recommended submission is not a total renunciation of future change: the fruit must be gathered from the tree, but only when the time is ripe. In bad times, he writes, "the example of Brutis rather than Cato is by many commended. Its safer (in this respect) to be a patient foole then an active mad malcontent" (300). Brutus concealed his resistance to Tarquin under a mask of madness, but he did take action when the time was ripe. This conditional submissiveness is captured in Overton's response when a cache of arms was discovered in his house in 1660: Overton acknowledged that he had purchased them, but denied that he intended to use them. His political language is informed by a Machiavellian register of civic prudence as well as by millenarian discourse.

Similar patterns can be found in the post-Restoration writings of another former supporter of Parliament—and a poet much admired by Overton—George Wither. In a work published at the time of the king's restoration, Wither expressed deep skepticism about whether any monarch would be able to rule justly, even if he were surrounded by ideal counselors—among whom he included Samson. He warned supporters of the Good Old Cause that

> We, lately, active were ev'n unto blood;
> But, now such *activenesse* will do no good,
> And, we must *passive* be, till GOD shall please
> Our sins to pardon and to give us ease.[20]

Here is the renunciation of action that has been found in Milton's later works, but once again it is couched in qualified terms: when God has decided the time is right, the godly will be active again. In 1661, imprisoned in the general panic about republican plots, Wither published a poem in which he dramatized his enemies as the World by whose weapon, the Flesh, he was "openly exposed (in some sort) / Like *Sampson* for a while, to make you sport," but warned that even if he were defeated, he would die nobly in his citadel, "And, that it will to thee (when batter'd down) / Prove like the House by *Sampson* overthrown."[21] Wither reiterated the comparison in a poem he published from prison after the plague struck London in 1665. Addressing God, he urges:

> Let Dagons temple then, be overthrown
> Though *Sampson* die, in pulling of it down:
> For, all thy Souldiers, seek their glorifying
> In conquering, although it be by dying.[22]

Both comparisons function as spiritual allegories rather than calls to overt imitation of Samson's exploits, and yet the threatening tone contributed to the suspicion with which the authorities regarded these writings. Wither did condemn Venner's rising, but only in highly qualified terms: Jael and Ehud had been justified in political assassinations of tyrants because they "had no doubt, secret warrants from GOD for these *irregular Actings,* by a divine impulse upon their spirits." The Fifth Monarchists had been deluded into believing they had such an impulse, but Wither does not explain beyond a perfunctory "no doubt" how we might distinguish justified from unjustified tyrannicide, and he goes on to use strongly military metaphors to describe the saints. He complains that he has been subject to "mis-interpretations" of his "free expressions," recalling that Christ himself was charged with sedition for innocent preaching.[23] It is not so surprising, however, that the authorities should have been worried by the menacing implications of claiming the combined authority of Samson and Christ, of a passivity that was consciously provisional.

If Samson fascinated Overton, the Hutchinsons, and Wither, it was not just because of his strength but because of his riddling. Republicans after 1660 were caught in a very complex hermeneutical web. On the one hand, they might want to pattern themselves on Brutus and Samson by concealing their political designs in equivocal language. On the other hand, they were constantly vulnerable to the attempts of agents provocateurs and informers to incriminate them in plots they rejected as imprudent. To this day, historians find it difficult to decide how far the voluminous documentation of plots and conspiracies after 1660 to be found in the state papers reflects actual activity, paranoid fantasy, or a deliberate attempt to discredit republicans by provoking them into illegal activities. Lucy Hutchinson relates an episode that illustrates the problem. When John Hutchinson was in prison, his writings were closely watched. His keeper searched his papers, and though he did not find a narrative of his imprisonment that he had composed, he did lay hands on a piece of paper on which he had chosen the text from Scripture that was to be the epigraph, "Judge me, O God, and plead my cause against an ungodly nation: O deliver me from the deceitful and unjust man" (Ps. 43.1). The keeper said that by the "unjust man" Hutchinson clearly intended the king, although, Lucy Hutchinson comments, "the application was of his owne making."[24] Perhaps it was, to the extent that Hutchinson was indicting the ungodly in general, but he was clearly using Scripture to claim an authority greater than that of worldly powers. In his personal Bible he in fact annotated quotations from the Psalms with specific reference to his keeper and to the political and ecclesiastical authorities. He was adopting a deliberately equivocal, indirect form of language to evade censorship; the risk he ran was that the authorities would take advantage of this indirection to implicate him, to claim that he was calling for more active and therefore treasonous resistance than he actually was. Hutchinson's keeper alleged that he had called out to some other prisoners to "take courage, they should yet have a day for it." Hutchinson indignantly denied this: it was a classic example of agent provocateur tactics. But it is nonetheless the kind of thing he might have said to keep his comrades' courage up without having to be too specific about what that "day" might be.

Such hermeneutic problems were intensified by the practice of legitimizing action by an appeal to biblical texts. It is possible to exaggerate the gulf between a more secular, prudent republicanism and an armed millenarianism if one reads some of the Fifth Monarchist declarations too literally. The manifesto for the 1660 rising, *A Door of Hope,* declared that even without Scripture their cause, which included a number of economic grievances, would be justified by the laws of nature and nations alone. While acknowledging that "we go a step above depraved reason and common understanding in representing things under the notion of the Kingdom of Christ," they warned that some might willfully mistake them, as if they meant by the term

some strange thing contrary to the sound hope of the Gospel, and Doctrine of the true Primitive Church, and not in Scripture and reason, were intended, as that Christ should immediately appear to head an Army. We shall therefore throw that stone out of your way by Declaring, that the Kingdom of Christ, or that part of it under the *Kingdome of the Stone,* which respects the Government of a well ordered Commonwealth, we mean, That we should have the best of men, of sound Principles, of known integrity, haters of Bribes and Covetousness, lovers of Mercy and Justice, that without Fees, and tedious vexatious delayes, should give you Justice, for our Magistrates and Governours.[25]

That kind of slippage between the literal kingdom and the represented kingdom went along with slippages between internal and external violence, between passivity and activism. Such debates recapitulated a dispute from the previous decade between Edmund Ludlow, whose political position was close to Hutchinson's, and the Fifth Monarchist Thomas Harrison. Harrison justified the army's dissolution of the Rump Parliament to set up the kingdom of Christ by appealing to Daniel 8:18: "the saints shall take the kingdom." Ludlow replied from verse 22 of the same chapter: "judgement was given to the saints." Both men were quite convinced that the Book of Daniel had great prophetic authority, but each of them was forced to read active verbs as if they were really passive or vice versa to establish a clear political line.[26]

Though Ludlow, like Milton and Hutchinson, was wary about premature military action, and after 1660 he constantly resisted pressure for involvement in a series of conspiracies, he never ruled out such an option if the time were right, asking God to "give us wisedome to know when to goe forward and when to stand still, that by making hast we may not strengthen the hand of the enemy, nor by standing still neglect the opportunity he puts into our hands . . . that when the Lord's tyme is come we may up and be doing."[27]

In Restoration oppositional discourse, then, there was no clear-cut opposition between the pacific Son and the riddling, violent Samson, between quietist withdrawal and violent action. For figures like Hutchinson, Overton, Wither, Ludlow, and Milton, the difficulty was to find the best way of reconciling millenarian hopes with civic prudence. They came to differing conclusions on particular issues: Ludlow criticized Hutchinson for becoming too submissive after 1660, Milton differed from Overton over the government of Cromwell. In many cases, however, these differences were on a knife-edge from identity: Overton's actions, as has been seen, were regarded as explicable only by his being a Fifth Monarchist, and critics are still debating how far Milton came to retract his own earlier support for Cromwell.[28] *Paradise Regained* and *Samson Agonistes* reflect this atmosphere of political equivocation and textual involution. Rather than offering a straightforward opposition between quietism and action, they present two different models of the relations between prudence and military action, of the proper way to read and seize the occasion, in such a way that individual human agency becomes subsumed under divine agency.

Neither occasion, to complicate matters further, can be translated immediately into the historical situation of post–1660 Puritans: the reader is asked, as it were, to engage in an exercise of triangulation, to find the points where these very different examples might throw light on the stresses and potentialities of the present. Milton criticism has tended to emphasize typological readings of the Bible, but some of the seventeenth century's most influential interpreters of biblical history, notably Sir Walter Raleigh, had absorbed the much more secular, political emphasis of humanist historiography even while retaining a providential framework. Raleigh's *History of the World* had many lessons to teach Oliver Cromwell about trusting in God and keeping his powder dry.[29] Milton's Jesus and Samson are faced with unique conjunctures, with which they engage with a sharp, adaptable eye for their immediate possibilities; the reader is being educated in their alertness to working within the frame of action allowed them, and being implicitly urged to do likewise in the present. Such alertness is more important than a particular preformulated set of prescriptions.

II

The hermeneutical position is especially complex in *Paradise Regained:* writing under the Restoration censorship, Milton is presenting a character who has to be vigilant about the authorities of his own day. Satan functions somewhat like a royalist agent provocateur trying to extort a seditious statement. We therefore need to be especially wary about taking any of the Son's defensive responses to Satan as direct statements of policy for the 1670s, and to focus more closely on the processes of dialectical exchange. Satan's speech of temptation to kingship (3.150–80) touches the sore spots that were felt by post–1660 republicans like John Hutchinson about sitting still: "think'st thou to regain / Thy right by sitting still or thus retiring?" Satan challenges Tiberius's right to rule Israel and indicts his government as intemperate, and he appeals to Judas Maccabeus as a precedent for a war of national liberation. The Son has already shown himself open to such an appeal, and in giving "heroic acts" to "words" still reserves the possibility of other forms of action (1.215– 26). Satan brings his speech to a climax by using the language of the *occasione:*

> Zeal and Duty are not slow;
> But on Occasion's forelock watchful wait.
> They themselves rather are occasion best,
> Zeal of thy Father's house, Duty to free
> Thy Country from her Heathen servitude. (172–76)

The play on an alternative sense of "occasion" as "cause" and the use of the iconographical motif draw particular attention to the word. Satan's words, however, in themselves indicate a need for the Son to be wary about this particular offer. The Maccabeus temptation is very specific: the Maccabees combined the roles of priest and king, and their deeds were chronicled in biblical books that Protestants consider apocryphal. There was also a contemporary resonance: Maccabeus had been the favorite model for Owen Roe O'Neill and other champions of Irish Catholic resistance to England, a model Milton would have rejected precisely because it did involve an alliance with priests.[30]

Jesus responds not with a direct negation but with a proverb, a conditional statement about God's purposes, and a series of questions. Their burden is to shift attention from time-bound to timeless kingships, but he does not lose contact with contemporary political idioms: in declaring that

> who best
> Can suffer, best can do; best reign, who first
> Well hath obey'd; just trial e'er I merit
> My exaltation without change or end, (3.194–97)

he uses a maxim, attributed to Solon, which was widely current in classical and early modern texts on government, and implied a meritocratic view of power (compare Marvell's "Horatian Ode," lines 83–84).[31] Not taking this hint, Satan declares that he needs to be schooled in "regal arts" and "Mysteries" by visiting "radiant Courts." These arts are Machiavellian, but with a strongly regal tinge. The Son can indeed know when the proper occasion is due: "prediction . . . supposes means," and he will not "engage / Thy Virtue" without ensuring his safety (3.347–56). "Virtue" here implies a Machiavellian *virtù,* a forceful engagement, and the Hutchinsons, Overton, and Ludlow would have agreed that acting on prophecy would be irresponsible without prudent means and forceful civic virtue. Satan's Machiavellianism, however, does not share their concern for civil liberty. "Means" for him involve a narrow form of reason of state, such as might be found in the "radiant Courts" (3.237) which he sees as the best schools of political virtue.

The advice to seek power through an alliance with the Parthians places Jesus' own short-term dynastic advantage over the people as a whole. There is a particular irony in this choice of example, for a debate over an alliance with the Parthians comes at a climactic moment of Lucan's republican epic, the *Pharsalia.* After the defeat at Pharsalia, Pompey urges a strategic alliance but is opposed in a passionate speech by Lentulus, who complains that such an external alliance would compromise the ideological purity of what at present is an internal war over political principles: why did he claim that his cause was the love of liberty? (8.339–40). The one mitigation of their sufferings was that they owed no obligations to a foreign ruler. Milton had echoed this part of the poem in *Paradise Lost* (6.436), a poem deeply informed by Lucan's influence; the relation of the later poem to the *Pharsalia* remains to be fully explored, but the parallels indicate that *Paradise Regained* does not completely repudiate secular republicanism.[32] Moreover, the detailed attention Milton gives to the first-century political and military situation, with his vivid evocation of the details of battle, illustrates how far he is from dealing with a timeless world of types and antitypes.

At the time the poem was published, the legitimacy of alliances with foreign monarchies of just the kind Satan proposes was a matter of active concern for English republicans. The exile Algernon Sidney was engaged in one of a series of intrigues in which he alternately courted the aid of Louis XIV to overthrow Charles and offered his services to Charles against the French. In each case, Sidney believed that seizing a short-term opportunity with pragmatic motives would in the long term revive the Good Old Cause.[33] Though Sidney indignantly rejected the "court maxims" of reason of state, like other republicans he was ready to engage in such negotiations if the occasion seemed right. The way Milton presents the debate in *Paradise Regained* suggests skepticism about the value of any such alliance, but the issues involved were very much of the present moment.

In his retort to Satan, the Son does not raise the same kind of ideological issue as Lucan's Lentulus—who of course is speaking in a republican forum— and contemptuously rejects Satan's notion of "means." That rejection, however, will prove to be provisional, and once again he touches on republican concerns. In having the Son remind Satan that he had incited King David to number his kingdom and thus brought plague on his people, Milton alludes to contemporary attacks on the restored monarchy, and warns his people, as David Quint has argued, against an "easy transition and slide from republican to royalist statism."[34] He ends with a vision of the future in which the lost tribes who had "wrought their own captivity" regain their sense of freedom and return to the Promised Land. The agency for this change is attributed to God alone, but implicit in the claim that they had brought about their captivity is the possibility that at least in some sense they themselves can seize the *occasione* of their freedom. The return of the Jews to the Holy Land had been a key issue for millennial Puritans, who expected that the Jews would be converted shortly before the millennium; Jesus is here voicing a position that had become indelibly associated with the radicalism of the mid-century.[35]

Satan now shifts attention to the throne of Rome. As Malcom Kelsall points out, Jesus is so careful to avoid open sedition that he does not himself attack Tiberius, merely alluding in a "thou say'st" to the speech in which Satan assembles a Tacitean indictment of his vices.[36] Once again he claims that the people have made their own servitude, and it would therefore be futile to redeem them now. However, he also suggests that redemption will come eventually:

> Know therefore when my season comes to sit
> On *David's* Throne, it shall be like a tree
> Spreading and overshadowing all the Earth,
> Or as a stone that shall to pieces dash
> All Monarchies besides throughout the world,
> And of my Kingdom there shall be no end:
> Means there shall be to this, but what the means,
> Is not for thee to know, nor me to tell.   (4.146–53)

This is the climactic moment in the dialogue over earthly means and divine providence, and after his initial hedging Jesus ends with a strong, menacing affirmation of means. The menace is of course confirmed by his allusion to Daniel 2:35: "the stone that smote the image became a great mountain, and

filled the whole earth." This passage was so strongly associated with Fifth
Monarchist sedition that its decoding as specifically republican would have
come with tremendous force. At the same time, Jesus takes the rhetorical
initiative by declaring that he is not telling what he might. Disclosing the
means would incriminate him, and this generalized threat draws attention to
his own control over the speech-act.

Satan has thus gradually pushed the Son from fairly bland statements of
nonresistance into more powerful expressions of prophetic longing for the
time when monarchy will be overthrown, yet he has still kept back from
preaching direct sedition. Satan now uses language very like that of a Restoration official dealing with a recalcitrant republican prisoner such as John
Hutchinson. He is being difficult and nice, nothing will please him but always
contradicting (4.157–58). And then, in an outrageous shift of register, he
offers Jesus all the kingdoms if he falls down and worships him. Behind all of
Satan's apparent falling in with the rhetoric of liberty and civic activism, he is
a self-idolater who wants Jesus merely to be his puppet.

Satan now turns from action to contemplation, but in fact his speech
works its way back to the temptation to kingship:

> These here revolve, or, as thou lik'st, at home,
> Till time mature thee to a Kingdom's weight;
> These rules will render thee a King complete
> Within thy self, much more with Empire join'd.   (4.281–84)

He here takes up Jesus' earlier Stoical speech in praise of self-kingship,
suggesting that this "more Kingly" (2.476) ideal would be made even more
kingly by adding kingship. Jesus' reply is a wry Miltonic joke that has taken on
more irony over time: "Think not but that I know these things; or think / I
know them not" (4.286–87). If Milton critics have until recently failed to
perceive the allusion to a passage of Lucan that would have been inspiring to
seventeenth-century republicans, it might be concluded that the protagonists
of the poem know "these things" better than many later readers. Chronologi-
cally, of course, Jesus could not have had access to the writings of Tacitus,
Seneca, or Lucan, but their discourse was being formed in response to the
growing tendency of the Roman Empire toward tyranny which Milton represents as being already in progress. The poem's Jesus has enough political
sensitivity to be able to preempt the most acceptable moral points of a nas-
cent anti-imperial politics. In many ways Jesus' heroism in the desert parallels that of the Stoic Cato, the last and most ethically exalted of the heroes of
the *Pharsalia,* and a hero both to first-century and seventeenth-century republicans. As Andrew Shifflett reminds us, however, Stoical ideas were politically ambiguous: they could point to passive or even active resistance or

to a quietist abstention from political action. As deployed by writers like Sir George Mackenzie, Senecanism was being used to urge external conformity to the Restoration church on the grounds that inward freedom would not be thus compromised.[37] Critics who describe post–1660 Puritans as turning inward risk losing sight of the degree to which, in the dissenting mentality, "conscience acts in the world."[38]

Puritan neo-Stoics, moreover, always rejected any attempt to make secular prudence independent of the Gospel. Sidney has a corrupt courtier declare that

at court we little trouble ourselves with the intricacies of the Bible. If any amongst us were known to read it he would be looked upon as a fanatic, to the utter ruin of his fortune. Our principal study is romances, playbooks, or poets. If we apply ourselves to anything more serious, we read Machiavelli and other books of that kind, which we find more useful to us than all that is contained in the Bible.[39]

Yet Sidney was ready to use Machiavelli for his own purposes; when engaging with a courtier, however, the emphasis is on the superiority of the Bible. The Son repudiates a quest for "virtue" that would appeal only to Fortune or Fate: a purely secular Stoicism or Machiavellianism is never Milton's ideal. However, he is very far from accepting a turn inward that makes political forms indifferent: classical orators are

> to our Prophets far beneath,
> As men divinely taught, and better teaching
> The solid rules of Civil Government
> In thir majestic unaffected style
> Than all the Oratory of *Greece* and *Rome*.
> In them is plainest taught, and easiest learnt,
> What makes a Nation happy, and keeps it so,
> What ruins Kingdoms, and lays Cities flat;
> These only, with our Law, best form a King.   (4.356–64)

This is his final retort to Satan's attempt to commandeer classical learning for monarchical ambition. If he acknowledges—as some republicans did—the possibility in principle of a good king, the king these prophets form is one who can ruin kingdoms.

On the final day of temptations, Satan reverts to the question of the right occasion for action:

> Did I not tell thee, if thou didst reject
> The perfect season offer'd with my aid
> To win thy destin'd seat, but wilt prolong
> All to the push of Fate, pursue thy way

> Of gaining *David's* Throne no man knows when,
> For both the when and how is nowhere told
>
> .   .   .   .
>
>   each act is rightliest done,
> Not when it must, but when it may be best.   (4.467–76)

Satan's statecraft, however, has already revealed itself as flawed, and he clinches his perversion of Machiavellianism when he acknowledges that he has seen his exchanges with the Son as seizing the *occasione:* "opportunity I here have had / To try thee, sift thee" (4.531–32)—and, he hopes, to pin him down. The temptation on the pinnacle produces a final riddling answer— "Tempt not the Lord thy God"—which condenses the double-edged quality of the Son's utterances through the poem. Satan the agent provocateur ends up like a victim of the Sphinx who was unable to solve the riddle. He has been confounded not by silence and evasion but by consistent skill and cunning of speech—speech which is also action. The answer to the Sphinx's riddle, of course, was "man," not "God" or "king." In a final indication that the poem does not so much repudiate classicism as reclaim and rework its republican traditions, the narrator compares Jesus in his moment of triumph to Hercules triumphing over Antaeus. Hercules was a contested figure in antiquity: Augustus had revived a cult of Hercules, heralded by Virgil in the *Aeneid,* but Seneca had countered with a Stoic Hercules, and Milton had quoted the tyrannicidal lines Seneca ascribed to his hero in his *First Defence* (YP 4:446). Seneca's nephew Lucan narrated the Hercules-Antaeus episode in Book Four of the *Pharsalia,* where it provides an ironic prelude to the defeat of the Caesarian Curio. Its Libyan setting provides a prelude to the Libyan scenes later in the epic where the republican Cato will reveal his affinity with the Stoic Hercules.[40] Jesus has regained Paradise not by ritualistic sacrifice but by an expert deployment of rhetoric: he, rather than Satan, is the master of seizing the occasions of argument, and he does so in order to proclaim a principled resistance to earthly monarchy without prematurely compromising his mission. As Milton wrote in the *First Defence,* he "took upon himself the form of a slave, but he never lost the heart of a liberator" (YP 4:374–75).

There are implications here for the present, but they are not clear-cut. The *occasione* Jesus faces in this early-imperial world is one well known to republican writers ancient and modern, who agreed that the Roman people had become corrupted by civil war, that even figures like Pompey who fought for the republic had become compromised in their ideals. Further attempts to destroy the empire were tactically and ethically highly debatable. That analysis was shared by some Restoration radicals: in 1663 the treatise *Mene Tekel,* a manifesto for the rising after which John Hutchinson was arrested, gave a purely prudential reason why Christ and Peter did not resist the government: the rest of the nation had accepted tyranny, and it would have been futile for them to resist though they had a perfect right to do so.[41] The author was far from believing that that particular example should be imitated in the present, when circumstances, he believed, were different. Similarly, while there are clear parallels between Milton's disillusioned views of the English and of the Romans, his deployment of the Daniel prophecy makes clear the difference: these, he was confident, were the last days, the time whose deferral the poem constantly dramatizes, with a sense of frustration and anticlimax. By the same token, *Paradise Regained* creates an expectation of a denouement in which resolution and restoration will come.

III

If *Paradise Regained* arouses a desire for closure, *Samson Agonistes* concludes the 1671 volume with what may seem an excess of closure, not only in its violence but in the way that violence is directed against the dramatic medium itself. Milton highlights the savagery of the conclusion to a degree that understandably makes modern readers uncomfortable. It is not clear that contemporaries with comparable political views would have shared the full degree of modern disquiet, but neither do we need to argue that Samson is an unequivocal role model. Whatever its resonance for Restoration England, this poem, too, is set at a different historical moment, and the contrast between it and *Paradise Regained* presents us with different responses to the question of action that may have been appropriate to each circumstance, rather than a clear contrast between godly passivity and ungodly action.

Here a further contemporary parallel with Samson can help illuminate the issues. Blair Worden has noted many possible echoes in *Samson Agonistes* of George Sikes's life of Sir Henry Vane; for the present argument what is of special interest is the way the Samson figure is interpreted.[42] Sikes writes that Vane "has more advantaged a good CAUSE and condemned a bad one, done his honest Countrey-men more service, and his enemies more disservice by his death, (as *Sampson* served the *Philistines*) then before in all his Life, though that also were very considerable" (119). Like John Hutchinson, Vane had been spared in 1660 but became involved in the authorities' anxieties after the Venner rising and was executed. Sikes was concerned to vindicate Vane from any complicity in plotting, and like Lucy Hutchinson he used the Samson analogy in a pacific, Christlike sense: "What he vigorously prosecuted when he was active, he ratified and sealed with his blood (and all the tendencies thereunto, *by witnessing a good Confession*) since he was passive" (106–7). Saints should "not antedate his season, but quietly wait till the set time for Sions deliverance be come, through the State-ministry of the mighty angels and Church-ministry of spiritual believers" (117). Peter had been too hasty to draw the sword against those who offered violence against his master; Christ had checked him, saying, "Thinkest thou that I cannot now pray to my father, and he shall presently give me more than twelve legions of angels?" (Matt. 26:53). Similarly, if Vane could have procured twelve legions of angels to lay all his brutish adversaries in the scaffold and around him dead at his feet, he would have forborne to desire it "till the proper season for that dispensation be come, which he reckoned to be very near" (117).

The tone, then, is pacific, and yet the vividness with which Sikes is ready to imagine angelic guerrillas coming to Vane's rescue on the scaffold is at least as striking as his repudiation of this strategy. As so often in post-Restoration Puritan republicanism, there is an almost immediate shift from denying violent intentions to saying that violence may be necessary at some time in the future. And in fact Sikes goes on to give a description of apocalyptic warfare which it is very hard to distinguish from the English civil war, "the late war, that was but a shadow to what this Angelical host and their performances upon the enemy will amount unto" (118). While it is yet a suffering season, the greatest conquest over our enemies is by death; Vane leaves open the possibility that the suffering season may change to one of action. He looks forward to the saints' final coming forth, and alludes to the familiar vision of the stone breaking the image from Daniel 2:35. Like so many Dissenters, Sikes draws attention to Christ as a parallel for the use of riddling and evasive political language. He had rejected the temptation to temporal kingship because it would be used against him, and he refused to give a more direct answer to the Pharisees, and thus stop slanders, because his actions would speak for themselves.

Sikes's book brings together key themes and images in *Paradise Regained* and *Samson Agonistes,* and it is also the place where Milton's first post-Restoration publication occurred. Sikes included the sonnet to Vane, which he had written but not published in 1652. Annabel Patterson has noted the significance of this oppositional speech-act[43]; it should further be emphasized how important the sonnet is to Sikes's argument. Though he never mentions the author, he takes the poem as a definitive analysis of Vane's life and character. He uses the sonnet's three parts as the basis for his division of Vane's career over the ensuing ten pages, and it marks the turning point from general theological discussions to politics, as an exemplary definition of "A Common-Wealths-Man . . . a dangerous Name to the Peace and Interest of Tyranny" (93). For all his notorious propensity to cloudy mysticism, Vane had been a ruthlessly effective manager of naval affairs, and Milton begins by comparing him to the senators of early, specifically republican, Rome, citing Cicero in the phrase "gowns not arms." Vane is then praised for his political

prudence in judging the right moment to pursue military rather than diplo-
matic options: in Machiavellian terms, he could judge the *occasione;* though
as the sonnet moves on to praise his skills in administering the war effort,
Machiavelli's rejection of the claim that money is the sinew of war is adapted
to emphasize the role of finance. In his comments on the sonnet, Sikes noted
that Vane had been uneasy about the war with the Dutch, whose champions
"too much turned War into a trade" (96), but had pursued the war resolutely
once the choice was made. It is in the sestet that Milton turns, "besides," to
the knowledge of the separation of civil and spiritual powers. Thus the sonnet, rather than leading readers away from politics into a timeless religious
realm, is seen as a way into concrete political analysis. Milton's sonnet, like
the later works, is finely poised between the demands of war and peace,
insisting on the need for careful judgment of the right moment. Its placement in Sikes's book gives valuable evidence of the way Milton's verse would
have been read by republicans.

In Sikes's portrayal of Vane, then, both Christ and Samson figure a kind
of nonresistance that has by no means unequivocally repudiated activism.
The same applies, I would argue, to the juxtaposition of these figures in the
1671 volume. Both men are inspired by the example of Gideon, the liberating
leader from earlier in the Book of Judges. Gideon's name had been on the
banner of the Fifth Monarchist rising in 1661, indicating his continuing
relevance as a type of nonresistor—even though Milton would have disap-
proved of the Fifth Monarchists' judgments about the right occasion.[44] The
period when "there was no king in Israel" (Judg. 17:6, 18:1) was particularly
attractive to republicans. As in *Paradise Regained,* Milton tries to imagine his
hero within a specific historical setting—in this case one of fluid and uncertain political structures in the face of repeated foreign invasions.[45] There are
great patterns of civic virtue, such as Gideon and Jephtha, but the people lack
the will to freedom that would allow their victories to be followed up, preferring "Bondage with ease than strenuous liberty" (271). When Israel does gain
a greater degree of political independence, it will soon lose civil liberty by
subordinating itself to a monarchy. As in the time of *Paradise Regained,* then,
the future does not offer a triumphant resolution; but, within the limits of his
time, Samson is able to score an important victory. He is a man of his times.
Criticism has tended to focus on the ways in which Samson is a self-portrait of
the blind poet, but this risks obscuring the extent to which Milton has imagined himself into a very different kind of figure, acutely conscious of his
physical bulk, finding pain in the process of enforced reflection and agony
over the impossibility of translating thought immediately into physical action.
Though sharing with his people a desire for liberty that has not yet yielded to
monarchy, Samson also resembles Milton's Britons in having great military

valor but a fatal lack of civil prudence. The Son excels in rhetorical skill; Samson has a common propensity for riddling speech, but he has allowed each of his wives in turn to guess his riddles and given up his "fort of silence." While Jesus is able to safeguard his aims with his ambiguous responses, Samson does not match his skill in understanding and using words, especially insofar as it goes with a skill in judging occasions.

Milton uses the word "occasion" in *Samson Agonistes* more than any of his biblical sources, although, interestingly, the word does occur more often in English versions than in the Vulgate. In the Latin version Samson's marriage at Timna is recognized as an "occasionem" against the Philistines (Judg. 14:4). The Geneva translation glosses this passage as "To fight against them for the deliuerance of Israel," and reuses the word in a gloss to Judges 15:3, where Samson begins to unleash the fiery foxes: "through his father in lawes occasion, he was moued againe to take vengeance of the Philistims." This was an episode that Milton included among his many plans for a tragedy derived from Judges. In a later passage, the Danites' "doe ye sit stil? be not slouthfull to goe and enter to possesse the lande" is glossed as "Lose ye this good occasion through your slouthfulnesse?"—terminology very close to the early modern iconography of occasion (18:9). The Authorized Version introduces the word "occasion" at 9:33, where it had not been used in earlier translations.

Taking up such hints, in *Samson Agonistes* Milton explores occasions in terms of civic prudence as well as divine providence. In his opening exchanges with the Chorus he echoes the Geneva text and gloss on the Timna marriage: "that by occasion hence / I might begin *Israel's* Deliverance" (224–25), and the Chorus praises him for "seeking just occasion to provoke / The *Philistine*, thy Country's Enemy," but observes that "*Israel* still serves with all his Sons" (237–40). Manoa ruefully points to what he sees as Samson's past misjudgments of occasions:

> thou didst plead
> Divine impulsion prompting how thou might'st
> Find some occasion to infest our Foes.
> I state not that; this I am sure; our Foes
> Found soon occasion thereby to make thee
> Thir Captive, and thir triumph.   (421–26)[46]

Samson acknowledges that his missed occasions stem from a disproportion of strength to judgment:

> Immeasurable strength they might behold
> In me, of wisdom nothing more than mean;
> This with the other should, at least, have paird,
> These two proportion'd ill drove me transverse.   (206–9)

Here it is not simply a question of saying that physical strength is bad and political wisdom good; rather, they need to be deployed together in a way appropriate to the occasion—as he has already said, strength needs a "double share" of wisdom (53–54).[47] The analysis of a need to combine military valor with civic prudence is very close to that in *Of Education* and the "Digression" to the *History of Britain*. In the course of the play we see Samson presented with an occasion. It is by no means ideal, and there is a lot of room for argument about whether it really helps the people. But it is the best that Samson can manage.

Blair Worden has shown how much of the play mirrors the situation of the imprisoned republicans. Like them, Samson is humiliated by his enforced passivity. Like John Hutchinson, however, he still prefers prison to a freedom brokered by Manoa in which he would merely be "sitting idle" (566). The whole episode of Manoa's trying to free Samson is Milton's addition to the story; it parallels the situation of many republicans in 1660, notably John Hutchinson. Samson maintains his honor to the extent of refusing a shabby compromise, but he lacks Jesus' rhetorical mastery. When he encounters Dalila and Harapha he loses his cool, and we can see the lack of self-control that made him blurt out his secrets; as he says, "my riddling days are over." When a Philistine officer comes to command him to take part in idolatrous revels, however, he finds his occasion. Importantly, the moment when he realizes this comes between the officer's two visits. At first the officer has merely commanded him to attend and he insists that he will not come: "Do they not seek occasion of new quarrels / On my refusal to distress me more, / Or make a game of my calamities?" (1329–31). Critics differ enormously over the inner processes that lead to Samson's change of mind as he obeys a "divine impulse." Some see this as a radically antinomian moment; others emphasize that Samson is shown to act in accordance with valid general principles.[48] Victoria Kahn has shown that these views can be reconciled to some degree by linking Milton with those Puritan theorists for whom reason of state offered a rationalization for moments that could not be subsumed under general principles. As has been seen, Hutchinson, Overton, and other contemporaries thought in these terms. Milton's foregrounding of the word "occasion" at this point in the drama brings this line of thinking to the fore, coloring the scene with connotations that bring together a sense of utter particularity and a possible convergence with divine purposes. Countering what the Philistines see as their occasion, he abruptly reverses their expectations. The inner impulse manifests itself in a new skill in speech: the riddler returns. He pretends this time to accept commands: "Masters' commands come with a power resistless / To such as owe them absolute subjection" (1404–5). These lines, of course, are ironic: it is only

God whose commands are absolute for Samson, a point he will take up in his last words:

> Hitherto, Lords, what your commands impos'd
> I have perform'd, as reason was, obeying,
> Not without wonder or delight beheld.
> Now of my own accord such other trial
> I mean to show you of my strength, yet greater;
> As with amaze shall strike all who behold.   (1640–45)

In the biblical account we are given a view of Samson's inward thoughts; Milton shifts the emphasis to his external, pragmatic use of language. As with the officer, he uses the language of commands and rational obedience to lull the Philistines into false security. His reference to striking them is his last grim riddle before he pulls down the temple. Samson's strength and his speech have come together again.

The gory ending of *Samson Agonistes* has understandably disquieted commentators, and defenders of an anti-Samson reading have pointed out that his act does not immediately liberate Israel. Neither the violence nor the lack of immediate consequence, however, is necessarily presented as discrediting the act altogether. In the realm of civil prudence within which the play is situated, occasions must be judged on their merits, and there may be no easy solution. Manoa comments that "To *Israel* / Honour [he] hath left, and freedom, let them but / Find courage to lay hold on this occasion" (1714–16). As appears from subsequent biblical narratives, they failed to do so; the judgment lies on them, not on Samson. The fact that we are invited to view the act in its historical perspective, however, draws attention to the fact that it is not a direct model for the present. Was Milton calling for republican activists to pull down the Drury Lane Theatre over the king's head? Insofar as he is narrating a past event, the moral does not have to be read so directly. The preponderance of brute strength over wisdom, of military force over civil prudence, in Samson falls short of the ideals Milton sketched in the *History,* and forms a clear contrast with Jesus. And yet within the constraints of the situation he faces, Samson has the options only of seizing or refusing the occasion, and readers are expected to derive a grim pleasure from the effectiveness with which he most literally seizes the occasion of revenge. That we are not offered this recourse as an immediate policy prescription need not, however, mean that Milton shared the outrage of a more liberal age. He had countenanced violence against civilians in his role as a public spokesman, notably in the aftermath of Cromwell's massacres in Ireland, and he showed no signs of later recantation. What can be said is that he consistently indicated a preference for political solutions before the last recourse of violence.

As we have seen, there is some equivocation in *Paradise Regained* over the role of physical force, while one thing that interests Milton in Samson is precisely the extent to which he is able to move away from mere physical force. As with *Paradise Regained,* the moral for Milton's own time is necessarily complex. A revolution led by figures like Samson would be likely to lurch from disaster to disaster unless strengthened by leaders more gifted in civil prudence. On the other hand, Samson's strength and resolution, once combined with a modicum of wisdom, would have been able to break through obstacles that might have seemed insuperable.

One thing the heroes of *Paradise Regained* and *Samson Agonistes* do have in common, and share with the author of the texts, is an ability to act appropriately through language, to seize the *occasione* with their speech-acts. As Radzinowicz has pointed out, Milton repeatedly uses the word "occasion" to refer to resourceful uses of language by a writer. In *Comus* the Attendant Spirit, one of the masque's figures of the artist, comes to "the present aid / Of this occasion" (89–90) to help, as Radzinowicz puts it, "a pilgrim unmistakably associated with an ideal of republicanism."[49] In 1642 he had thanked an opponent for giving him an "apt occasion" to vindicate himself (YP 1:884). In his 1645 note to *Lycidas,* he wrote that he "by occasion foretells the ruin of our corrupted Clergy then in their height." As John Beale had feared, the 1671 volume formed in itself a republican speech-act that seized the kind of *occasione* open to the blind poet, summoning the spirits of his political allies under difficult circumstances. It was for the nation to lay hold on that occasion as it best could.

Merton College, Oxford

NOTES

    1. Nicholas von Maltzahn, "Laureate, Republican, Calvinist: An Early Response to Milton and *Paradise Lost* (1667)," in *Milton Studies* 29, ed. Albert C. Labriola (Pittsburgh, 1992), 181–98.

    2. Michael Fixler, *Milton and the Kingdoms of God* (London, 1964); Michael Wilding, *Dragons Teeth: Literature in the English Revolution* (Oxford, 1987), 149–58; Irene Samuel, "*Samson Agonistes* as Tragedy," in *Calm of Mind,* ed. J. A. Wittreich Jr. (Cleveland, 1971), 235–57; Joseph Wittreich, *Interpreting "Samson Agonistes"* (Princeton, 1986). Christopher Hill, "*Samson Agonistes* Again," *Literature and History,* 2d ser., 1 (1990): 25–39, points out that Wittreich's book overwhelmingly uses comparisons with royalists, and omits consideration of parliamentarians, in trying to decide Milton's own view of Samson. Hill notes in passing the references by Lucy Hutchinson and George Wither which I here explore further.

    3. See, for example, Richard L. Greaves, *Deliver Us from Evil: The Radical Underground in*

Britain, 1660–1663 (New York, 1986); Tim Harris, Paul Seaward, and Mark Goldie, eds., *The Politics of Religion in Restoration England* (Oxford, 1990).

4. Laura Lunger Knoppers, *Historicizing Milton: Spectacle, Power, and Poetry in Restoration England* (Athens, Ga., 1993), 63, 123–41.

5. David Loewenstein, *Representing Revolution in Milton and His Contemporaries: Religion, Politics, and Polemics in Radical Puritanism* (Cambridge, 2001), 295.

6. Stanley Fish, "Spectacle and Evidence in *Samson Agonistes*," *Critical Inquiry* 15 (1988–89): 556–86, and *How Milton Works* (Cambridge, Mass., 2001), 391–473; David Loewenstein, "The Revenge of the Saint: Radical Religion and Politics in *Samson Agonistes*," in *Milton Studies* 33, *The Miltonic Samson*, ed. Albert C. Labriola and Michael Lieb (Pittsburgh, 1997), 133–58.

7. Martin Dzelzainis, "Milton's Classical Republicanism," in *Milton and Republicanism*, ed. David Armitage et al. (Cambridge, 1995), 3–24, esp. 10–15.

8. Nicholas von Maltzahn, *Milton's "History of Britain": Republican Historiography in the English Revolution* (Oxford, 1991).

9. *The History of Britain*, in *The Complete Prose Works of John Milton*, 8 vols., ed. Don M. Wolfe et al. (New Haven, 1953–82), 5:449–51; subsequent references to Milton's prose are taken from this edition and designated as YP and cited parenthetically by volume and page number in the text.

10. Charles D. Moseley, *A Century of Emblems: An Introductory Anthology* (Aldershot, 1989), 41–42, 109, 135, 149, 227.

11. Hanna Fenichel Pitkin, *Fortune Is a Woman: Gender and Politics in the Thought of Niccolò Machiavelli* (Berkeley and Los Angeles, 1984), 143–53.

12. Verse quotations are from *John Milton: Complete Poems and Major Prose*, ed. Merritt Y. Hughes (New York, 1957).

13. Jonathan Scott, *Algernon Sidney and the English Republic, 1623–1677* (Cambridge, 1988), 30.

14. Mary Ann Radzinowicz, *Toward "Samson Agonistes": The Growth of Milton's Mind* (Princeton, 1978), 167.

15. Victoria Kahn, "Political Theology and Reason of State in *Samson Agonistes*," *South Atlantic Quarterly* 95 (1996): 1076; see further her *Machiavellian Rhetoric: From the Counter-Reformation to Milton* (Princeton, 1994).

16. *A Door of Hope* ([London, 1660]), 4, 7; on Fifth Monarchism as continuing some of the themes of secular radicalism, see James Holstun, *Ehud's Dagger: Class Struggle in the English Revolution* (London, 2000), 275–304.

17. Lucy Hutchinson, *Memoirs of the Life of Colonel Hutchinson* (London, 1973), 234, 242, 41; Nottinghamshire Archives, DD/HU4, p. [420]. Hutchinson uses the word "occasion" frequently, though not in the specifically political sense here considered. For further discussion of Samson in the Restoration, see Blair Worden, "Milton, *Samson Agonistes*, and the Restoration," in *Culture and Society in the Stuart Restoration: Literature, Drama, History*, ed. Gerald MacLean (Cambridge, 1995), 111–36, and Janel Mueller, "The Figure and the Ground: Samson as a Hero of London Nonconformity, 1662–1667," in *Milton and the Terms of Liberty*, ed. Graham Parry and Joad Raymond (Cambridge, 2002), 137–62.

18. Hutchinson, *Memoirs*, 255, 216, 269; Hutchinson, "Elegies," in David Norbrook, "Lucy Hutchinson's 'Elegies' and the Situation of the Republican Woman Writer," *English Literary Renaissance* 27 (1997): 468–521; quote on 498.

19. Barbara Taft, "'They that persew perfection on earth': The Political Progress of Robert Overton," in *Soldiers, Writers, and Statesmen of the English Revolution*, ed. Ian Gentles,

John Morrill, and Blair Worden (Cambridge, 1998), 298; hereafter cited in the text by page number.

20. George Wither, *Speculum Speculativum* (London, 1660), 56; reprinted in *Miscellaneous Works of George Wither,* 6 vols. (1872–78; reprint, New York, 1967), vol. 5; hereafter cited as *MW* in the text.

21. George Wither, *A Triple Paradox* (London, 1661), in *MW,* 2:3–4.

22. George Wither, *A Single Sacrifice* (London, 1663), in *MW,* 4:62.

23. George Wither, *Fides-Anglicana* (London, [1661]), in *MW,* 5:21–26.

24. Hutchinson, *Memoirs,* 260

25. *A Door of Hope,* 4–5.

26. *The Memoirs of Edmund Ludlow,* 2 vols., ed. C. H. Firth (Oxford, 1894), 2:7–8.

27. Edmund Ludlow, *A Voyce from the Watch Tower,* ed. A. B. Worden (London, 1978), 309–10.

28. For a recent contribution to an ongoing debate, see Robert Thomas Fallon, "*A Second Defence:* Milton's Critique of Cromwell," in *Milton Studies* 39, ed. Albert C. Labriola (Pittsburgh, 2000), 167–83.

29. Christopher Hill, *Intellectual Origins of the English Revolution* (Oxford, 1965), 180–93, 202–3, 209–10; Anna Beer, *Sir Walter Ralegh and His Readers in the Seventeenth Century: Speaking to the People* (Houndmills, 1997), 150–52.

30. Jerrold Casway, "Gaelic Maccabeanism: The Politics of Reconciliation," in *Political Thought in Seventeenth-Century Ireland: Kingdom or Colony,* ed. Jane Ohlmeyer (Cambridge, 2000), 176–88; Barbara Kiefer Lewalski, *Milton's Brief Epic: The Genre, Meaning, and Art of "Paradise Regained"* (Providence, R.I., 1966), 262–63. In the *First Defence* Milton praised the Maccabees for rebelling against King Antiochus but immediately went on to censure the ensuing return to monarchical government (YP 4:409).

31. John M. Wallace, *Destiny His Choice: The Loyalism of Andrew Marvell* (Cambridge, 1968), 88.

32. On the *Pharsalia* and *Paradise Lost,* see David Norbrook, *Writing the English Republic: Poetry, Rhetoric, and Politics, 1627–1660* (Cambridge, 1999), 438–67; on *Paradise Regained,* see David Quint, "David's Census: Milton's Politics and *Paradise Regained*," in *Re-membering Milton: Essays on the Texts and Traditions,* ed. Mary Nyquist and Margaret W. Ferguson (New York, 1987), 128–30. Milton's continuing interest in Lucan is one reason I disagree with Blair Worden's argument that the later Milton "withdraws from politics into faith." See Blair Worden, "Milton's Republicanism and the Tyranny of Heaven," in *Machiavelli and Republicanism,* ed. Gisela Bock, Quentin Skinner, and Maurizio Viroli (Cambridge, 1990), 244.

33. Jonathan Scott, *Algernon Sidney and the English Republic, 1623–1677* (Cambridge, 1988), 232–35.

34. Quint, "David's Census," 141.

35. N. I. Matar, "Milton and the Conversion of the Jews," *SEL* 27 (1987): 109–24. Fixler, *Milton and the Kingdoms of God,* 266, comments that Milton refuses to make Jesus speculate about the time of the Jews' return, but raising the question in the poem at all was bound to arouse such speculation.

36. Malcolm Kelsall, "The Historicity of *Paradise Regained*," in *Milton Studies* 12, ed. James D. Simmonds (Pittsburgh, 1978), 243.

37. Andrew Shifflett, *Stoicism, Politics, and Literature in the Age of Milton: War and Peace Reconciled* (Cambridge, 1998), 147–48.

38. Sharon Achinstein, "*Samson Agonistes* and the Drama of Dissent," in *Milton Studies* 33, *The Miltonic Samson,* ed. Albert C. Labriola and Michael Lieb (Pittsburgh, 1997), 149.

39. Algernon Sidney, *Court Maxims,* ed. Hans W. Blom, Eco Haitsma Mulier, and Ronald Janse (Cambridge, 1996), 39.

40. Kelsall, "The Historicity of *Paradise Regained,*" 242–45; Virgil, *Aeneid,* 6:801–3, 8:288–305; Lucan, *Pharsalia,* 4:593–665.

41. Laophilus Misotyrannus [Roger Jones?], *Mene Tekel* (London, 1663), 54–55; on this text in relation to *Paradise Regained,* see Loewenstein, *Representing Revolution,* 250–51.

42. Worden, "Milton, *Samson Agonistes,* and the Restoration," passim; citations in the text are from [George Sikes], *The Life and Death of Sir Henry Vane, Kt.* (London, 1662).

43. Annabel Patterson, *Early Modern Liberalism* (Cambridge, 1997), 84–87.

44. Compare Loewenstein, *Representing Revolution,* 256.

45. Mary Ann Radzinowicz, " 'In those days there was no king in Israel': Milton's Politics and Biblical Narrative," *Yearbook of English Studies* 21 (1991): 242–52.

46. This kind of erroneous divine impulse, in which God presents occasions of sin, is analyzed in *De doctrina Christiana;* see Albert C. Labriola, "Divine Urgency as a Motive for Conduct in *Samson Agonistes,*" *Philological Quarterly* 50 (1971): 100, and YP 6:331–35.

47. Wittreich writes that this latter phrase, as cited by Adlai Stevenson, was the germ of *Interpreting "Samson Agonistes"* (xxvii), but in Samson's usage, and it would seem in Stevenson's, the phrase does not imply the repudiation, only the temperate use, of force.

48. Norman T. Burns, " 'Then Stood up Phineas': Milton's Antinomianism, and Samson's," in *Milton Studies* 33, *The Miltonic Samson,* ed. Albert C. Labriola and Michael Lieb (Pittsburgh, 1996), 133–58, emphasizes antinomianism, and Fish, *How Milton Works,* 477, writes of the play's "indeterminacy and indecipherability"; see also Barbara Kiefer Lewalski, "Milton's *Samson* and the 'New Acquist of True [Political] Experience,' " in *Milton Studies* 24, ed. James D. Simmonds (Pittsburgh, 1989), 233–51; Loewenstein, *Representing Revolution,* 281–91; and Achinstein, "*Samson Agonistes* and the Drama of Dissent," 151–54.

49. Radzinowicz, *Toward "Samson Agonistes,"* 127.

PACIFIST, QUIETIST, OR PATIENT MILITANT? JOHN MILTON AND THE RESTORATION

John Coffey

"All things are best fulfilled in their due time."
Paradise Regained, 3.182

PETER ACKROYD'S NOVEL, *Milton in America,* is based on a delightful conceit. In 1660, faced with the prospect of an imminent Restoration of the Stuarts, the great defender of the regicide decides to emigrate. He sails to Puritan New England, where his fame among the godly enables him to establish New Milton, an ideal commonwealth named in his honor. But the purity of New Milton is soon threatened by another settlement, Mary Mount, founded by a happy-go-lucky papist from Virginia, Sir Ralph Kempis. As the fun-loving culture of Mary Mount begins to make inroads into his own austere utopia, Milton becomes increasingly belligerent. He tours New England, assembling a Puritan confederacy against Mary Mount, and destroys it in a climactic crusade.[1]

Ackroyd's fantasy perpetuates crude stereotypes of grim Roundheads and easygoing Cavaliers, which stand in curious contrast to political realities in post-Restoration England, where Anglican Cavaliers instigated a fierce persecution of Puritan Dissenters.[2] Yet Ackroyd's fictional Milton—militant, bellicose, and wrathful—is recognizably the man who defended the regicide, praised the New Model Army, and celebrated Cromwell's victories over the Irish and the Scots. Despite the Restoration, Milton remains as belligerent as ever.

A number of scholars, however, have offered us a very different picture of the post-Restoration Milton. In Milton's epic poems they detect disillusionment with political violence and war, a turn toward inner spirituality, apolitical quietism, and even pacifism. James Freeman and others have argued that *Paradise Lost* is a powerful satirical attack on the practice of war.[3] According to Stephen Marx, *Paradise Regained* suggests that Milton had adopted the pacifism espoused by Restoration Quakers. Joseph Wittreich has maintained that *Samson Agonistes* is a pacifist work that mocks and unmasks

149

its macho hero. For Michael Wilding the later poems expose the satanic character of violence, and reveal Christ's alternative of "patience and heroic martyrdom."[4] Other scholars stop short of presenting a "pacifist Milton," but they still suggest that the major poems display a new quietism and register a sharp discontinuity with Milton's earlier political prose. Blair Worden has argued that after 1660 Milton "withdraws from politics into faith," and M. L. Donnelly maintains that the civil war forced Milton to reevaluate and eventually repudiate "the heroic celebration of military virtue."[5]

These pacifist or quietist interpretations of the post-Restoration Milton have attracted some strong criticism. Robert Fallon alleges that the pacifist Milton is an anachronism; the seventeenth-century Puritan who supported Cromwell's armies has been replaced by "a late twentieth-century, liberally oriented university don." Michael Lieb has written about Milton's "sparagmatic sensibility," his belief that violence could be a redemptive force, and a source of renewal. David Loewenstein presents a Milton who was immersed in a radical Puritan culture that was violent, iconoclastic, and apocalyptic. For all of these scholars, Milton's epic poems stand in continuity with his revolutionary prose.[6]

I want to reassess the debate on Milton's post-Restoration politics by examining the treatment of war and violence in *Paradise Regained* and Milton's other epic poems. Does Milton come to regret the Puritan revolution? Does he turn from politics to a quietist faith? Do his later works really suggest pacifism or hostility toward war? I will begin by describing the reactions of some of Milton's radical contemporaries to the Restoration. This will provide us with valuable points of reference as we consider Milton's later poems. Above all, it will demonstrate that in the 1660s veterans of the revolution were preoccupied by questions that are central to *Paradise Regained*—questions concerning the *timing* and the *means* of their deliverance. Having established this intellectual context, I will then move on to Milton's later poems. After discussing the treatment of violence and force in *Paradise Lost,* I will concentrate on *Paradise Regained* and *Samson Agonistes,* the two poems that Milton published together in 1671.

MILTON'S CONTEMPORARIES AND THE EXPERIENCE OF DEFEAT

Elsewhere in this volume, David Norbrook has introduced us to some of Milton's contemporaries: John Hutchinson, Robert Overton, and George Wither.[7] I want to complement Norbrook's study by examining the post-Restoration outlook of four other godly republicans who shared much in common with Milton: John Goodwin, Sir Henry Vane the younger, Algernon

Sidney, and Edmund Ludlow.[8] None of these figures gave up hope of ultimate victory for the Good Old Cause, but each was deeply exercised by questions of the timing and means of that victory.

John Goodwin was among the most prolific and controversial pamphleteers of the Puritan revolution.[9] Like Milton, Goodwin had been educated at Cambridge before becoming minister of the parish of Coleman Street in London, not far from Aldersgate Street and the Barbican where Milton lived during the 1640s. Both men became Independents in the mid-1640s and were active in the toleration controversy, and both published in defense of the regicide and the Protectorate. Goodwin became disillusioned with Cromwell around 1657, as (probably) did Milton. Moreover, both were Puritan Arminians who had abandoned Calvinism during the revolution. At the Restoration, Goodwin and Milton were the twin targets of a royal proclamation in August 1660 which called for their regicide tracts to be confiscated and burned. Yet both escaped execution or incarceration, partly because they had Anglican admirers who appreciated Milton's literary genius and Goodwin's status as a learned, Arminian divine.

Historians have overlooked Goodwin's response to the Restoration, but it is illuminating. Gilbert Burnet mistakenly claimed that Goodwin was a leader of the Fifth Monarchists, a confusion that probably arose from the fact that Thomas Venner led one of several sectarian congregations to meet in the Coleman Street district. But Goodwin had always rejected Fifth Monarchist militancy. In "An Admonition" to his flock in the mid-1650s, Goodwin had analyzed the various sects of the day, including the Fifth Monarchy Men, or the "Quinto-Monarchians" as he called them. The problem with the Fifth Monarchists, Goodwin explained, arose "not so much from their opinion concerning the said Monarchie"; as a millenarian, Goodwin did not deny the future reign of Christ and his saints upon the earth. The error of the Fifth Monarchists lay not in the end they sought, but in their violent spirit, their godless means, and their premature timing. They sought "by that fierce and restless spirit which worketh in them" to bring in the Fifth Monarchy "by uncouth and unhallowed methods and ways, and this before the times of the other Monarchies be fulfilled."[10]

In the wake of Venner's ill-fated rising in 1661, Goodwin's congregation published a declaration reiterating this analysis, and explaining that their own principles were "diametrically repugnant" to those of Venner. They accused the Fifth Monarchy Men of three fundamental errors: First, they had tried "to accelerate and hasten" Christ's Second Coming "by force and violence," rather than accepting that no man could predict the timing of his return. Second, Goodwin's people rejected "their unchristian and unman-like principle, after the custome of Mahomet, to propagate Religion by the sword: The Gospel we own and profess, is not *Evangelium armatum,* an armed Gospel; the weapons of that warfare, wherein we serve as Christians, are not carnal, but spiritual." Third, Goodwin's congregation declared, "we are far from disowning the present Powers and Dominions of the earth, and in particular that of his Majesty, utterly renouncing that principle, whether appropriately Papal, or by whomsoever owned or professed, That all temporal power is founded in grace."[11]

Goodwin's own response to the Restoration is most clearly revealed in his one major (though anonymous) work of the 1660s, *A Door Opening unto the Christian Religion* (1662). This six-hundred-page catechism was a summary of Goodwin's theology. It shows that Goodwin retained a millenarian hope, and saw three signs of the last days around him: first, "an extraordinary Spirit of security, sensualitie, and earthly-mindednesse working at an high rate in the generality of men"; second, "A great despondency and fainting of heart in the generality of the Saints, and people of God, by reason of that low and most sad condition, unto which they shall be brought by their enemies"; and third, "a triumphant confidence amongst the enemies of the Saints and Servants of God, that . . . the world is now become theirs." Yet though he saw these as signs of the last days, Goodwin was reluctant to push speculation too far—he affirmed his faith in a coming millennium, but warned that dating the end "is a matter of very great difficulty, and which hath not prospered in the hand of any undertaker, that I know of."[12]

A Door did contain the occasional defiant aside attacking kings. Goodwin wrote,

That God in the heighth of his glory, and unconceivable Splendor and brightnesse of his Majesty, is altogether unlike the generality of those that are called Gods upon Earth, Kings, Princes, Potentates, and Grandees of the World, who are more ready to tread and trample upon, to grind the faces, and to break the bones of those that are beneath them, and under their power; especially, if they have at any time provoked them, or been disobedient to them, than to commiserate or relieve them in their distresse. (*A Door,* 95–96)

But when Goodwin came to discuss the crucial Fifth Commandment, he refused to endorse active resistance.

Such laws of [magistrates], unto which they cannot, without sin, or a doubting conscience, yield a practicall obedience; they ought to subject themselves unto passively, that is, patiently and with a meek spirit, accept of that punishment, which they impose upon the non-observers of them. The persons of their Magistrates, yea though they be none of the best, they ought to reverence and honour, as being set over them by the providence of God, under him to rule and govern them for their good. (*A Door,* 432)

Thus Goodwin in the 1660s was apparently a changed man. He still looked forward to a coming millennium, but he was not willing to encourage armed resistance against the powers that be.

Sir Henry Vane had been the leading republican politician in 1659–1660, and he had confidently predicted that the new Commonwealth would usher in the millennium. He was arrested in 1660, but rather than abandoning his apocalypticism, he embarked on an intensive study of Daniel and Revelation in order to make sense of this sudden twist of fate. Vane argued that the 1260 years of the Beast's reign had begun around 400 A.D. and were now drawing to a close. But the godly had been unprepared for the Beast's final fling. The suffering they were now enduring was the final persecution of the witnesses predicted in Revelation, chapter 11. According to that passage, the witnesses would be miraculously resurrected after lying in the streets of the great city for three and a half days (often interpreted as years by students of eschatology). Vane himself believed that the great events of the last days would take place in England, and he had penciled in 1666 as the year when the witnesses would arise. He taught that onlookers, who had seen the witnesses' corpses lie in the streets for three and a half years, would be transfixed with terror. Before their eyes, the witnesses would ascend to heaven. Endowed with miraculous powers, they would minister the Spirit to the godly and pour out judgment on the wicked. Babylon would fall, the Beast would be destroyed, and the millennium would then begin.[13] In 1662, Vane was sentenced to death for treason—as one of the most potent symbols of the Puritan revolution he was seen as too dangerous to be left alone. His writings during his final months suggest that he viewed his own death in an apocalyptic context and regarded himself as one of the witnesses slaughtered in the great city. If this reading is correct, Vane went to the scaffold in 1662 anticipating a spectacular vindication three and a half years later in 1666—the very year he had identified as the moment of the resurrection of the witnesses. Vane was quite clear about both timing and means—the godly would be delivered by miraculous intervention from the heavens within a few years.

Milton was one of Vane's ardent admirers, having written a sonnet in praise of Vane's defense of religious liberty in the 1650s. The sonnet first appeared in a biography of Vane published in 1662, and David Norbrook speculates that Milton may have been involved in the publication.[14] Another republican who revered Vane was Algernon Sidney, but Sidney concluded that the defenders of the Good Old Cause could not wait around for heaven-sent miracles; they had to be prepared to act themselves. Blair Worden has written that "No two seventeenth-century republicans are closer in their ideas than Sidney and Milton,"[15] so it is worth taking Sidney's views seriously. Like Milton, Sidney was friendly with Quakers, and in 1681, William Penn was to seek his advice about the constitution of Pennsylvania. In his *Court Maxims* composed in the early 1660s, Sidney wrote sympathetically about Quaker pacifism. "The Quakers indeed get some credit to this doctrine of not repelling force with force," he said, "because they practise it in patiently suffering all injuries, though mistaken in that doctrine." Yet although he acknowledged that early church fathers like Tertullian endorsed pacifism, Sidney went on to write, "At this day we find none to espouse those opinions but our Quakers, some few Anabaptists in Holland and Germany, and some of the Socinians in Poland. It is most generally known all christian churches have rejected the opinion of those that thought no use of the sword lawfull, having made use of it against such princes and their ministers as have governed contrary to law."[16] Sidney was to go to the scaffold in 1683 for defending this lawful use of the sword against princes; in the wake of the Rye House Plot to assassinate Charles II and his brother James, his unpublished *Discourses concerning Government* were used as evidence against him.

Edmund Ludlow was a close friend of Sidney and an admirer of Vane, and he combined Vane's apocalypticism with Sidney's stress on republican activism. After the Restoration, Ludlow the regicide escaped to Switzerland, but he did not lose faith in a revival of the Puritan and republican cause. In his *Memoirs* written in the 1660s, Ludlow continually returned to the question of timing and means. Although he sympathized with the Fifth Monarchist rebels of 1661, he believed it "very adviseable in matters of so great weight . . . to be carefull we make not haste," but rather "make use of such means as God approves of, and directs unto." The "poore well-meaning" Fifth Monarchists had been rash and naive; instead of meticulously planning the timing and means of their coup, they had simply trusted in God to get them through. Ludlow himself, by contrast, belonged to the trust-in-God-and-keep-your-powder-dry school. He believed that the saints would need to bide their time. "This is the day of the patience of the Lord and his Saints," he wrote; the strength of the godly "sometymes consists in quietness and confidence." The present persecution of the saints by "the Nimrods of the earth" was punishment for their divisions and self-interest, and they must patiently submit to divine discipline. Eventually, however, God would "certeinly lift them up and bringe them to honour."[17]

Goodwin, Vane, Sidney, and Ludlow did not react to the Restoration in exactly the same way. Goodwin mixed a certain contempt for kings with a commitment to obedience; Vane expected a spectacular, supernatural vindication. Sidney was the only one of the four who seems to have actively plotted against the Restoration regime. The exiled Ludlow, however, did look forward to the day when the godly would rise up to throw off their own chains.[18] Yet despite their differences, these four veterans of the Puritan revolution had much in common. None had given up hope of ultimate deliverance. All saw contemporary political events within an apocalyptic framework. Most importantly, all four were absorbed by questions concerning the timing and means of their deliverance—when and how would the defeated saints be liberated? Finally, each would, I think, have distanced himself from both the rashness of Thomas Venner, and the new "peace principle" of George Fox. As defenders of the Good Old Cause, they stood between Fifth Monarchist belligerence and Quaker pacifism.

Milton had worked alongside Goodwin, Vane, Sidney, and Ludlow in the years following the regicide and the establishment of the Commonwealth, and I want to suggest that after the Restoration he had more in common with these figures than with either the Fifth Monarchists or the Quakers. I will try to show that *Paradise Regained* displays the same concern with timing and means that we find in Milton's contemporaries, a concern that is also evident in *Samson Agonistes*. But before turning to these poems, I need to address briefly the treatment of war and violence in Milton's *Paradise Lost*.

PARADISE LOST

In *Milton and the Martial Muse*, James Freeman argues that "Milton habitually distrusted war." *Paradise Lost*, he suggests, subverts and satirizes war by presenting Satan as the conventional martial hero and then ruthlessly deconstructing him. The poem "speaks against war with such learning, complexity and humaneness that it still towers over other statements in our long Western tradition."[19]

Freeman's case builds on Milton's famous condemnation of earlier epics for glorying in war and battles. In introducing the tale of the Fall, Milton declares that he is not inclined to write of

> Wars, hitherto the only argument
> Heroic deemed, chief mastery to dissect
> With long and tedious havoc fabled knights
> In battles feigned; the better fortitude
> Of patience and heroic martyrdom
> Unsung.   (9.28–33)

Freeman argues that Milton's own treatment of war is essentially satirical—by militarizing the fallen angels, the poet makes war seem reprehensible. Satan, the model general, is exposed in all his ugliness.

We can assess the validity of Freeman's argument by attending closely to the poem's discussion of "violence" and "force." Milton is at pains to trace the origins of *violence* to rebellion against God. By stressing the original peace and harmony of heaven, *Paradise Lost* emphasizes that violence is not an eternal principle, but an intruder in God's creation, and that Satan is the original peace-breaker. Although the biblical references to the fall of Satan were both very brief and highly oblique, Milton goes out of his way to elaborate in order to drive this point home. In Book Five, the angel Raphael tells Adam the story of Satan's rebellion. Infuriated by the Father's appointment of the Son as "Messiah King," Satan draws his legions into rebellion, shatters the harmony and tranquillity of heaven, and precipitates the war described in Book Six. Even Death, Satan's offspring, later describes him as "that traitor angel," "Who first broke peace in heav'n and faith, til then / Unbroken" (2.689–91).

The violence of the rebels is underlined in Books One and Two, where Milton identifies the rebel leaders as those who will later seduce men away from God. The first is Moloch, "horrid king, besmeared with blood / of human sacrifice, and parents' tears" (1.392–93). The last is Belial, associated with "Eli's sons, who filled / With lust and violence the house of God" (1.495–96), and with the fatal rape of the matron in Gibeah described in the Book of Judges (1:503–5).[20] The violent fruits of sin are also graphically illustrated by Sin's own description of the birth of her son, Death. Impregnated by Satan, Sin tells us of how "this odious offspring," "breaking violent way / Tore through my entrails," emerging from the womb "brandishing his fatal dart" (2.781–86). Death is soon "inflamed with lust" for his own mother, and pursues her until in "embraces forcible and foul" he rapes her and engenders "yelling monsters" (2.790–802).

In his description of the war in heaven, Milton takes care to emphasize the "violence" of the fallen angels. When Michael confronts the rebellious "Author of evil" (6.262), he (like Death) rebukes Satan for disturbing "Heav'n's blessed peace" (6.267), and declares that "Heav'n the seat of bliss / Brooks not the works of violence and war" (6.273–74). During the first day of battle, the good angel Abdiel redoubles his blows and overthrows "the violence / Of Ramiel" (6.371–72). Despite being "from their place by violence moved" (6.405), the good angels put their enemies to flight. Exasperated, Satan resolves to find "Weapons more violent" (6.439).

But it is in Books Eleven and Twelve that the violence engendered by sin is revealed most fully. Here Michael gives Adam a preview of the history of the world. He begins by showing him his eldest son Cain smiting his brother Abel, and Abel "Rolling in dust and gore" (11.460). He goes on to explain that "violence / Proceeded, and oppression, and sword-law" (11.671–72). Adam laments "Death's ministers, not men, who thus deal death / Inhumanly to men, and multiply / Ten-thousandthfold the sin of him who slew / His brother" (11.676–79). Michael explains that after the Fall,

> might only shall be admired,
> And valor and heroic virtue called;
> To overcome in battle, and subdue
> Nations, and bring home spoils with infinite
> Manslaughter, shall be held the highest pitch
> Of human glory.   (11.689–94)

We are then introduced to Nimrod, commonly identified as the first tyrant, "Hunting (and men not beasts shall be his game) / With war and hostile snare such as refuse / Subjection to his empire tyrannous" (12.30–32).

Yet while *Paradise Lost* can be read as an attack on "violence," this does not mean that Milton is endorsing pacifism. In *The Tenure of Kings and Magistrates,* Milton had laid out the standard Reformed account of the origins of government—that following the sudden eruption of "violence" after the Fall, men "saw it needful to ordaine som authoritie, that might restraine by force and punishment what was violated against peace and common right."²¹ *Paradise Lost* seems to confirm the assumption that the violence of a fallen world necessitates the use of force by the just. In Book Six especially, the illegitimate "violence" of fallen angels and fallen men is contrasted with the legitimate "force" exercised by God and his agents. Milton, along with most of his contemporaries, accepted a "legitimist" definition of violence, according to which violence is the illegitimate use of force.²² When Milton employed the term "violence" it always carried pejorative connotations— "violence" was practiced by persecuting clergy, oppressing tyrants, and demonic beings.²³ It was, in other words, something done by others. The legitimate use of force was simply not violence. Thus Milton's good angels were armed and uniformed like their evil counterparts. Even before Satan's rebellion, heaven resembles a military camp—the angels carry "ensigns" and "standards" (5.588–89), and are organized in "legions," "bands and files" (5.669, 651). For Milton, a military presence is not a threat to peace, but the means of securing and maintaining it. Later in the poem, the archangels Raphael, Gabriel, and Michael are presented as military commanders with formidable weaponry and legions of "flaming warriors."

Moreover, Milton is less averse to describing war than he himself suggests, and Fallon contends that the war in heaven in Book Six is "in the classic tradition of Homer and Virgil." Out of the poem's ten thousand lines, nine hundred are devoted to actual battle. When we consider Satan's review of his forces in Book One and his council of war in Book Two, around a quarter of *Paradise Lost* concerns war in the widest sense.²⁴ Milton seems to relish the task of describing the sound and fury of the war in heaven, though throughout Book Six he never fails to distinguish unrighteous violence from righteous force. God sends his angels "to subdue / By force" those who reject his authority (6.40–41). On the third and final day of the war in heaven, the Son enters the fray, "in his right hand / Grasping ten thousand thunders" (6.835–36); at the very sight of him, Satan's forces lose all courage and drop their weapons. When the Son defeats the evil angels, he drives them "as a herd / Of goats or timorous flock together thronged," "for he meant / Not to destroy, but root them out of heav'n" (6.854–58). Thus the war fought by the Son and the angels is a just war, a defensive war, a classic example of the use of force against violence.

Rather than condemning or satirizing warfare in general, *Paradise Lost* can be seen as presenting the prototype of all just wars. The war in heaven waged by the faithful angels meets all the criteria established by the Christian just war tradition.[25] It is authorized by proper authority, indeed by the ultimate proper authority, the Creator himself. It is a war with a just cause, a defensive war fought against violent aggressors, and a war of last resort, fought only because Satan's forces are massing for attack. It is a war waged with a right intention and a just end in view, the goal being the restoration of harmony and peace. Since it is a war waged with the full support of the Almighty, it clearly has a reasonable hope of success. Finally, the righteous army observes the principle of proportionality; they exercise restraint, and the fallen angels are not subjected to wholesale slaughter, but to eviction from heaven. It is difficult to imagine a conflict that better fulfills the standards set by the doctrines of *jus ad bellum* (governing the right to go to war) and *jus in bello* (governing conduct in war).

It makes sense, therefore, to conclude that both before and after the Restoration Milton accepted the standard seventeenth-century view of war as a tragic but unavoidable feature of a fallen universe. If his Christian humanism produced in him an Erasmian distaste for warmongering and chivalric heroism, his classical republicanism and Puritan zeal led him to appreciate virtuous citizen armies. *Paradise Lost* (the writing of which straddled the Restoration), does not suggest that Milton had abandoned his republican values and commitments. As a significant body of recent scholarship has demonstrated, the epic poem echoes Milton's polemical prose works and shows the basic continuity in Milton's political attitudes.[26] The contemporary royalist John Beale had no doubts that Milton "holds to his old Principle." Beale particularly objected to the passages on Nimrod and other tyrants in the final books. The thought that Milton had suddenly turned pacifist never crossed his mind.[27] Milton's treatment of war and violence in *Paradise Lost* was still republican or civic humanist rather than pacifist. Milton still condemns violent tyrants, he still defends just wars, and he still admires the virtue, valor, and discipline of a godly army.

PARADISE REGAINED

But if *Paradise Lost* does not yield a pacifist Milton, *Paradise Regained* does seem to offer more hope, and it naturally lies at the heart of the debate over the politics of the post-Restoration Milton. Here Milton embroiders the story of the Son's temptation in the wilderness, devoting extended attention to the second temptation, where Satan shows the Son the kingdoms of the world. In Milton's account, the Son's temptation becomes the temptation to take things into his own hands, to act violently like Judas Maccabeus, and deliver his people from Roman oppression, and in doing so to imitate the glory and violence of Rome itself.

Even before Satan issues this temptation in Book Three, we know that Jesus has already experienced it. In Book One he explains that as a young man he had felt this temptation and rejected it:

> victorious deeds
> Flamed in my heart, heroic acts, one while
> To rescue Israel from the Roman yoke,
> Then to subdue and quell o'er all the earth
> Brute violence and proud tyrannic power,
> Till truth were freed, and equity restored:
> Yet held it more humane, more heavenly first
> By winning words to conquer willing hearts,
> And make persuasion do the work of fear;
> At least to try, and teach the erring soul
> Not wilfully misdoing, but unaware
> Misled; the stubborn only to subdue. (1.215–26)

The Son's words implicitly reinforce the distinction between force and violence that we detected in *Paradise Lost,* for he imagines himself quelling "Brute violence" with righteous force. Moreover, although he comes to see that he must first use "winning words" rather than military might, he also recognizes that these will only work on "willing hearts." "The stubborn," by contrast, will need to be subdued by force.

However, at this point in the Son's ministry, there is no doubt that military conquest is a temptation to be resisted. When Satan urges the Son "Quench not the thirst for glory," Jesus refuses to succumb, and exposes the violence on which glorious empires are built:

> They err who count it glorious to subdue
> By conquest far and wide, to overrun
> Large countries, and in field great battles win,
> Great cities by assault: what do these worthies,

> But rob and spoil, burn, slaughter, and enslave
> Peaceable nations.   (3.71–76)

Instead, glory is to be attained "by means far different. . . . Without ambition, war, or violence; / By deeds of peace, by wisdom eminent, / By patience, temperance" (3.89–92). Instead of imitating Satan's "Great Julius" (3.39), Jesus will honor "patient Job" and "poor Socrates," both of whom suffered death for the sake of truth (3.95–96). When Satan parades mighty armies before the Son of God, Jesus is not impressed:

> Much ostentation vain of fleshy arm,
> And fragile arms, much instrument of war
> Long in preparing, soon to nothing brought,
> Before mine eyes thou hast set; and in my ear
> Vented much policy, and projects deep
> Of enemies, of aids, battles and leagues,
> Plausible to the world, to me worth naught.   (3.387–93)

Although Satan warns that the Son's refusal to employ these means will lead to "scorns, reproaches, injuries / Violence and stripes and lastly cruel death" (4.387–88), the Son has already prepared himself for his fate. He recognizes that God has first decreed to try him "By tribulations, injuries, insults, / Contempts, and scorns, and snares, and violence" (3.190–91).

The Son's rejection of violence in *Paradise Regained* has occasioned much speculation, not least because Milton may have been prompted to write the poem by the Quaker, Thomas Ellwood. In 1662, Ellwood became Milton's student and also took on the responsibility of reading to the blind poet. In 1665, when Milton wished to leave the city to escape the plague, Ellwood found him a cottage in the Quaker village of Chalfont St. Giles, close to where he himself lived. In his autobiography, Ellwood wrote that after he had read Milton's manuscript of *Paradise Lost,* he asked the poet "what hast thou to say about Paradise found?" When Ellwood visited Milton in London some time later, he claimed that Milton showed him *Paradise Regained* and said, "this is owing to you, for you put it into my head by the question you put to me at Chalfont."[28]

Milton's Quaker connection is significant given the fact that the main body of Quakers had embraced pacifism after the Restoration. Branded as seditious, and imprisoned in the thousands in the early 1660s, Quakers were determined to distance themselves from sectarian revolutionaries like the Fifth Monarchists who had organized a failed rising in London in 1661. These Fifth Monarchist rebels were activist millenarians who believed that the millennium would be ushered in by the decisive armed action of the saints.[29] Following this rising, George Fox and other Quakers issued *A Decla-*

ration from the Harmless and Innocent People of God called Quakers, against all Sedition, Plotters, and Fighters in the World (1661), in which they enunciated their famous "peace principle."

Stephen Marx argues that Ellwood's role in inspiring *Paradise Regained*, and Christ's firm repudiation of violent means in the poem itself, suggests that Milton had come to share the Quakers' "peace principle." Although he agrees that Milton was no pacifist during the Puritan revolution, he maintains that the Restoration caused "a dramatic shift of the poet's point of view over time from a militarist to a pacifist outlook." Milton's "affirmation of Quaker pacifist principles," he writes, "seems unmistakeable."[30]

Whatever the attractions of this interpretation, it is not as compelling as Marx suggests. To begin with, recent studies of the Quaker movement have called into question the simple assumption that 1660 was a "pacifist fulcrum" for the movement, transforming Quakers from belligerent supporters of the New Model Army to complete pacifists. As Meredith Weddle has pointed out, Quaker attitudes toward violence (before and after 1660) were complex. There were Quaker pacifists before the Restoration, and Quaker belligerents after it, such as the Rhode Island Quakers who fought with their fellow colonists against Native Americans in King Philip's War of 1675–1676. There were ambiguities in the "peace testimony": Quakers continued to use the fiery rhetoric of "the Lamb's war"; the God Quakers worshiped was no pacifist; there were instances of Quakers fighting back against persecution; and the early Quakers accepted that nonviolence was for the redeemed, and that magistrates had to employ force to protect society from violent men. "Both before and after 1660," Weddle states, "Quaker comments show clearly that Quakers by no means universally observed peace principles even in their most basic, simple form."[31]

Moreover, there is no evidence that Milton himself ever became a Quaker, and the pacifism of *Paradise Regained* is by no means "unmistakeable." It seems likely that the poem's primary concern is with how the godly respond to the persecuting regime of the 1660s. The Son is tempted to deliver his people like another Judas Maccabeus, to usher in his kingdom by violence, and he refuses. But this is not necessarily a pacifist position. Is Jesus teaching that his followers can never bear arms, or serve as magistrates, or fight in defensive wars, or is the point that Satan is tempting the Son to employ force before the appointed time?

As David Norbrook shows in his essay on "Republican Occasions" in this volume, the Puritan revolutionaries displayed an acute awareness of the need to "seize the *occasione*." In his defenses of the civil war and revolution, for example, John Goodwin repeatedly appealed to a sense of "opportunitie and occasion," "crisis or juncture of time," or "a peculiar juncture of circumstances."[32] The Puritan concern to seize the providential moment merged with the republican desire to take advantage of the fortuitous occasion. Whether one followed *Providentia* or *Fortuna,* one was alert to the "peculiar juncture of circumstances" Goodwin identified. Historians now believe that Cromwell's brilliant opportunism stemmed from his providentialism, but contemporaries often attributed it to his Machiavellianism.[33]

Yet this obsession with occasion did not merely lead to a stress on seizing the moment. It also fostered patience, a willingness to wait until the time was right. The question of timeliness is central to *Paradise Regained,* with its references to "due time" (3.182) and "fullness of time" (4.380).[34] In Book Two, the fishermen Andrew and Simon express their concern at the disappearance of Jesus, and they recall their earlier expectations of imminent deliverance for their country:

> Now, now, for sure, deliverance is at hand,
> The kingdom shall to Israel be restored:
> Thus we rejoiced, but soon our joy is turned
> Into perplexity and new amaze:
> For whither is he gone, what accident
> Hath rapt him from us? will he now retire
> After appearance, and again prolong
> Our expectation? God of Israel,
> Send thy Messiah forth, the time is come;
> Behold the kings of the earth how they oppress
> Thy chosen, to what height their power unjust
> They have exalted, and behind them cast
> All fear of thee, arise and vindicate
> Thy glory, free thy people from their yoke,
> But let us wait.   (2.35–49)

In putting these words into the mouths of the disciples, Milton is going well beyond the biblical text, and going out of his way to make a point. For the experience of the disciples corresponds almost exactly to that of the godly during the late 1650s and 1660s. Hopes were raised by the revival of the Good Old Cause, and then dashed by the Restoration. Even after the Restoration, some Puritan leaders like Sir Henry Vane continued to believe fervently that their victory was still imminent. By highlighting the mistaken expectations of Andrew and Simon, Milton may well be commenting on the earnest but questionable anticipations of the godly. Yet his is not a counsel of despair, for the disciples rest in the assurance that God will fulfill his promises—that one day the nation will be delivered.

But what of the Son's rejection of military revolt? Does this not dash all hopes of political deliverance? Even here, the issue is one of discerning God's timing. In Book One the Son recalls that as a young man he was fired by dreams of crushing Roman power, but concluded that it is "more humane, more heavenly *first* / By winning words to conquer willing hearts" (1.221–22). Tempted to follow in the steps of Judas Maccabeus, he replies:

> All things are best fulfilled in their due time,
> And time there is for all things, truth hath said:
> If of my reign prophetic writ hath told,
> That it shall never end, so when begin
> The Father in his purpose hath decreed,
> He in whose hand all times and seasons roll.
> What if he hath decreed that I shall first
> Be tried in humble state. (3.182–89)

When Satan recommends instruments of war, the Son responds:

> Means I must use thou say'st, prediction else
> Will unpredict and fail me of the throne:
> My time I told thee (and that time for thee
> Were better farthest off) is not yet come. (3.394–97)

When his time does come, Christ explains, he will not need "that cumbersome / Luggage of war there shown me" (3.400–401)—the implication being that he will be able to smash his enemies without the aid of human machinery. In a later passage, Christ declares that "when my season comes to sit / On David's throne," it shall be "as a stone that shall to pieces dash all monarchies besides throughout the world" (4.146–50). The reference is to the Book of Daniel, and to one of the favorite texts of the Fifth Monarchists. It reminds us that Milton's disapproval of the Fifth Monarchist rising in 1661 did not rest on a rejection of millenarianism. Rather Milton (like Goodwin) was appalled by Venner's timing, his carnal means, and his determination to build dominion on grace by excluding all but the saints from government. Instead of waiting on the Lord, Venner had tried to do things in his own way and in his own time, to accelerate the onset of the millennium. But that the Son would one day crush persecuting religion, destroy tyrants, and bruise the Serpent's head was not in doubt. This was only a matter of time.

The problem with many interpretations of *Paradise Regained* is that they do not attend to the place of the Son's temptation in the wilderness within the grand narrative of salvation history, a narrative with a beginning, a middle, and an end. The biblical story begins with Creation and Fall, centers on Christ's atoning death on the cross, and culminates in his Second Coming. The point of the temptation story is that Christ is being tempted to preempt the Apocalypse and to bypass the cross. This temptation was the very one facing the godly in Milton's day, for had not the Fifth Monarchists in their presumption tried to avoid the suffering and persecution of the Restoration by attempting the premature overthrow of worldly monarchy? *Paradise Regained* is a sharp reminder to the godly that they should be willing to live with the mysteries of divine providence and follow the Son on the road of "patience and heroic martyrdom" that led to the cross. Yet the poem is emphatic in its insistence that one day the Son will come in glory and in power to crush the satanic forces.[35]

SAMSON AGONISTES

If the destruction of Satan's kingdom and the deliverance of the saints is foretold in *Paradise Regained,* it is most fully imagined in *Samson Agonistes*. Samson himself is in many ways the personification of the defeated Puritan and republican cause. Like the godly, he is imprisoned, "Eyeless in Gaza" (41), seemingly crushed. His enemies, he confesses, "come to stare / at my affliction" and insult him to add to his bitterness (112–14). In the words of the Chorus, Samson is "The glory late of Israel, now the grief" (179); and this, no doubt, is how Milton saw himself and his fellow revolutionaries. The painful contrast between the past glories of the Commonwealth and its present abject state is powerfully captured in Manoa's shock on first seeing his captured son:

> O miserable change! Is this the man,
> That invincible Samson, far renowned,
> The dread of Israel's foes, who with a strength
> Equivalent to angel's walked their streets,
> None offering fight; who single combatant
> Duelled their armies ranked in proud array,
> Himself an army, now unequal match
> To save himself against a coward armed
> At one spear's length.   (340–48)

Samson's experience directly parallels that of England's Puritans, secure and honored at one moment, cast into prison the next:

> Select, and sacred, glorious for awhile,
> The miracle of men: then in an hour
> Ensnared, assaulted, overcome, led bound,
> Thy foes' derision, captive, poor, and blind
> Into a dungeon thrust.   (363–67)

In the course of the poem, Samson (like Andrew and Simon in *Paradise Regained*) reflects on the incomprehensible mystery of God's providence:

> God of our fathers, what is man!
> That thou towards him with hand so various,
> O might I say contrarious,
> Temper'st thy providence through his short course,
> Not evenly.   (667–71)

Samson's bewilderment at the downturn in his fortunes parallels the confusion of the godly at the Restoration. And as he continues, he wonders at the sudden fall of good and virtuous men:

>   such as thou hast solemnly elected,
> With gifts and graces eminently adorned
> To some great work, thy glory,
> And people's safety, which in part they effect:
> Yet toward these thus dignified, thou oft
> Amidst their height of noon,
> Changest thy countenance, and thy hand with no regard
> Of highest favours past
> From thee on them, or them to thee of service.
> Nor only dost degrade them, or remit
> To life obscured, which were a fair dismission,
> But throw'st them lower than thou didst exalt them high,
> Unseemly falls in human eye,
> Too grievous for the trespass or omission,
> Oft leav'st them to the hostile sword
> Of heathen and profane, their carcasses
> To dogs and fowls a prey, or else captived:
> Or to the unjust tribunals, under change of times,
> And condemnation of the ingrateful multitude.   (678–96)

In this passage, Milton may well be reflecting on the disinterment of Bradshaw, Cromwell, and Ireton; the imprisonment of Lambert and Vane; and the execution of Sir Henry Vane in 1662. Vane was indeed eminently adorned with gifts and graces as Milton had acknowledged in his sonnet of 1652, and he was wholly committed to both the glory of God and the "people's safety," to reformation and republic. In 1659–1660, he had been at his "height of noon," the most charismatic leader of England's republicans, a man with a wide appeal among the godly. Yet suddenly he was brought before "unjust tribunals, under change of times," and left "to the hostile sword / Of heathen and profane."

Yet in Milton's eyes, Vane was unusual in his impeccable virtue. While the Restoration could be put down to the dark and inexplicable providence of God, Milton also believed that it was due to the failings of the godly themselves and of the English people. His explanation of why Samson has fallen coincides with his own understanding of why the Puritan revolution failed. Manoa is clear that Samson's fall has come about because he trusted in his own strength rather than in God's empowerment: "O ever-failing trust / In mortal strength! and O what not in man / Deceivable and vain!" (348–50). Samson himself reflects, "But what is strength without a double share / Of wisdom, vast, unwieldly, burdensome, / Proudly secure, yet liable to fall" (53–55). He has been "like a foolish pilot" who has "shipwrecked, / My vessel trusted from above, / Gloriously rigged" (198–200). He can only look back bitterly on the opportunity he has squandered. Had he only added virtue to his strength he "Might have subdued the earth, / Universally crowned with highest praises" (174–75).

Significantly, Milton's Samson only laments his lack of virtue, not his strength—his sin is not that of destroying Philistines, but of failing to acknowledge the source of his power. Indeed, the Chorus makes it clear that God empowers mighty deliverers to overthrow tyrants:

> O how comely it is and how reviving
> To the spirits of just men long oppressed!
> When God into the hands of their deliverer
> Puts invincible might
> To quell the mighty of the earth, the oppressor,
> The brute and boisterous force of violent men.   (1268–73)

The language here closely parallels that used in Book One of *Paradise Regained,* when the Son recalls his youthful ambition "to subdue and quell o'er all the earth / Brute violence and proud tyrannic power" (1.218–19). For Milton, this desire to see tyranny quelled is perfectly legitimate, even noble. But as in *Paradise Regained,* he stresses the priority of virtue over force, and the necessity of patience. The Chorus continues:

> But patience is more oft the exercise
> Of saints, the trial of their fortitude,
> Making them each his own deliverer,
> And victor over all
> That tyranny or fortune can inflict,
> Either of these is in thy lot,
> Samson, with might endued
> Above the sons of men; but sight bereaved
> May chance to number thee with those
> Whom patience finally must crown.   (1287–96)

It is hard to resist the thought that Milton here is speaking to himself and to the godly oppressed by the Restoration regime. Providence will determine their "lot," and they must be prepared to embrace whatever God dictates, be it might or martyrdom. However "comely" and "reviving" the thought of a mighty deliverance, the reality may be that they are numbered "with those / whom patience finally must crown."

And yet there remains the possibility that deliverance may be close at hand. While Samson is at the temple of Dagon to perform for the Philistines, the Chorus hears a thunderous noise and speculates

> What if his eyesight (for to Israel's God
> Nothing is hard) by miracle restored
> He now be dealing dole among his foes,
> And over heaps of slaughtered walk his way?   (1527–30)

We soon learn that Samson himself is among the slaughtered. Placed between the central pillars of the temple, he has destroyed the entire structure:

> straining all his nerves he bowed,
> As with the force of winds and waters pent,
> When mountains tremble, those two massy pillars
> With horrible convulsion to and fro,
> He tugged, he shook, till down they came and drew
> The whole roof after them, with burst of thunder
> Upon the heads of all who sat beneath,
> Lords, ladies, captains, counsellors, or priests,
> Their choice nobility and flower.   (1646–54)

The violent ending of *Samson Agonistes* has troubled many readers and led some to argue that the poem was composed before the Restoration. Stephen Marx follows W. R. Parker in proposing a pre-Restoration date for the poem, since this allows him to salvage the case for the pacifism of the later Milton. But as we have already seen, there are good grounds for dating the composition of *Samson Agonistes* after 1660, and the case for its Restoration context has been persuasively made in recent scholarship.[36]

However, those who wish to maintain that Samson's violence does not win the approval of the later Milton can still argue that Samson is not being presented as a noble and heroic figure. Instead, he is being contrasted unfavorably with the patient and peaceful Son of *Paradise Regained*. In his major study of *Samson Agonistes*, Joseph Wittreich has argued that "*Samson* is no sabre-rattling poem but rather an enquiry into why sabre-rattling should cease." He argues that Milton's Samson succumbs to the very temptations the Son resists. Whereas Jesus turns his back on violence and glory to take the path of the cross, Samson does the opposite: "*Samson* is a human tragedy recounting the tragedy of civilisation and of its supposedly civilising religions."[37] By placing *Samson Agonistes* after *Paradise Regained* in the 1671

168 JOHN COFFEY

volume, Milton shows how tempting it is to reject the example of the Son in favor of more conventional routes to deliverance. Milton's reader was faced with a choice: would they follow Jesus or Samson?

Wittreich's argument is appealing, but it is hard to reconcile with Milton's apparent defense of Samson's action in the poem. Milton goes out of his way to exonerate Samson from accusations of "self-violence," explaining that his death was accidental rather than suicidal. He also alters the biblical record so that the people escape the catastrophe and only the ruling classes are destroyed, thus making Samson's action seem more defensible. The poem concludes with Samson's father assuring us that his death was "noble" and "heroic," and the Chorus declaring that he was God's "faithful champion" (1751). Wittreich detects deep irony here, but this is unlikely. Although Samson *is* a deeply flawed character, this makes him all the more appropriate as the personification of the redeemed sinner. As Loewenstein has demonstrated, Samson displays many of the key characteristics of the Puritan saint: inwardness, providentialism, patient waiting on God, openness to the "rousing motions" of the Spirit, and apocalypticism.[38] Alongside the Son, Samson's failings are manifest, but it would be wrong to posit a dichotomy between a patient Jesus and a vengeful Samson. As we have seen, the Son of *Paradise Regained* looks forward to an ultimate destruction of Satan, and Samson learns the importance of patience and the futility of strength without wisdom and virtue. Samson's final act of pulling down the temple of Dagon dramatizes the destruction of Stuart monarchy and Anglican persecution that the defenders of the Good Old Cause continued to seek after 1660.

CONCLUSION

David Loewenstein has argued that Milton's decision to publish *Paradise Regained* and *Samson Agonistes* in one volume in 1671 was "a deeply ambivalent or double-edged response" to the politics of the Restoration. *Paradise Regained* imagined what it might be like to "repudiate all temporal kingdoms and establish the inward kingdom of Jesus through humble actions and 'winning words,'" while *Samson Agonistes* "envisioned what it would be like, in a spectacular act of holy violence and revenge, to destroy the idols and theatre of Dagon and his worshippers." It is a mistake to assume that Milton's radicalism "can be firmly aligned with one prophetic poem and its heroic vision more than with the other." Rather, there is a "profound indeterminacy" about the 1671 volume, which "enabled Milton to juxtapose two distinctive representations of radical religious and political sainthood without necessarily suggesting that one model is altogether preferable to the other."[39]

This interpretation perhaps exaggerates the incompatibility and "radical indeterminacy" of Milton's final poems. Milton is not, I think, presenting his readers with an either/or proposition; the poems do not offer alternative routes to liberation. Instead, there is a striking consistency between the two poems. The Son resists the temptation to bypass the cross, and Samson learns to endure suffering and persecution. Both poems stress the incomprehensible ways of Providence. Just as Satan is taken aback by a Jesus who dismisses the "cumbersome / Luggage of war" (*PR* 3.400–401), so Harapha is outraged by a Samson who has the temerity to "disparage glorious arms" (*SA* 1130). Both Christ and Samson recognize that what matters most is not might or arms, but patience, wisdom, and virtue. Christ knows that one day he will bruise Satan's head, and Samson brings down the temple of Dagon. In both poems, the question is one of timing. Deliverance will come, and the enemies of God will be forcibly overthrown, but in the meantime the godly must wait, patiently, and be prepared to suffer.

Although some critics have suggested that the Old Testament Samson is superseded by the New Testament Jesus,[40] the place of the two within salvation history can be construed very differently. Early modern Christians thought of history as a grand narrative, with a beginning (Creation and Fall), a middle (Christ's life, death, and Resurrection), and an end (the Apocalypse). *Paradise Lost* clearly concerns the beginning of salvation history, and it develops the themes of Genesis—Creation and Fall. *Paradise Regained* turns to the middle of salvation history, the life of the Messiah. Many critics have been surprised that Milton chose to write about the Son's temptation in the wilderness rather than about the Passion, but in a sense the story of the Passion is at the heart of the poem. The Son is being tempted to take another route to glory; by resisting Satan's temptation, he sets his face toward Calvary. But the poem also looks forward to the end of the Christian story—the Apocalypse, the final defeat of Satan, and the establishment of the Son's kingdom in glory and power. For many seventeenth-century English Protestants, especially Puritans, the end of history was imminent,[41] and there is ample evidence that Milton shared this apocalyptic or millenarian outlook.[42] But publishing an epic poem about the Apocalypse in Restoration England would have been almost impossible for Milton—how could the notorious supporter of the regicide have written about such a politically explosive topic? Instead, Milton publishes *Samson Agonistes*, where the final destruction of tyranny is imagined in the poem's apocalyptic climax. By placing it after *Paradise Regained* in the 1671 volume, he perhaps hinted at the poem's eschatological subject matter. Together with *Paradise Lost,* the two poems can be seen as forming a triptych, telling the story of salvation from Creation and Fall, through redemption, to the Apocalypse.

With its accent on the sufferings of the saints, the mysteries of Providence, and the hope of dramatic deliverance, *Samson Agonistes* reflects the apocalyptic mentality of the defeated Puritans in the early 1660s, a mentality displayed so vividly in the writings of Vane, Sidney, and Ludlow at this time. Despite its ending, the poem is not glibly gung-ho or triumphalist in its outlook. The last thing Milton wanted was another Venner—a hotheaded, narrow-minded zealot who presumptuously preempted God's apocalyptic timetable rather than waiting patiently and enduring the trial of persecution. The poem invites the saints to compare themselves to Samson, a flawed character whose might had not been matched by his wisdom, and a man who only acquired virtue through the bitter experience of crushing defeat. It asks the saints to contemplate the sobering possibility that "chance" may "number thee with those / Whom patience finally must crown." As Achinstein has suggested, *Samson Agonistes* is not simply concerned with what will happen in the end; it also tackles the problem of what to do in the meantime, a problem acutely faced by Dissenters.[43] Nevertheless, in its apocalyptic climax, the poem does seem to imagine the final destruction of the Antichrist, as it looks forward to the day when God "unexpectedly returns" to bear witness to "his faithful champion" (1750–51).

Yet there is still a puzzle over the form of deliverance Milton expects. One can read Samson as a type of Christ. Standing between the pillars of the temple with his arms outstretched, he recalls the Crucifixion, but also points forward to the vengeance and deliverance of the Second Coming. This would fit with the pessimistic view of church history offered at the close of *Paradise Lost* in which the suffering of the saints is only ended by the Parousia, and it would place Milton in the company of Sir Henry Vane, who predicted an imminent and supernatural deliverance from above. Milton, however, had always been far more cautious in his eschatological speculation than Vane, and it seems unlikely that he spent the 1660s waiting with bated breath for the two witnesses to be revealed. As a man of the Renaissance as well as the Reformation, Milton's outlook was closer to that of John Goodwin, a Puritan divine famous for his "elegant and learned sermons."[44] Milton may have admired Vane while also sharing Goodwin's skepticism about attempts to date the Apocalypse. Moreover, as someone who had gone through the same traumatizing experience as Goodwin in 1660, Milton had also decided to keep his head down, and submit to the governing authorities.

But Goodwin and Milton were not simply passive, submissive, and cooperative, and the authorities kept a watchful eye on both men. In March 1664, Roger L'Estrange was granted a warrant to apprehend Goodwin with all his papers and writings, and Milton, too, was regarded with suspicion.[45] If both men knew that it was folly to engage in open resistance, their very productivity after 1660 testified to a quieter defiance. They would, I think, have sympathized with the patient militancy of Algernon Sidney and Edmund Ludlow, who believed that the defenders of the Good Old Cause would one day be the agents of their own deliverance. If we take Milton's Samson as a paradigm for the saints, rather than a type of Christ, the moral of the tale is clear. By retelling the story of Samson, Milton reminds the saints that whatever their previous failings, God can still use them as the means to destroy oppressive and idolatrous power. Instead of passively expecting deliverance from on high, the saints must patiently await the moment when they themselves can act.

In the mid-1660s, Edmund Ludlow gave the following advice to Dissenters and supporters of the Good Old Cause oppressed by the "Nimrodian power" of their adversaries:

The Lord therefore unite us in his feare, that by suffering we may be fitted for the doing of his will, and give us wisdome to know when to goe forward and when to stand still, that by making hast we may not strengthen the hand of the enemy, nor by standing still neglect the opportunity he puts into our hands, but that, being on our Watch Tower, and living by faith, we may see our duty so plainly, that when the Lords tyme is come we may be up and be doing, and the Lord may appeare to be with us and to owne us.[46]

Ludlow's exhortation could almost be a commentary on *Paradise Regained* and *Samson Agonistes*. The saints are to expect "suffering," and they must cultivate "wisdom," but they must also be on their watchtower, waiting for their opportunity "to goe forward." After 1660, Milton and Ludlow did not turn their backs on the Puritan revolution, or conclude that they should never employ force to achieve their ends. Instead, they regarded the present suffering times as a purifying trial that would purge the saints and prepare them for a final onslaught against anti-Christian tyranny. That trial might be long and bitter. The saints must learn that virtue took priority over force, and they must be willing to face "heroic martyrdom." But Milton and Ludlow continued to believe that political force could be a source of renewal, and they looked forward to another revolutionary upheaval. They did not retreat into apolitical quietism. They were biding their time. They were waiting for "the Lord's tyme."

University of Leicester

NOTES

An earlier version of this paper was given at the University of Leicester's Early Modern Seminar and at the British Milton Seminar. I am especially grateful to Gordon Campbell, Tom Corns, David Loewenstein, and Blair Worden for their helpful comments.

1. Peter Ackroyd, *Milton in America* (London, 1997).

2. See John Coffey, *Persecution and Toleration in Protestant England, 1558–1689* (Harlow, 2000), chap. 7.

3. James A. Freeman, *Milton and the Martial Muse: "Paradise Lost" and European Traditions of War* (Princeton, 1980). A similar interpretation is presented by B. A. Wright, *Milton's "Paradise Lost"* (London, 1962), 128–37; and by Stella Revard, *The War in Heaven* (Ithaca, N.Y., 1980), both of which see the war in heaven as a satire on war in general.

4. Stephen Marx, "The Prophet Disarmed: Milton and the Quakers," *SEL* 32 (1992): 111–28. E. Wagenknecht, *The Personality of Milton* (Norman, Okla., 1970), 93, declares that *Paradise Regained* "is certainly one of the great pacifist books of all time." Joseph Wittreich, *Interpreting "Samson Agonistes"* (Princeton, 1986); Michael Wilding, *Dragons Teeth: Literature in the English Revolution* (Oxford, 1987), chaps. 7–9, esp. 249–57.

5. Blair Worden, "Milton's Republicanism and the Tyranny of Heaven," in *Machiavelli and Republicanism*, ed. Gisela Bock, Quentin Skinner, and Maurizio Viroli (Cambridge, 1990), 244. M. L. Donnelly, " 'Ostentation Vain of Fleshly Arm': Milton's Reevaluation of the Heroic Celebration of Military Virtue," in *The English Civil Wars in the Literary Imagination*, ed. Claude J. Summers and Ted-Larry Pebworth (Columbia, 1999), 202–19.

6. Robert Fallon, *Captain or Colonel: The Soldier in Milton's Life and Art* (Columbia, 1984), 14. Michael Lieb, *Milton and the Culture of Violence* (Ithaca, N.Y., 1994); Lieb, " 'A Thousand Fore-Skins': Circumcision, Violence, and Selfhood in Milton," in *Milton Studies* 38, *John Milton: The Writer in His Works*, ed. Albert C. Labriola and Michael Lieb (Pittsburgh, 2000), 198–219. David Loewenstein, *Milton and the Drama of History: Historical Vision, Iconoclasm, and the Literary Imagination* (Cambridge, 1990); David Loewenstein, *Representing Revolution in Milton and His Contemporaries: Religion, Politics, and Polemics in Radical Puritanism* (Cambridge, 2001). Other scholars who stress the persistence of a militaristic Milton include G. Wilson Knight, *Chariot of Wrath: The Message of John Milton to Democracy at War* (London, 1942); Jackie Di Salvo, " 'The Lord's Battles': *Samson Agonistes* and the Puritan Revolution," in *Milton Studies* 4, ed. James D. Simmonds (Pittsburgh, 1972), 39–62.

7. Norbrook, "Republican Occasions in *Paradise Regained* and *Samson Agonistes*," in this volume.

8. Vane, Sidney, and Ludlow have previously been used as points of reference by Blair Worden, "Milton, *Samson Agonistes*, and the Restoration," in *Culture and Society in the Stuart Restoration*, ed. Gerald Maclean (Cambridge, 1995), 111–36.

9. I am currently working on an intellectual biography of Goodwin, entitled *John Goodwin and the Puritan Revolution* (Woodbridge, Suffolk, forthcoming).

10. John Goodwin, "An Admonition to the Sheep of Christ," sec. 10, *Cata-Baptism; or, New Baptism, Waxing Old, and Ready to Vanish Away* (London, 1655).

11. *A Declaration on the behalf of the Church of Christ usually meeting in Coleman-street, in Communion with Mr John Goodwyn, against the late insurrection made in the City of London* ([London], 1661), 3–4.

12. [Goodwin], *A Door*, 74–76. Hereafter cited in the text by page number.

13. Henry Vane, *Two Treatises* (London, 1662), esp. 53–58, 68–81; Vane, *A Pilgrimage into the Land of Promise* (London, 1664), 104–9; "A letter of Sr H:V:s to Mr H:C:y," Forster MS F.48.D.41, Victoria and Albert Museum, ff. 264–308. I plan to discuss Vane's apocalypticism in much greater depth in "The Martyrdom of Sir Henry Vane," in *Martyrdom in Early Modern Britain*, ed. Tom Freeman (Woodbridge, Suffolk, forthcoming).

14. Norbrook, *Writing the English Republic: Poetry, Rhetoric, and Politics, 1627–1660* (Cambridge, 1999), 435.

15. Worden, "Milton, *Samson Agonistes,* and the Restoration," 113–14.

16. Algernon Sidney, *Court Maxims,* ed. Hans W. Blom, Eco H. Mulier, and Ronald Janse (Cambridge, 1996), 103–5.

17. Edmund Ludlow, *A Voyce from the Watch Tower, Part Five: 1660–1662,* ed. A. Blair Worden (London, 1978), 279.

18. The political attitudes and activities of Sidney and Ludlow after the Restoration are admirably elucidated in Blair Worden, *Roundhead Reputations: The English Civil Wars and the Passions of Posterity* (London, 2001), chaps. 1–6.

19. Freeman, *Milton and the Martial Muse,* 61, 223.

20. Discussed in Lieb, *Milton and the Culture of Violence,* chap. 6.

21. John Milton, *The Tenure of Kings and Magistrates,* in *The Complete Prose Works of John Milton,* 8 vols., ed. Don M. Wolfe et al. (New Haven, 1953–82), 3:198–99; hereafter designated YP and cited parenthetically by volume and page number in the text. The Scottish Covenanter, Samuel Rutherford, also argued that the institution of government (with its authority to punish and wage war) had been established after the Fall, "as a remedy for violence and injustice." See *Lex, Rex; or, The Law and the Prince* (London, 1644), 213.

22. See C. A. J. Coady, "The Idea of Violence," in *Violence and Its Alternatives: An Interdisciplinary Reader,* ed. Manfred B. Steger and Nancy S. Lind (London, 1999), chap. 3: Coady rejects the "legitimist" and "wide" definitions of violence in favor of a "restricted" definition concentrated on "positive interpersonal acts of force usually involving the infliction of personal injury." This definition of violence is employed in this essay.

23. F. A. Patterson, *An Index to the Columbia Edition of the Works of John Milton* (New York, 1940), 2.2036–37, s.v. "violence."

24. Robert Fallon, "Michael Murrin's Milton and the 'Epic without War': A Review Essay," *Milton Quarterly* 31 (1997): 119–23.

25. On the just war tradition, see James Turner Johnson, *Ideology, Reason, and the Limitation of War: Religious and Secular Concepts, 1200–1740* (Princeton, 1975).

26. On the republicanism of *Paradise Lost,* see David Norbrook, *Writing the English Republic,* chaps. 9–10; Barbara Lewalski, "*Paradise Lost* and Milton's Politics," in *Milton Studies* 38, ed. Albert C. Labriola and Michael Lieb (Pittsburgh, 2000), 141–68; Loewenstein, *Representing Revolution,* chap. 7; Roger Lejosne, "Milton, Satan, Salmasius, and Abdiel," in *Milton and Republicanism,* ed. David Armitage, Armand Himy, and Quentin Skinner (Cambridge, 1995), chap. 6.

27. Norbrook, *Writing the English Republic,* 467.

28. See Lewalski, *The Life of John Milton: A Critical Biography* (Oxford, 2000), 443–44.

29. On Milton and Venner's rising, see Laura Lunger Knoppers, *Historicizing Milton: Spectacle, Power, and Poetry in Restoration England* (Athens, Ga., 1994), chap. 5.

30. Marx, "The Prophet Disarmed," 112, 126.

31. Meredith B. Weddle, *Walking the Way of Peace: Quaker Pacifism in the Seventeenth Century* (Oxford, 2001), 59 and passim. See also Peter Brock, *The Quaker Peace Testimony, 1660–1914* (New York, 1980), 1–31.

32. Goodwin, *Anti-Cavalierisme* (London, 1642), 50–51; [Goodwin], *The Army Harmlesse* (London, 1647), 4; Goodwin, *Might and Right Well Met* (London, 1649), 14.

33. Compare Blair Worden, "Providence and Politics in Cromwellian England," *Past and Present* 109 (1985): 55–99, with William Prynne, *The Machiavellian Cromwellist and Hypocritical New Statist* (London, 1648).

34. See Loewenstein, *Representing Revolution,* 262–65.

35. As Knoppers, *Historicizing Milton,* observes, "*Paradise Regained* is not a simple renun-

ciation of force—past or present—against Rome or self-styled Roman conquerors. Force is renounced for the time being only because it is inappropriate and ineffectual. And this is so because the real threat to Israel is not any external empire but the Israelites themselves" (137).

36. C. Hill, *The Experience of Defeat: Milton and Some Contemporaries* (London, 1984), 301–10; Worden, "Milton, *Samson Agonistes,* and the Restoration"; Loewenstein, *Representing Revolution,* chap. 9; Knoppers, *Historicizing Milton,* chap. 2; Achinstein, "*Samson Agonistes* and the Drama of Dissent," in *Milton Studies* 33, *The Miltonic Samson,* ed. Albert C. Labriola and Michael Lieb (Pittsburgh, 1996), 133–58.

37. Wittreich, *Interpreting "Samson Agonistes,"* 379, 369.

38. See esp. Loewenstein, *Representing Revolution,* chap. 9.

39. Ibid., 292–95.

40. Wittreich, *Interpreting "Samson Agonistes"*; Wilding, *Dragons Teeth,* 253–57.

41. This has been demonstrated by scholars like William Lamont, Paul Christianson, David Katz, and Bryan Ball, but see especially Christopher Hill, *Antichrist in Seventeenth-Century England* (Oxford, 1971).

42. On Milton's apocalypticism, see C. A. Patrides, " 'Something like Prophetick strain': Configurations of the Apocalypse in Milton," in *The Apocalypse in English Renaissance Thought and Literature,* ed. Patrides and Joseph Wittreich (Manchester, 1984), chap. 8; Crawford Gribben, *The Puritan Millennium: Literature and Theology, 1550–1682* (Dublin, 2000).

43. Achinstein, "*Samson Agonistes* and the Drama of Dissent," 136.

44. [Stephen Nye], *The Life of Thomas Firmin* (1698), 6. Firmin had attended Goodwin's church in the 1650s before falling under the spell of the Socinian John Biddle. As a wealthy merchant, well known for his Socinianism, he later became a close friend of John Locke.

45. On Goodwin, see *Calendar of State Papers Domestic, 1663–1664,* 103; on suspicions about Milton, see Lewalski, *The Life of John Milton,* 399–415; Lewalski, "*Paradise Lost* and Milton's Politics," 147–48.

46. Ludlow, *A Voyce from the Watch Tower,* 309–11.